LEARNING THREADS FOR THE EYFS

FOR THE

Practical activities for 3–5 year olds

ELEANOR HOSKINS

Learning Matters
An imprint of SAGE Publications Ltd
1 Oliver's Yard
55 City Road
London EC1Y 1SP

SAGE Publications Inc.
2455 Teller Road
Thousand Oaks, California 91320

SAGE Publications India Pvt Ltd
B 1/I 1 Mohan Cooperative Industrial Area
Mathura Road
New Delhi 110 044

SAGE Publications Asia-Pacific Pte Ltd
3 Church Street
#10-04 Samsung Hub
Singapore 049483

Editor: Amy Thornton
Senior project editor: Chris Marke
Project management: Deer Park Productions
Marketing manager: Lorna Patkai
Cover design: Wendy Scott
Typeset by: C&M Digitals (P) Ltd, Chennai, India
Printed in the UK

Library of Congress Control Number: 2018961089

British Library Cataloguing in Publication Data

A catalogue record for this book is available from the
British Library

ISBN 978-1-5264-5005-0
ISBN 978-1-5264-5006-7 (pbk)

At SAGE we take sustainability seriously. Most of our products are printed in the UK using responsibly sourced
papers and boards. When we print overseas we ensure sustainable papers are used as measured by the PREPS
grading system. We undertake an annual audit to monitor our sustainability.

Contents

About the Author

Eleanor (Elly) Hoskins works in initial teacher training at Manchester Metropolitan University teaching early years and primary trainees. Prior to this role, she taught early years and primary children for several years and gained additional experience as a school improvement teacher, assistant head and deputy head teacher. Within her school management roles, she led many changes within early years. For example, creating and organising a new, open-plan foundation stage unit and trialling unique approaches to continuous provision learning that ensured a thorough transition for children between EYFS and KS1.

Introduction

The learning threads and practical activities in this book embrace early years play and exploration while recognising the preparation needed for Key Stage 1, Year 1. This book aims to save you planning time by offering clear and concise practical activities that are detailed and closely linked to early years specifications and requirements.

Purpose and practicalities

Planning guidance

A core element of *Learning Threads for EYFS: Practical Activities for 3–5 Year Olds* is 'how' to interpret early years guidance and goals to develop these in practice. Therefore this book contains many suggested activities with accompanying planning guidance grids that clearly link activity and outcomes/goals alongside notes about *actual practice* displayed in blue brackets.

ESSENTIAL LITERACY AND MATHEMATICS DEVELOPMENT				
PRIME AREAS		**Development guidance**	**SPECIFIC AREAS**	**Development guidance**
COMMUNICATION AND LANGUAGE	Listening and attention	**30-50 months** *Focusing attention - still listen and do, but can shift own attention (listening to others whilst exploring shells)* **40-60+ months** *Two channelled attention- can listen and do for short span* **ELG** *They give their attention to what others say and respond appropriately, while engaged in another activity (simultaneous listening and exploring of shells in boxes or bags)*	**LITERACY** / Reading	**30-50 months** *Knows information can be relayed in the form of print (texture adjectives on shell word wall)* **40-60+ months** *Can segment sounds in simple words and blend them together and knows which letters represent some of them. Begins to read words* **ELG** *They use phonic knowledge to decode regular words and read them aloud accurately (texture adjectives on shell word wall)*
	Related outcomes and goals from Early years outcomes, Development Matters in the Early Years Foundation Stage and Statutory Framework for the Early Years Foundation Stage		Writing	**30-50 months** *Sometimes give meaning to marks as they draw (some children may add mark making to post it notes)* **40-60+ months** *Uses some clearly identifiable letters to communicate meaning, representing some sounds correctly and in sequence.* **ELG** *Children use their phonic knowledge to write words in ways, which match their spoken sounds. (sounding out phonetically plausible texture adjectives to add to Post it notes)*
			The interpretation of the outcome/goal in practice is highlighted in blue.	
	Understanding	**30-50 months** *Understands use of objects. Shows understanding of prepositions such as 'under', 'on top', 'behind' (understanding how to locate shells in box or bag)* **40-60+ months** *Listens and responds to ideas expressed by others in conversation or discussion* **ELG** *Children follow instructions involving several ideas and actions (responding to others ideas whilst exploring shells and following basic instructions about feeling shells in box or bag)*	**MATHEMATICS** / Numbers	**30-50 months** *Uses some number names and number language spontaneously (spontaneous use of number language related to shells, e.g. counting of starfish legs)* **40-60+ months** *Estimates how many objects they can see and checks by counting them (estimation and spontaneous counting of shells in the box or bag while exploring)*
	Speaking	**30-50 months** *Using vocabulary focused on objects ...* *Builds up vocabulary that that reflects the breadth of their experiences (development and use of vocabulary related to shells and textures)* **40-60+ months** *Extends vocabulary, especially by grouping and naming, exploring the meaning and sounds of new words (vocabulary related to shells and textures)* **ELG** *Children express themselves effectively, showing awareness of listeners' needs (while exploring shells alongside others)*	Shape, space and measure	**30-50 months** *Beginning to talk about shapes of everyday objects (while feeling shell shapes in box or bag)* **40-60+ months** *Can describe their relative position such as 'behind' or 'next to'* **ELG** *They explore characteristics of everyday objects and shapes and use mathematical language to describe them (while exploring and feeling shell shapes in box or bag)*
	Clear 30-50 months, 40-60+ months and ELG age expectation headings.			

Planning support

All activities are grouped in chapters while linked to a clear **learning thread.** The **learning thread** of each chapter is the overarching inspiration and interest: the 'thread' that runs through all activities to build cohesion and provide a structured framework for you to follow.

This book aims to support you with the everyday planning burden by outlining clear activities connected to a learning thread and matched to early years outcomes, goals and other important information ready to be instantly used.

Following DfE reviews regarding how to reduce teacher workload one aspect suggests, *Teachers spend an undue amount of time planning and resourcing lessons* (DfE, 2016, p.5). Therefore this book aims to save you the 'undue' planning and resourcing time and to release this precious time for use elsewhere.

Planning essentials

Within early years, it is imperative that children explore and learn across all areas with interconnected prime and specific areas to develop the child holistically. Essential to this equation are the 'Characteristics of Effective Learning', which underpin how the children engage with other people and their activities. With this in mind, all activities in this book also include a 'Characteristics of Effective Learning' planning grid which highlight *how* the characteristics relate to the actual activity in practice:

CHARACTERISTICS OF EFFECTIVE LEARNING	Suggested outcomes
Playing and exploring –*engagement*	**Using sense of touch to explore and describe shells**
Active learning – *motivation*	**Persistence while exploring shells in feely box or bag**
Creating and thinking critically – *thinking*	**Making links between touch, textures and describing vocabulary**

The main planning guidance grids also begin with 'Essential Literacy and Mathematics Development', which firstly outline the specific Literacy and Mathematics outcomes/Early Learning Goals (ELG's) alongside the prime area of Communication and Language:

ESSENTIAL LITERACY AND MATHEMATICS DEVELOPMENT					
PRIME AREAS		Development guidance	SPECIFIC AREAS		Development guidance
COMMUNICATION AND LANGUAGE	Listening and attention	**30-50 months** *Focusing attention - still listen and do, but can shift own attention (listening to others while exploring shells)* **40-60+ months** *Two-channelled attention - can listen and do for short span* ***ELG** They give their attention to what others say and respond appropriately, while engaged in another activity (simultaneous listening and exploring of shells in boxes or bags)*	LITERACY	Reading	**30-50 months** *Knows information can be relayed in the form of print (texture adjectives on shell word wall)* **40-60+ months** *Can segment sounds in simple words and blend them together and knows which letters represent some of them. Begins to read words* ***ELG** They use phonic knowledge to decode regular words and read them aloud accurately (texture adjectives on shell word wall)*
				Writing	**30-50 months** *Sometimes give meaning to marks as they draw (some children may add mark making to Post-it notes)* **40-60+ months** *Uses some clearly identifiable letters to communicate meaning, representing some sounds correctly and in sequence* ***ELG** Children use their phonic knowledge to write words in ways, which match their spoken sounds (sounding out phonetically plausible texture adjectives to add to Post it notes)*
	Understanding	**30-50 months** *Understands use of objects. Shows understanding of prepositions such as 'under', 'on top', 'behind' (understanding how to locate shells in box or bag)* **40-60+ months** *Listens and responds to ideas expressed by others in conversation or discussion* ***ELG** Children follow instructions involving several ideas and actions (responding to others' ideas while exploring shells and following basic instructions about feeling shells in box or bag)*	MATHEMATICS	Numbers	**30-50 months** *Uses some number names and number language spontaneously (spontaneous use of number language related to shells, e.g. counting of starfish legs)* **40-60+ months** *Estimates how many objects they can see and checks by counting them (estimation and spontaneous counting of shells in the box or bag while exploring)*
	Speaking	**30-50 months** *Uses vocabulary focused on objects and people that are of particular importance to them (development and use of vocabulary related to shells and textures)* **40-60+ months** *Extends vocabulary, especially by grouping and naming, exploring the meaning and sounds of new words (vocabulary related to shells and textures)* ***ELG** Children express themselves effectively, showing awareness of listeners' needs. They use past, present and future forms accurately when talking about events that have happened or are to happen in the future. They develop their own narratives and explanations by connecting ideas or events (while exploring shells alongside others)*		Shape, space and measure	**30-50 months** *Beginning to talk about shapes of everyday objects (while feeling shell shapes in box or bag)* **40-60+ months** *Can describe their relative position such as 'behind' or 'next to'* ***ELG** They explore the characteristics of everyday objects and shapes and use mathematical language to describe them (while exploring and feeling shell shapes in box or bag)*

The reasoning for this organisation is to focus planning and learning development towards the requirements of Key Stage 1, as there is a growing expectation for staff in Reception to prepare children for the demands of Year 1, including the increased expectations of the 2014 national curriculum (Ofsted, 2017, p.12) but without losing the essential exploratory approach from EYFS.

Structure and support

Chapter layout

Each chapter relates to a **learning thread** such as 'Beaches and Blue Seas' or 'Dangerous Dinosaurs' providing you and the children with overarching inspiration and interest whilst adding a cohesive 'thread' that runs through all activities. *How* each **learning thread** links to the children's learning and development is also clearly outlined at the beginning of each chapter. Also listed are related role-play area suggestions to provide you with ideas and inspiration.

Activities

All the activities will fit within independent continuous provision exploration with some requirement of adult supervision to direct and clarify. The activities link to the idea that an adult in your setting will be supervising the whole of continuous provision and within this role will take 'seized opportunities' similar to teachable moments to informally pause and gather children to initiate interest or steer thinking. This is different to structured, guided, focus activities, formally led by a specified adult at a planned time. However, these activities are flexible and could easily be adapted if a structured, guided approach is preferred.

Activity outline and preparation

Each activity begins with 'Activity outline and preparation', which provides you with a brief explanation of the activity and highlights any resources you will need. Preparation tips are also bullet pointed to offer clear support and guidance about items that need creating or gathering prior to the activity commencing.

Activity development

This section within the activity lists the planning guidance grids that clearly match activity to goals and actual practice to help you with planning. There is also a 'Characteristics of effective learning' planning grid, which further consolidates planning support and links to early years guidance.

Activity guidance

The 'Activity guidance' focuses the activity with a clear aim and suggests how you and other adults can initiate or sustain children's interest in the activity.

Activity in practice

This section provides further detail (additional to comments already provided on the planning guidance grid) about *how* the activity should look like in practice and *how* the activity develops the children within all prime and specific areas in practice. Again, this embraces the practical element of the book which aims to provide you with hands-on ideas and support.

Possible next steps and opportunities for further development

In the 'Possible next steps and opportunities for further development' section, suggestions about future links that will consolidate the initial activity are detailed. Again, further comments about these activities in practice and ideas for supporting children are listed in additional boxes.

Final thoughts and reflections

This section encourages you to engage with contemplative considerations, reflections and further thoughts about the activity. It helps you identify the activity within a bigger picture and consider the educational journey that children in your setting have been or will be engaged with prior to and beyond the activity.

Resource support

Some activities have an example 'Resource support' at the end if applicable. This section provides resource examples to support the activity for you to photocopy or copy and adapt.

References

DfE (2016) *Eliminating Unnecessary Workload Around Planning and Teaching Resources: Report of the Independent Teacher Workload Review Group*. London: DfE.

Ofsted (2017) *Bold Beginnings: The Reception Curriculum in a Sample of Good and Outstanding Primary Schools*. London: DfE.

References to key documents used throughout the text

DfE (2013) *Early years outcomes: A non-statutory guide for practitioners and inspectors to help inform understanding of child development through the early years*. London: DFE.

DfE (2017) *Statutory framework for the early years foundation stage: Setting the standards for learning, development and care for children from birth to five*. London: DFE.

Early Education (2012) *Development Matters in the Early Years Foundation Stage (EYFS)*. London: Early Education.

CHAPTER 1

LEARNING THREAD
BEACHES AND BLUE SEAS

Beaches and Blue Seas

In this chapter

In this chapter, you will find activities related to beaches, holidays and underwater sea worlds. This learning thread links to:

- sensory discovery and exploration through activities such as 'secret shells' and 'mysteries of the sea'

- imaginative discovery via 'underwater world'

- exploration and construction through 'splendid sand'

- reflections upon experiences from the children's world through 'happy holidays!' and 'wish you were here' activities.

The activities in this chapter will help you to work towards:

- encouraging children to reflect upon experiences from the world around them and express this imaginatively and creatively

- developing children's sensory processing and skills through exploration and discovery.

Activities

Activity		Page	Provision
1	Secret shells	3	Continuous provision indoors or outdoors
2	Underwater world	9	Continuous provision indoors or outdoors
3	Happy holidays!	15	Continuous provision indoors
4	Splendid sand	21	Continuous provision indoors or outdoors
5	Wish you were here!	27	Continuous provision indoors or outdoors
6	Mysteries of the sea	33	Continuous provision indoors or outdoors

Role-play area links:

- Travel agents

- Under the sea play area with blue voile curtains so children can 'swim' in and out, pebbles, sea creature toys, sea creature masks, mask and snorkels

- Beach area (outdoors) with sand, deckchairs, windbreak, parasol, etc.

Activity 1 Secret shells

Activity outline and preparation

This sensory activity encourages the children to predict and discover through their sense of touch using a feely bag or box. The feely box or bag needs to be big enough so the children can easily touch and feel (with both hands if possible) a selection of shaped shells. The activity is intended to develop children's descriptive vocabulary in relation to what they 'feel' therefore aim to secure the box or bag so the children are not tempted to 'look' instead.

Resources

- Secure feely box/es or bag/s
- Selection of different shaped and sized shells to place inside the box/bag – try to source starfish and sea urchins as well as these have unusual textures and shapes
- Shell word wall and Post-it notes
- Pencils

Preparation

- Create a secure feely box or bag so the children can place one or two hands inside and feel but not see. Add different sized and shaped shells.
- Create a shell word wall with pre-labelled 'texture' adjectives (feely words) e.g. smooth, spiky, soft, etc. on Post-it notes (30-50 months) or blank Post-it notes (40-60+ months).

Activity development

ESSENTIAL LITERACY AND MATHEMATICS DEVELOPMENT

PRIME AREAS		Development guidance	SPECIFIC AREAS		Development guidance
COMMUNICATION AND LANGUAGE	Listening and attention	**30-50 months** *Focusing attention - still listen and do, but can shift own attention (listening to others while exploring shells)* **40-60+ months** *Two-channelled attention - can listen and do for short span* **ELG** *Children listen attentively in a range of situations. They listen to stories, accurately anticipating key events and respond to what they hear with relevant comments, questions or actions. They give their attention to what others say and respond appropriately, while engaged in another activity. (simultaneous listening and exploring of shells in boxes or bags)*	**LITERACY**	Reading	**30-50 months** *Knows information can be relayed in the form of print (texture adjectives on shell word wall)* **40-60+ months** *Begins to read words and simple sentences. (texture adjectives on shell word wall)* **ELG** *Children read and understand simple sentences. They use phonic knowledge to decode regular words and read them aloud accurately. They also read some common irregular words. They demonstrate understanding when talking with others about what they have read. (texture adjectives on shell word wall)*
				Writing	**30-50 months** *Sometimes gives meaning to marks as they draw and paint. (some children may add marks to Post-it notes)* **40-60+ months** *Uses some clearly identifiable letters to communicate meaning, representing some sounds correctly and in sequence.* **ELG** *Children use their phonic knowledge to write words in ways which match their spoken sounds. They also write some irregular common words. They write simple sentences, which can be read by themselves and others. Some words are spelt correctly and others are phonetically plausible. (sounding out phonetically plausible texture adjectives to add to Post-it notes)*
	Understanding	**30-50 months** *Shows understanding of prepositions such as 'under', 'on top', 'behind' by carrying out an action or selecting correct picture. (understanding how to locate shells in box or bag)* **40-60+ months** *Listens and responds to ideas expressed by others in conversation or discussion.* **ELG** *Children follow instructions involving several ideas or actions. They answer 'how' and 'why' questions about their experiences and in response to stories or events. (responding to others' ideas while exploring shells and following basic instructions about feeling shells in box or bag)*	**MATHEMATICS**	Numbers	**30-50 months** *Uses some number names and number language spontaneously (spontaneous use of number language related to shells, e.g. counting of starfish legs)* **40-60+ months** *Estimates how many objects they can see and checks by counting them (estimation and spontaneous counting of shells in the box or bag while exploring)*
	Speaking	**30-50 months** *Uses vocabulary focused on objects and people that are of particular importance to them.* *Builds up vocabulary that reflects the breadth of their experiences. (development and use of vocabulary related to shells and textures)* **40-60+ months** *Extends vocabulary, especially by grouping and naming, exploring the meaning and sounds of new words (vocabulary related to shells and textures)* **ELG** *Children express themselves effectively, showing awareness of listeners' needs. They use past, present and future forms accurately when talking about events that have happened or are to happen in the future. They develop their own narratives and explanations by connecting ideas or events. (while exploring shells alongside others)*		Shape, space and measure	**30-50 months** *Beginning to talk about shapes of everyday objects (while feeling shell shapes in box or bag)* **40-60+ months** *Can describe their relative position such as 'behind' or 'next to'* **ELG** *Children use everyday language to talk about size, weight, capacity, position, distance, time and money to compare quantities and objects and to solve problems. They recognise, create and describe patterns. They explore characteristics of everyday objects and shapes and use mathematical language to describe them. (using everyday and some mathematical language whilst exploring and feeling shell shapes in box or bag)*

CHARACTERISTICS OF EFFECTIVE LEARNING	Suggested outcomes
Playing and exploring – *engagement*	**Using sense of touch to explore and describe shells**
Active learning – *motivation*	**Persistence while exploring shells in feely box or bag**
Creating and thinking critically – *thinking*	**Making links between touch, textures and describing vocabulary**

PRIME AREAS		Development guidance	SPECIFIC AREAS		Development guidance
PHYSICAL DEVELOPMENT	Moving and handling	**40-60+ months** *Begins to form recognisable letters.* *Uses a pencil and holds it effectively to form recognisable letters, most of which are correctly formed (while adding texture adjectives to Post-it notes)*	UNDERSTANDING THE WORLD	People and communities	
				The world	**30-50 months** *Comments and asks questions about aspects of their familiar world such as the place where they live or the natural world (shells from their natural world)* **40-60+ months** *Looks closely at similarities, differences, patterns and change* **ELG** *Children know about similarities and differences in relation to places, objects, materials and living things. They talk about the features of their own immediate environment and how environments might vary from one another. They make observations of animals and plants and explain why some things occur, and talk about changes. (recognition of similarities and differences in shell textures)*
				Technology	
	Health and self-care		EXPRESSIVE ARTS AND DESIGN	Exploring and using media and materials	**30-50 months** *Beginning to be interested in and describe the texture of things (interested and describing shell textures)* **ELG** *Children sing songs, make music and dance, and experiment with ways of changing them. They safely use and explore a variety of materials, tools and techniques, experimenting with colour, design, texture, form and function. (exploration of materials via shell textures and form in feely box or bag)*
				Being imaginative	
PERSONAL, SOCIAL AND EMOTIONAL DEVELOPMENT	Making relationships	**30-50 months** *Initiates play, offering cues to peers to join them (encouraging others to join in exploring shells in feely boxes or bags)* **40-60+ months** *Initiates conversations, attends to and takes account of what others say.* **ELG** *Children play co-operatively, taking turns with others. They take account of one another's ideas about how to organise their activity. They show sensitivity to others' needs and feelings, and form positive relationships with adults and other children. (conversations while exploring when taking turns with feely boxes or bags)*			
	Self-confidence and self-awareness	**30-50 months** *Confident to talk to other children when playing (confidence discussing shell textures)* **ELG** *Children are confident to try new activities, and say why they like some activities more than others. They are confident to speak in a familiar group, will talk about their ideas, and will choose the resources they need for their chosen activities. They say when they do or don't need help. (confidence exploring shells in feely boxes or bags)*			
	Managing feelings and behaviour	**30-50 months** *Begins to accept the need to and can take turns and share resources, sometimes with support from others (while sharing feely boxes or bags)* **40-60+ months** *Aware of the boundaries set and behavioural expectations in the setting (aware of behaviour while exploring shells and boxes/bags)* **ELG** *Children talk about how they and others show feelings, talk about their own and others' behaviour, and its consequences, and know that some behaviour is unacceptable. They work as part of a group or class, and understand and follow the rules. They adjust their behaviour to different situations, and take changes of routine in their stride. (working within a group sharing feely boxes or bags and discussing ideas about shells and textures)*			

Activity guidance

This is a continuous provision activity that aims to develop children's descriptive vocabulary through sensory exploration.

Organise the feely boxes or bags and prepare the shell word wall with Post-it notes nearby.

To initiate interest ask some children to try the feely box/bag and talk about what they can feel inside. Scaffold their description by asking questions such as 'what does it feel like?' 'What words would describe the object?' Encourage the children to feel and describe as opposed to guessing what the object is.

After children have independently explored for a while, return to the activity to encourage some children to record on Post-it notes and add to the shell word wall.

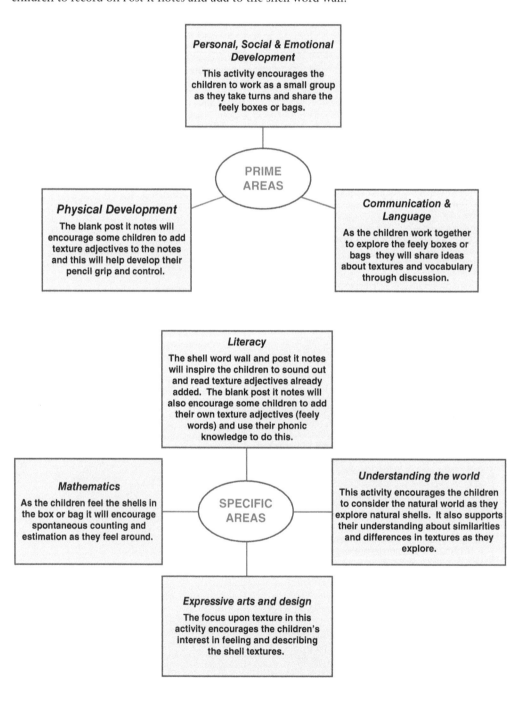

Personal, Social & Emotional Development

This activity encourages the children to work as a small group as they take turns and share the feely boxes or bags.

PRIME AREAS

Physical Development

The blank post it notes will encourage some children to add texture adjectives to the notes and this will help develop their pencil grip and control.

Communication & Language

As the children work together to explore the feely boxes or bags they will share ideas about textures and vocabulary through discussion.

Literacy

The shell word wall and post it notes will inspire the children to sound out and read texture adjectives already added. The blank post it notes will also encourage some children to add their own texture adjectives (feely words) and use their phonic knowledge to do this.

SPECIFIC AREAS

Mathematics

As the children feel the shells in the box or bag it will encourage spontaneous counting and estimation as they feel around.

Understanding the world

This activity encourages the children to consider the natural world as they explore natural shells. It also supports their understanding about similarities and differences in textures as they explore.

Expressive arts and design

The focus upon texture in this activity encourages the children's interest in feeling and describing the shell textures.

Possible next steps and opportunities for further development

Feely trays

To consolidate textures and feeling further, repeat the activity using trays or baskets to add variety and focus upon new objects to discover. Fruits and vegetables are good for textures and shapes.

Some children will benefit from other sensory activities that encourage feeling textures such as exploration of sensory baskets.

Creative textures

Explore textures further through creative activities such as shell and fruit printing (pineapples and avocadoes are great for this) or rubbings.

Final thoughts and reflections

Observation and observational skills are crucial but consider how this sense can also dominate. This activity encourages the children to 'feel' instead of 'look' (observe) and this develops the children's sense of touch without the influence of sight.

Consider the impact of developing early vocabulary to ensure language gaps do not occur. This activity focuses upon feeling and describing while the shell word wall helps to capture some of the vocabulary.

9

Activity 2 Underwater world

Activity outline and preparation

This sensory activity encourages the children to play imaginatively as they create and explore an underwater world in the water tray.

It is a good idea to share an underwater story with the children before they begin in order to ignite their interest and imagination.

To create the underwater world, the children will need a water tray or water tanks as well as sea creature plastic toys, pebbles and foliage.

Resources

- Water tray or water tanks (you can use cheap, plastic fish tanks)

- Plastic sea creatures (labelled)

- Foliage (real pond weed works well or use artificial foliage)

- Pebbles and small rocks

- Food colouring (if you wish to change the colour of the water)

- Paper, pencils, crayons

- Underwater stories such as *Fidgety Fish*, *Smiley Shark*, Octonaut stories or poems such as 'Commotion in the Ocean'

Preparation

- Half fill the water tray or small tanks with water and add colouring if you wish to add colour to the water.

- Label plastic sea creatures and ensure pebbles and rocks are clean. Organise foliage (wash if using real foliage) and any other resources for the children to choose and use. Arrange these resources in baskets near the water tray.

- Arrange paper, pencils and crayons next to the activity so children can create underwater pictures.

Activity development

ESSENTIAL LITERACY AND MATHEMATICS DEVELOPMENT				
PRIME AREAS		**Development guidance**	**SPECIFIC AREAS**	**Development guidance**
COMMUNICATION AND LANGUAGE	Listening and attention	**30-50 months** *Listens to stories with increasing attention and recall (underwater sea story before children explore activity)* *Listens to others one to one or in small groups, when conversation interests them (as they explore and play imaginatively)* **40-60+ months** *Two-channelled attention – can listen and do for short span* **ELG** *Children listen attentively in a range of situations. They listen to stories, accurately anticipating key events and respond to what they hear with relevant comments, questions or actions. They give their attention to what others say and respond appropriately, while engaged in another activity. (simultaneous listening and underwater imaginative play)*	LITERACY / Reading	**30-50 months** *Listens and joins in with stories and poems, one to one and also in small groups.* *Listens to stories with increasing attention and recall (underwater stories or poems shared before activity begins)* **40-60+ months** *Hears and says the initial sound in words.* *Can segment sounds in simple words and blend them together and knows which letters represent some of them* **ELG** *Children read and understand simple sentences. They use phonic knowledge to decode regular words and read them aloud accurately. They also read some common irregular words. They demonstrate understanding when talking with others about what they have read. (segmenting and using other phonic skills to read plastic sea creature labels)*
			Writing	**30-50 months** *Sometimes gives meaning to marks as they draw and paint. (some children may add mark making to underwater sea picture)* **40-60+ months** *Gives meaning to marks they make as they draw, write and paint.* **ELG** *Children use their phonic knowledge to write words in ways which match their spoken sounds. They also write some irregular common words. They write simple sentences which can be read by themselves and others. Some words are spelt correctly and others are phonetically plausible. (mark making and sounding out phonetically plausible words to underwater sea picture)*
	Under-standing	**30-50 months** *Understands use of objects (understanding of objects to recreate underwater world)* **40-60+ months** *Listens and responds to ideas expressed by others in conversation or discussion* **ELG** *Children follow instructions involving several ideas or actions. They answer 'how' and 'why' questions about their experiences and in response to stories or events. (responding to others' ideas while creating an underwater world inspired by an underwater story)*	MATHEMATICS / Numbers	**30-50 months** *Knows that numbers identify how many objects are in a set (links between numbers and counting of sea creatures in set)* **40-60+ months** *Estimates how many objects they can see and checks by counting them (estimation and spontaneous counting of pebbles, rocks and sea creatures while imaginatively playing with an underwater world)* **ELG** *Children count reliably with numbers from one to 20, place them in order and say which number is one more or one less than a given number. Using quantities and objects, they add and subtract two single-digit numbers and count on or back to find the answer. They solve problems, including doubling, halving and sharing. (counting reliably to 20 whilst arranging sea creatures and other resources in an underwater world.)*
	Speaking	**30-50 months** *Uses vocabulary focused on objects and people that are of particular importance to them.* *Builds up vocabulary that reflects the breadth of their experiences. (development and use of vocabulary related to story and underwater)* **40-60+ months** *Uses language to imagine and recreate roles and experiences in play situations (language inspired by an underwater story during imaginative play in an underwater world)* **ELG** *Children express themselves effectively, showing awareness of listeners' needs. They use past, present and future forms accurately when talking about events that have happened or are to happen in the future. They develop their own narratives and explanations by connecting ideas or events. (connections between an underwater story and imaginative play in an underwater world)*	Shape, space and measure	**30-50 months** *Shows an interest in shape and space by playing with shapes or making arrangements with objects (exploring shapes while building an underwater world)* **40-60+ months** *Can describe their relative position such as 'behind' or 'next to'* **ELG** *Children use everyday language to talk about size, weight, capacity, position, distance, time and money to compare quantities and objects and to solve problems. They recognise, create and describe patterns. They explore characteristics of everyday objects and shapes and use mathematical language to describe them. (using everyday language to talk whilst positioning objects in underwater world and exploring all object shapes)*

CHARACTERISTICS OF EFFECTIVE LEARNING	Suggested outcomes
Playing and exploring – *engagement*	**Engaging in open ended imaginative water play**
Active learning – *motivation*	**Paying attention to detail while arranging underwater world**
Creating and thinking critically – *thinking*	**Making links between story ideas and imaginative water play**

PRIME AREAS		Development guidance	SPECIFIC AREAS		Development guidance
PHYSICAL DEVELOPMENT	Moving and handling	**30-50 months** *Holds pencil between thumb and two fingers, no longer using whole-hand grasp. (while mark making and drawing underwater picture)* **40-60+ months** *Begins to form recognisable letters.* *Uses a pencil and holds it effectively to form recognisable letters, most of which are correctly formed.* **ELG** *Children show good control and co-ordination in large and small movements. They move confidently in a range of ways, safely negotiating space. They handle equipment and tools effectively, including pencils for writing. (handling equipment whilst mark making and word-writing on underwater sea picture)*	UNDERSTANDING THE WORLD	People and communities	
				The world	**30-50 months** *Can talk about some of the things they have observed such as plants, animals, natural and found objects (plastic sea creatures, rocks, pebbles and foliage to create underwater world)* **40-60+ months** *Looks closely at similarities, differences, patterns and change* **ELG** *Children know about similarities and differences in relation to places, objects, materials and living things. They talk about the features of their own immediate environment and how environments might vary from one another. They make observations of animals and plants and explain why some things occur, and talk about changes. (observations and recognition of some similarities/differences of plastic sea creatures, rocks and foliage whilst creating underwater world)*
				Technology	
	Health and self-care	**30-50 months** *Understands that equipment and tools have to be used safely (awareness about playing safely in the water and trying to keep the floor dry)* **40-60+ months** *Practises some appropriate safety measures without direct supervision (understanding about playing safely in the water and not leaving wet toys or other resources on the floor where others could slip)*	EXPRESSIVE ARTS AND DESIGN	Exploring and using media and materials	**30-50 months** *Beginning to be interested in and describe the texture of things (interested and describing pebble, rock and foliage textures)* **40-60+ months** *Constructs with a purpose in mind, using a variety of resources (using variety of resources for creation of underwater world, inspired by story and using imagination)*
				Being imaginative	**30-50 months** *Uses available resources to create props to support role-play (use of resources to create underwater world to play with)* **40-60+ months** *Introduces a storyline or narrative into their play (while imaginatively playing with underwater world)*
PERSONAL, SOCIAL AND EMOTIONAL DEVELOPMENT	Making relation-ships	**30-50 months** *Initiates play, offering cues to peers to join them (encouraging others to join in exploring shells in feely boxes or bags)* **40-60+ months** *Initiates conversations, attends to and takes account of what others say* **ELG** *Children play co-operatively, taking turns with others. They take account of one another's ideas about how to organise their activity. They show sensitivity to others' needs and feelings, and form positive relationships with adults and other children. (conversations whilst exploring and taking turns with feely boxes or bags)*			
	Self-confidence and self-awareness	**30-50 months** *Confident to talk to other children when playing, and will communicate freely about own home and community. (confidence when discussing shell textures and ideas related to this)* **ELG** *Children are confident to try new activities, and say why they like some activities more than others. They are confident to speak in a familiar group, will talk about their ideas, and will choose the resources they need for their chosen activities. They say when they do or don't need help. (confidence trying the activity and when exploring shells in feely boxes or bags)*			
	Managing feelings and behaviour	**30-50 months** *Begins to accept needs and can take turns and share resources, sometimes with support from others (while sharing feely boxes or bags)* **40-60+ months** *Aware of the boundaries set and behavioural expectations in the setting (aware of behaviour while exploring shells and boxes/bags)* **ELG** *Children talk about how they and others show feelings, talk about their own and others' behaviour, and its consequences, and know that some behaviour is unacceptable. They work as part of a group or class, and understand and follow the rules. They adjust their behaviour to different situations, and take changes of routine in their stride. (working within a group sharing feely boxes or bags sensibly)*			

Activity guidance

This is a continuous provision sensory activity that aims to develop children's imaginative play.

Prepare the water tray and organise labelled plastic sea creatures, pebbles, rocks, foliage and other items in baskets nearby. Ensure blank paper, pencils and crayons are available near the activity.

To initiate interest gather a small group of children to share an underwater story such as *Fidgety Fish* or *Smiley Shark*. While sharing the story, draw attention to the underwater sea environment. Once the story is complete, ask the children whether they could create an underwater world similar to the story. Show the children the resources and explain that paper and crayons are available to capture a picture afterwards.

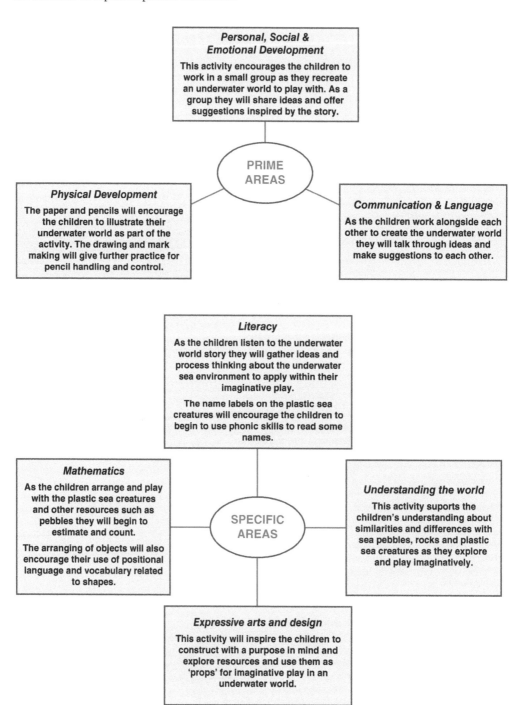

Personal, Social & Emotional Development

This activity encourages the children to work in a small group as they recreate an underwater world to play with. As a group they will share ideas and offer suggestions inspired by the story.

PRIME AREAS

Physical Development

The paper and pencils will encourage the children to illustrate their underwater world as part of the activity. The drawing and mark making will give further practice for pencil handling and control.

Communication & Language

As the children work alongside each other to create the underwater world they will talk through ideas and make suggestions to each other.

Literacy

As the children listen to the underwater world story they will gather ideas and process thinking about the underwater sea environment to apply within their imaginative play.

The name labels on the plastic sea creatures will encourage the children to begin to use phonic skills to read some names.

Mathematics

As the children arrange and play with the plastic sea creatures and other resources such as pebbles they will begin to estimate and count.

The arranging of objects will also encourage their use of positional language and vocabulary related to shapes.

SPECIFIC AREAS

Understanding the world

This activity suports the children's understanding about similarities and differences with sea pebbles, rocks and plastic sea creatures as they explore and play imaginatively.

Expressive arts and design

This activity will inspire the children to construct with a purpose in mind and explore resources and use them as 'props' for imaginative play in an underwater world.

Possible next steps and opportunities for further development

Further imaginative play

To consolidate imaginative play within the water further, explore adding new resources such as a cave or castle (use fish tank toys or familiar sea toys such as Octonaut toys) to encourage the children to play out new ideas and stories. Another twist on this activity is to replace the water tray with a paddling pool so children can explore with shoes and socks off. This will need closer supervision for safety though!

The sensory element to the underwater play will benefit some children more than others. For those who are ready, consider the vocabulary and writing that can develop from repeated consolidation of imaginative play within a common theme.

Links to events

Imaginative play can also take a new turn when linked to events from the world around us. Consider stories from the news, e.g. an oil spillage in the sea, to pose a problem for the children to solve. Add black food colouring to the water and encourage the children to work as a group to save and clean the sea creatures from the underwater, now polluted, world.

Final thoughts and reflections

Reflect upon children engaging in imaginative play inspired by stories. In addition to this, consider how the use of 'props' helps to recreate story ideas, adding direction and opportunities to develop related vocabulary.

Consider the importance of imaginative play linked with problem-solving and real-life events. Adding real-life purpose will often capture the children's interest and build in new motivation.

Activity 3 Happy holidays!

Activity outline and preparation

This activity inspires the children to reflect upon a happy holiday or other family times and to share these memories. It involves creating a group or class photo album so children can add their own family holiday photo alongside illustrations and marks. If there are children in the setting who do not have any family holiday photos then encourage a photo related to another family time, e.g. a day visit to a zoo, theme park or a trip to the cinema or theatre.

Resources

- Group or class blank photo album – use a blank scrapbook so there is plenty of space on each page for children to add their photos alongside illustrations or other marks

- Complete the first page/s with a WAGOLL ('What A Good One Looks Like') by adding a/ some staff family photos with simple illustrations and words/simple sentences to begin

- Pencils, crayons

- Glue, scissors

Preparation

- Organise or create the group/class photo album.

- Ask the children to bring in one holiday family photo/other family visit photo or request emailed photos. Set time aside to collect the photos or print these off with the children in preparation for the activity.

Activity development

ESSENTIAL LITERACY AND MATHEMATICS DEVELOPMENT				
PRIME AREAS		**Development guidance**	**SPECIFIC AREAS**	**Development guidance**
COMMUNICATION AND LANGUAGE	Listening and attention	**30-50 months** *Listens to stories with increasing attention and recall (shared discussion stories about family holidays in conjunction with photos)* **ELG** *Children listen attentively in a range of situations. They listen to stories, accurately anticipating key events and respond to what they hear with relevant comments, questions or actions. They give their attention to what others say and respond appropriately, while engaged in another activity. (listening and sharing discussion stories about family times in conjunction with photos)*	LITERACY / Reading	**30-50 months** *Holds books the correct way up and turns pages (handling of class photo album)* **40-60+ months** *Begins to read words and simple sentences* **ELG** *Children read and understand simple sentences. They use phonic knowledge to decode regular words and read them aloud accurately. They also read some common irregular words. They demonstrate understanding when talking with others about what they have read. (reading of others' words or simple sentences in class photo album)*
			Writing	**30-50 months** *Sometimes give meaning to marks as they draw and paint (some children may add mark-making and illustrations alongside family photo)* **40-60+ months** *Gives meaning to marks they make as they draw, write and paint* **ELG** *Children use their phonic knowledge to write words in ways which match their spoken sounds. They also write some irregular common words. They write simple sentences which can be read by themselves and others. Some words are spelt correctly and others are phonetically plausible. (mark making and sounding out phonetically plausible words or simple sentences alongside family photo in album).*
	Understanding	**30-50 months** *Responds to simple instructions (instructions/guidance - sticking photo in album and adding an illustration or marks)* **ELG** *Children follow instructions involving several ideas or actions. They answer 'how' and 'why' questions about their experiences and in response to stories or events. (following simple instructions/guidance regarding sticking photo in album and adding illustrations, words or simple sentences)*	MATHEMATICS / Numbers	**30-50 months** *Uses some number names and number language spontaneously (while looking at photos in album, e.g. these are my 'two' sisters)* **40-60+ months** *Recognise some numerals of personal significance. (while discussing own and others' family photos in the album, e.g. these are my 'two' sisters)*
	Speaking	**30-50 months** *Beginning to use more complex sentences to link thoughts (while talking a little about family photo)* **40-60+ months** *Uses talk to organise, sequence and clarify thinking, ideas, feelings and events (while talking about family photo)* **ELG** *Children express themselves effectively, showing awareness of listeners' needs. They use past, present and future forms accurately when talking about events that have happened or are to happen in the future. They develop their own narratives and explanations by connecting ideas or events. (talking about family photo and future related events)*	Shape, space and measure	**30-50 months** *Shows awareness of similarities of shapes in the environment (while discussing their own and others' photos in the album)* **40-60+ months** *Orders and sequences familiar events.* *Uses everyday language related to time.* **ELG** *Children use everyday language to talk about size, weight, capacity, position, distance, time and money to compare quantities and objects and to solve problems. They recognise, create and describe patterns. They explore characteristics of everyday objects and shapes and use mathematical language to describe them. (in relation to time whilst discussing own family photo)*

CHARACTERISTICS OF EFFECTIVE LEARNING	Suggested outcomes
Playing and exploring – *engagement*	**Showing curiosity about other children's families and their family events.**
Active learning – *motivation*	**Maintaining focus while adding their photo to the album.**
Creating and thinking critically – *thinking*	**Thinking of memories and ideas to accompany family photo in album.**

PRIME AREAS		Development guidance	SPECIFIC AREAS		Development guidance
PHYSICAL DEVELOPMENT	Moving and handling	**30-50 months** *Holds pencil between thumb and two fingers, no longer using whole-hand grasp (while mark making and drawing alongside family photo in album)* **40-60+ months** *Begins to form recognisable letters.* *Uses a pencil and holds it effectively to form recognisable letters, most of which are correctly formed* **ELG** *Children show good control and co-ordination in large and small movements. They move confidently in a range of ways, safely negotiating space. They handle equipment and tools effectively, including pencils for writing. (using equipment whilst illustrating, mark making and writing simple word/sentences alongside family photo in album)*	UNDERSTANDING THE WORLD	People and communities	**30-50 months** *Remembers and talks about significant events in their own experience. (recall and discussion of family happy memories).* **ELG** *Children talk about past and present events in their own lives and in the lives of family members. They know that other children don't always enjoy the same things, and are sensitive to this. They know about similarities and differences between themselves and others, and among families, communities and traditions. (discussion about happy family memories)*
				The world	
				Technology	**30-50 months** *Knows that information can be retrieved from computers. (supporting children with retrieval of photos to print from emails)* **ELG** *Children recognise that a range of technology is used in places such as homes and schools. They select and use technology for particular purposes. (supported retrieval of photos from emails)*
PHYSICAL DEVELOPMENT	Health and self-care		EXPRESSIVE ARTS AND DESIGN	Exploring and using media and materials	
				Being imaginative	
PERSONAL, SOCIAL AND EMOTIONAL DEVELOPMENT	Making relation-ships	**30-50 months** *Initiates play, offering cues to peers to join them (encouraging others to add to the photo album and sharing their photos)* **40-60+ months** *Initiates conversations, attends to and takes account of what others say* **ELG** *Children play co-operatively, taking turns with others. They take account of one another's ideas about how to organise their activity. They show sensitivity to others' needs and feelings, and form positive relationships with adults and other children. (taking turns co-operatively with the photo album)*			
	Self-confidence and self-awareness	**30-50 months** *Can select and use activities and resources with help (adding to the album with some help if required)* **ELG** *Children are confident to try new activities, and say why they like some activities more than others. They are confident to speak in a familiar group, will talk about their ideas, and will choose the resources they need for their chosen activities. They say when they do or don't need help. (confidence adding photo to the album and associated illustrations and mark makings. Asking for help if they need it.)*			
	Managing feelings and behaviour	**30-50 months** *Begins to accept the need and can take turns and share resources, sometimes with support from others (sharing of photo album and resources, taking turns to add their photo)* **ELG** *Children talk about how they and others show feelings, talk about their own and others' behaviour, and its consequences, and know that some behaviour is unacceptable. They work as part of a group or class, and understand and follow the rules. They adjust their behaviour to different situations, and take changes of routine in their stride. (taking turns with photo album and understanding behaviour expectations with the album e.g. not to write on other children's photos/illustrations)*			

Activity guidance

This is a continuous provision activity that encourages children to reflect upon events from their own and others' family lives.

Organise the class/group photo album and begin by adding an example or some examples of staff family photos and simple words or short sentences. Work with children individually to print out any photos from emails after sending requests to parents and carers.

Set up the photo album with glue, scissors, pencils and crayons nearby.

To initiate interest chat to children about happy family holidays and use the photos you have received to structure this brief discussion. Encourage children to talk about their family photo and memories from the photo. Share the album with inserts from staff to provide an encouraging WAGOLL and explain how children can stick a photo on their own page and add drawings and words if they wish.

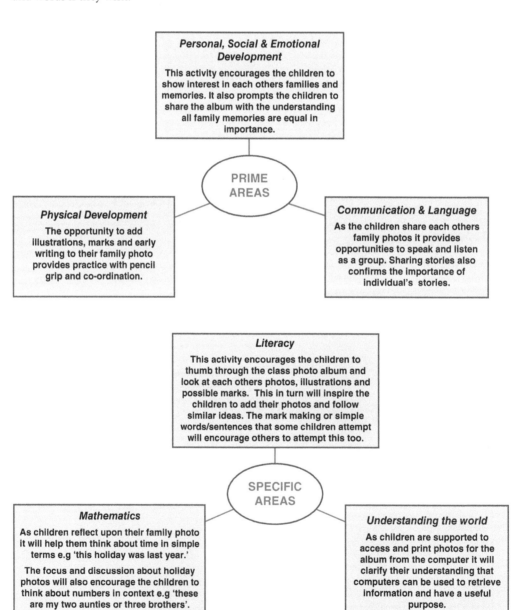

Personal, Social & Emotional Development

This activity encourages the children to show interest in each others families and memories. It also prompts the children to share the album with the understanding all family memories are equal in importance.

PRIME AREAS

Physical Development

The opportunity to add illustrations, marks and early writing to their family photo provides practice with pencil grip and co-ordination.

Communication & Language

As the children share each others family photos it provides opportunities to speak and listen as a group. Sharing stories also confirms the importance of individual's stories.

Literacy

This activity encourages the children to thumb through the class photo album and look at each others photos, illustrations and possible marks. This in turn will inspire the children to add their photos and follow similar ideas. The mark making or simple words/sentences that some children attempt will encourage others to attempt this too.

SPECIFIC AREAS

Mathematics

As children reflect upon their family photo it will help them think about time in simple terms e.g 'this holiday was last year.'

The focus and discussion about holiday photos will also encourage the children to think about numbers in context e.g 'these are my two aunties or three brothers'.

Understanding the world

As children are supported to access and print photos for the album from the computer it will clarify their understanding that computers can be used to retrieve information and have a useful purpose.

Possible next steps and opportunities for further development

Family stories

To further encourage children to talk about their family photo and associated memories, record their individual comments via short video shots. These can then be displayed via a video loop alongside the photo album.

Consider the impact of opportunities for further talk associated with the photos. Encouraging the children to keep talking about their photos will continue to develop their communication skills through the sharing of special family memories alongside a constant recap over mathematics in context via language associated with time and quantities.

Holidays in the past

To cement an understanding about families and build further upon the strong community links within the original activity, consider inviting grandparents into the setting to share their childhood holiday memories. Talk and photos from holidays 'long ago' will help the children make links with families in the past and further develop their mathematical understanding of time.

Final thoughts and reflections

Consider the strong links with people and communities within this activity. Making firm links with home and the children's familiar world not only adds comfort and familiarity for the children but taps into core principles of early years.

Value the impact of encouraging the children to talk alongside a familiar, structured photo. This will support the children to remember detail and memorable information that can prove difficult for some children from memory alone.

Activity 4 Splendid sand

Activity outline and preparation

This activity encourages the children to explore shape creation and construction with sand by building different sized and shaped sandcastles. It requires a sand pit or large sand tray and can link to current phonics and mathematics learning through choice of sand play resources – see list below.

Resources

- Sand pit or large sand tray and play sand

- Water to mix with sand - this often works well with water spray bottles. This encourages the children to spray and wet the sand but not soak it

- Different shaped sand buckets

- Flags to add to sandcastles – link this to mathematics by adding numbers to flags. To stretch further consider also adding in flags with + or – and = so number sentences can be constructed on top of the sandcastles. If addition or subtraction flags are used, consider providing counting apparatus also

- Spades, scoops, sieves and other sand play equipment

- Alphabet sand moulds – link this to phonics by adding in letter sand moulds that will spell some simple words related to the current phonic focus

Preparation

- Prepare the sand pit or sand tray with fresh sand and fill water spray bottles.

- Create and laminate number flags.

- Source and organise buckets, spades, scoops and other sand play equipment as well as alphabet sand moulds.

- Consider which alphabet sand moulds to use and ensure correct letters are available to spell words. Consider children's confidence with phonics: do you need to display a list of words they can copy and create?

Activity development

ESSENTIAL LITERACY AND MATHEMATICS DEVELOPMENT

PRIME AREAS		Development guidance	SPECIFIC AREAS		Development guidance
COMMUNICATION AND LANGUAGE	Listening and attention	**30-50 months** Is able to follow directions (if not directly focused on own choice of activity) *(following of simple directions about building sandcastles)* **40-60+ months** Two-channelled attention – can listen and do for short span **ELG** Children listen attentively in a range of situations. They listen to stories, accurately anticipating key events and respond to what they hear with relevant comments, questions or actions. They give their attention to what others say and respond appropriately, while engaged in another activity. *(listening to others around them whilst building sandcastles responding if they choose)*	LITERACY	Reading	**30-50 months** Knows information can be relayed in the form of print *(displayed list of simple phonic words that children can copy and create with sand moulds)* **40-60+ months** Begins to read words and simple sentences. **ELG** Children read and understand simple sentences. They use phonic knowledge to decode regular words and read them aloud accurately. They also read some common irregular words. They demonstrate understanding when talking with others about what they have read. *(using phonic knowledge to decode and words from displayed list or words created by sand moulds)*
				Writing	**30-50 months** Ascribes meanings to marks that they see in different places *(ascribe some meaning to words/partial words moulded in sand by others)* **ELG** Children use their phonic knowledge to write words in ways which match their spoken sounds. They also write some irregular common words. They write simple sentences which can be read by themselves and others. Some words are spelt correctly and others are phonetically plausible. *(using phonic knowledge to spell out words created with sand moulds)*
	Understanding	**30-50 months** Understands use of objects *(understands and uses correct equipment for digging, moulding and dampening sand)* **ELG** Children follow instructions involving several ideas or actions. They answer 'how' and 'why' questions about their experiences and in response to stories or events. *(following instructions/guidance about how to build sandcastles, add number flags and spell out words)*	MATHEMATICS	Numbers	**30-50 months** Uses some number names accurately in play *(while using number flags to display on sandcastles)* **ELG** Children count reliably with numbers from one to 20, place them in order and say which number is one more or one less than a given number. Using quantities and objects, they add and subtract two single-digit numbers and count on or back to find the answer. They solve problems, including doubling, halving and sharing. *(counting and ordering number flags on sandcastles. Some children will also add and subtract two single-digit numbers if number sentence flags are also provided)*
	Speaking	**30-50 months** Uses vocabulary focused on objects and people that are of particular importance to them *(use of vocabulary related to sandcastle building)* **40-60+ months** Uses talk to organise, sequence and clarify thinking, ideas, feelings and events *(talking through ideas whilst sandcastle building)* **ELG** Children express themselves effectively, showing awareness of listeners' needs. They use past, present and future forms accurately when talking about events that have happened or are to happen in the future. They develop their own narratives and explanations by connecting ideas or events. *(using narratives and explanations to connect previous experiences of building sandcastles with current activity)*		Shape, space and measure	**30-50 months** Shows an interest in shape and space by playing with shapes or making arrangements with objects *(playing with shapes as moulding and constructing with sand and equipment)* **40-60+ months** Uses familiar objects and common shapes to create and recreate patterns and build models *(using sand to build models and create shapes)*

CHARACTERISTICS OF EFFECTIVE LEARNING	Suggested outcomes
Playing and exploring – *engagement*	**Engaging in open-ended sandcastle building and construction**
Active learning – *motivation*	**Paying attention to detail as they mould sand carefully to create shapes**
Creating and thinking critically – *thinking*	**Solving problems and developing ideas until sand is correct moulding consistency**

PRIME AREAS		Development guidance	SPECIFIC AREAS		Development guidance
PHYSICAL DEVELOPMENT	Moving and handling	**30-50 months** Uses one-handed tools and equipment *(sand play equipment).* **40-60+ months** Uses simple tools to effect changes to materials Handles tools, objects, construction and malleable materials safely and with increasing control *(sensible use of sand equipment to construct with control)* **ELG** Children show good control and co-ordination in large and small movements. They move confidently in a range of ways, safely negotiating space. They handle equipment and tools effectively, including pencils for writing. *(effective handling of sand play equipment)*	UNDERSTANDING THE WORLD	People and communities	
				The world	**30-50 months** Talks about why things happen and how things work. *(talk whilst mixing sand with water and moulding)* **40-60+ months** Looks closely at similarities, differences, patterns and change. **ELG** Children know about similarities and differences in relation to places, objects, materials and living things. They talk about the features of their own immediate environment and how environments might vary from one another. They make observations of animals and plants and explain why some things occur, and talk about changes. *(exploring similarities and differences whilst exploring dry sand, wet sand, sand moulds and shapes)*
				Technology	
	Health and self-care	**30-50 months** Understands that equipment and tools have to be used safely *(sand play equipment)* **40-60+ months** Shows understanding of how to transport and store equipment safely *(sand play equipment)*	EXPRESSIVE ARTS AND DESIGN	Exploring and using media and materials	**30-50 months** Realises tools can be used for a purpose *(sand play equipment and tools)* **40-60+ months** Manipulates materials to achieve a planned effect Uses simple tools and techniques competently and appropriately Selects tools and techniques needed to shape, assemble and join materials they are using **ELG** Children sing songs, make music and dance, and experiment with ways of changing them. They safely use and explore a variety of materials, tools and techniques, experimenting with colour, design, texture, form and function. *(competently and safely exploring sand design, texture and form with sand play equipment and tools)*
				Being imaginative	
PERSONAL, SOCIAL AND EMOTIONAL DEVELOPMENT	Making relationships	**30-50 months** Keeps play going by responding to what others are saying or doing *(keeps sand play going by sharing ideas and imitating others)* **40-60+ months** Explains own knowledge and understanding and asks appropriate questions of others *(own knowledge and understanding about mixing sand carefully to carefully mould)* **ELG** Children play co-operatively, taking turns with others. They take account of one another's ideas about how to organise their activity. They show sensitivity to others' needs and feelings, and form positive relationships with adults and other children. *(sharing sand play equipment, flags and taking turns.)*			
	Self-confidence and self-awareness	**30-50 months** Confident to talk to other children when playing, and will communicate freely about own home and community *(confident chat while playing alongside other children in the sand)* **ELG** Children are confident to try new activities, and say why they like some activities more than others. They are confident to speak in a familiar group, will talk about their ideas, and will choose the resources they need for their chosen activities. They say when they do or don't need help. *(confident working within a group and choosing resources whilst playing in the sand).*			
	Managing feelings and behaviour	**30-50 months** Begins to accept the needs and can take turns and share resources, sometimes with support from others *(sharing of sand play equipment and resources).* **ELG** Children talk about how they and others show feelings, talk about their own and others' behaviour, and its consequences, and know that some behaviour is unacceptable. They work as part of a group or class, and understand and follow the rules. They adjust their behaviour to different situations, and take changes of routine in their stride. *(taking turns with sand play equipment and playing sensibly)*			

Activity guidance

This continuous provision activity aims to encourage children to construct and build while problem-solving about how to manipulate and mould sand successfully.

Prepare the sand pit or tray with fresh, soft sand. Organise and arrange water spray bottles, sand play equipment, flags and alphabet letter moulds in baskets or boxes nearby.

To initiate interest gather interested children around the sand pit/tray and talk through the available sand play equipment. Explain that children must explore how to 'create the best sand for moulding'. Show the number flags and alphabet letter moulds and encourage the children to use these resources too. Suggest a reward for the best sandcastles or moulded shapes.

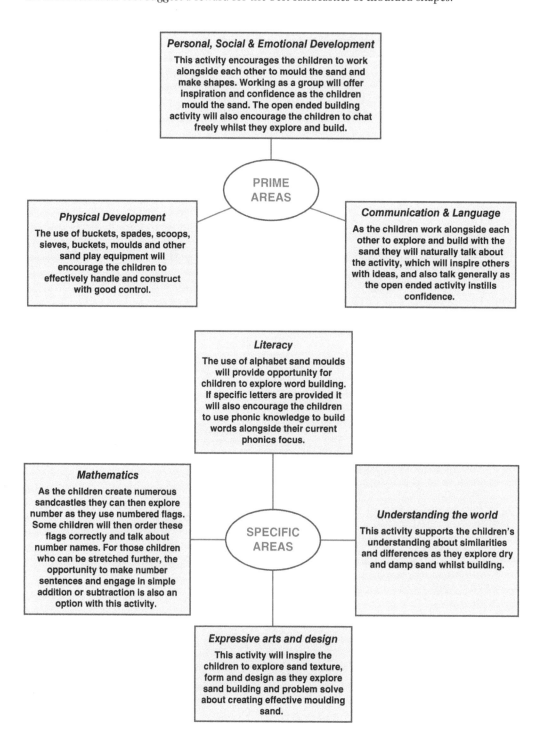

Personal, Social & Emotional Development

This activity encourages the children to work alongside each other to mould the sand and make shapes. Working as a group will offer inspiration and confidence as the children mould the sand. The open ended building activity will also encourage the children to chat freely whilst they explore and build.

PRIME AREAS

Physical Development

The use of buckets, spades, scoops, sieves, buckets, moulds and other sand play equipment will encourage the children to effectively handle and construct with good control.

Communication & Language

As the children work alongside each other to explore and build with the sand they will naturally talk about the activity, which will inspire others with ideas, and also talk generally as the open ended activity instils confidence.

Literacy

The use of alphabet sand moulds will provide opportunity for children to explore word building. If specific letters are provided it will also encourage the children to use phonic knowledge to build words alongside their current phonics focus.

Mathematics

As the children create numerous sandcastles they can then explore number as they use numbered flags. Some children will then order these flags correctly and talk about number names. For those children who can be stretched further, the opportunity to make number sentences and engage in simple addition or subtraction is also an option with this activity.

SPECIFIC AREAS

Understanding the world

This activity supports the children's understanding about similarities and differences as they explore dry and damp sand whilst building.

Expressive arts and design

This activity will inspire the children to explore sand texture, form and design as they explore sand building and problem solve about creating effective moulding sand.

Possible next steps and opportunities for further development

Mathematics and sand

Continue with the links to mathematics and consider adding different flags to completed sand-castles to support other learning in mathematics. This will open up opportunities to explore other areas such as 2D shapes, doubling, halving and simple money additions as well as positional language.

Consider how the practical links with sand building and mathematical concepts will help children grasp the mathematical content and cement understanding.

Sand art

To continue the exploration with sand, consider using different coloured sand for the children to explore and mix. Link this to creative activities as children create sand art pictures using different coloured sands and glue.

This further exploration and creation with coloured sand will help children who need further support with sensory development. The use of coloured sand is also good for encouraging children to use descriptive vocabulary as they mix and explore.

Final thoughts and reflections

Reflect upon the opportunities for problem-solving within this activity. It is important the children mix the correct consistency of sand to successfully build and mould and this is something they will solve through trial and error.

Consider how this activity encourages the children to develop their fine motor skills through repetitive play. For example, they will quickly understand that filled moulds/buckets will need to be tapped carefully and lifted with caution to ensure the moulded sand does not break apart.

Resource support: *Photocopiable examples of number flags*

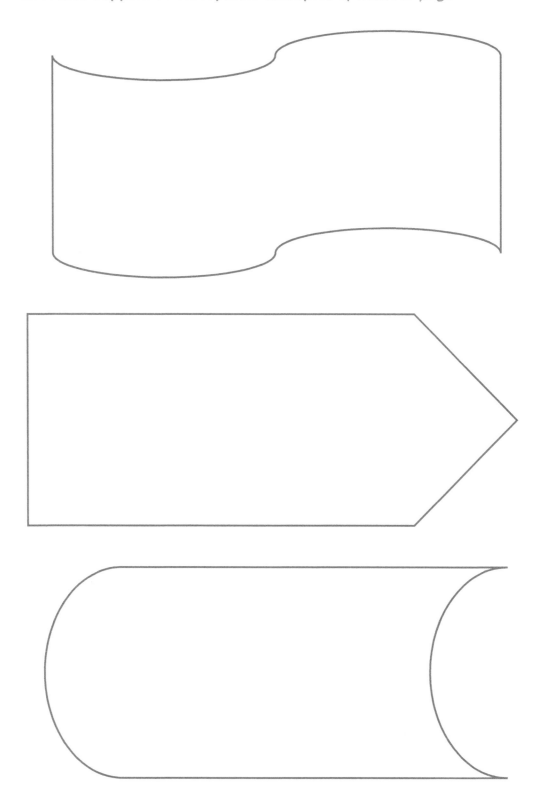

Activity 5 Wish you were here!

Activity outline and preparation

This activity encourages the children to reflect upon family special times, including holidays and day trips (not all children will have experienced full holidays) to create a postcard memory. It involves the children looking at holiday postcards and pictures to inspire their own postcard paintings.

Resources

- Selection of completed postcards (with stamps) or holiday images online or from magazines, brochures

- A3 paper

- Paints, brushes, easels and other painting equipment

Preparation

- Collect completed postcards and magazines from different holiday locations.

- Organise paints, brushes and other painting equipment.

- Collect sheets of A3 paper – this allows the children to paint in large-scale.

Activity development

ESSENTIAL LITERACY AND MATHEMATICS DEVELOPMENT

PRIME AREAS		Development guidance	SPECIFIC AREAS		Development guidance
COMMUNICATION AND LANGUAGE	Listening and attention	**30-50 months** *Focusing attention – still listen or do, but can shift own attention (focusing upon painting postcard)* **40-60+ months** *Two-channelled attention – can listen and do for short span* ***ELG** Children listen attentively in a range of situations. They listen to stories, accurately anticipating key events and respond to what they hear with relevant comments, questions or actions. They give their attention to what others say and respond appropriately, while engaged in another activity. (able to paint postcard and listen to conversation around them simultaneously)*	LITERACY	Reading	**30-50 months** *Knows information can be relayed in the form of print (writing on postcards)* **40-60+ months** *Begins to read words and simple sentences* ***ELG** Children read and understand simple sentences. They use phonic knowledge to decode regular words and read them aloud accurately. They also read some common irregular words. They demonstrate understanding when talking with others about what they have read. (reading of simple words and sentences on postcards)*
				Writing	**30-50 months** *Ascribes meanings to marks that they see in different places (words on completed postcards)* **40-60+ months** *Uses some clearly identifiable letters to communicate meaning, representing some sounds correctly and in sequence* ***ELG** Children use their phonic knowledge to write words in ways, which match their spoken sounds. They also write some irregular common words* *They write simple sentences which can be read by themselves and others. Some words are spelt correctly and others are phonetically plausible. (using phonic knowledge to spell out words while writing a sentence on the back of their painted postcard)*
	Understanding	**30-50 months** *Understands use of objects (paintbrushes and other painting equipment)* **40-60+ months** *Listens and responds to ideas expressed by others in conversation or discussion.* ***ELG** Children follow instructions involving several ideas or actions. They answer 'how' and 'why' questions about their experiences and in response to stories or events. (answering questions in response to holiday stories inspired by postcards)*	MATHEMATICS	Numbers	**30-50 months** *Shows curiosity about numbers by offering comments and asking questions (curiosity in numbers of postcard stamps)* **40-60+ months** *Recognises numerals 1 to 5 (numerals on postcard stamps)*
	Speaking	**30-50 months** *Uses talk to connect ideas, explain what is happening and anticipate what might happen next, and to recall and relive past experiences (talk about holidays or family days out while painting postcard)* ***ELG** Children express themselves effectively, showing awareness of listeners' needs. They use past, present and future forms accurately when talking about events that have happened or are to happen in the future. They develop their own narratives and explanations by connecting ideas or events. (children express themselves about past, future holidays or family days out whilst painting postcard)*		Shape, space and measure	**30-50 months** *Beginning to talk about the shapes of everyday objects (comments about shapes on postcards)* **40-60+ months** *Orders and sequences familiar events (children order and sequence events whilst painting own postcard.)*

CHARACTERISTICS OF EFFECTIVE LEARNING	Suggested outcomes
Playing and exploring – *engagement*	**Showing curiosity about completed holiday postcards**
Active learning – *motivation*	**Paying attention to detail when creating postcard**
Creating and thinking critically – *thinking*	**Thinking about correct paint colours on postcard and experimenting with ideas**

PRIME AREAS		Development guidance	SPECIFIC AREAS		Development guidance
PHYSICAL DEVELOPMENT	Moving and handling	**30-50 months** *Draws lines and circles using gross motor movements (large-scale painting of postcard)* **ELG** *Children show good control and co-ordination in large and small movements. They move confidently in a range of ways, safely negotiating space. They handle equipment and tools effectively, including pencils for writing. (good control and co-ordination of paintbrushes)*	UNDERSTANDING THE WORLD	People and communities	**30-50 months** *Recognises and describes special times or events for family or friends (while painting family holiday or day trip postcard)* **ELG** *Children talk about past and present events in their own lives and in the lives of family members. They know that other children don't always enjoy the same things, and are sensitive to this. They know about similarities and differences between themselves and others, and among families, communities and traditions. (children talk about their family and events whilst painting family holiday or day trip postcard)*
				The world	**30-50 months** *Comments upon and asks questions about aspects of their familiar world such as the place where they live or the natural world (comments upon natural world from holiday/other locations while painting postcard, e.g. beach, sea)* **40-60+ months** *Looks closely at similarities, differences, patterns and change.* **ELG** *Children know about similarities and differences in relation to places, objects, materials and living things. They talk about the features of their own immediate environment and how environments might vary from one another. They make observations of animals and plants and explain why some things occur, and talk about changes. (children recognise similarities and differences in relation to places as they are painting their postcard)*
				Technology	
	Health and self-care		EXPRESSIVE ARTS AND DESIGN	Exploring and using media and materials	**30-50 months** *Explores colour and how colours can be changed* *Realises tools can be used for a purpose (colour exploration while painting postcard)* **40-60+ months** *Explores what happens when they mix colours.* *Uses simple tools and techniques competently and appropriately (exploring colour, tools and techniques while painting postcard)*
				Being imaginative	**30-50 months** *Captures experiences and responses with a range of media such as music, dance and paint and other materials or words (capture of family experiences through postcard painting)* **40-60+ months** *Chooses particular colours to use for a purpose (while painting their postcard)*
PERSONAL, SOCIAL AND EMOTIONAL DEVELOPMENT	Making relationships	**30-50 months** *Initiates play, offering cues to peers to join them (showing their postcard painting and encouraging others to have a go)* **40-60+ months** *Explains own knowledge and understanding and asks appropriate questions of others (own knowledge and understanding about postcard painting locality and information)*			
	Self-confidence and self-awareness	**30-50 months** *Shows confidence in asking adults for help (while painting or adding mark making to back of postcard painting)* **ELG** *Children are confident to try new activities, and say why they like some activities more than others. They are confident to speak in a familiar group, will talk about their ideas, and will choose the resources they need for their chosen activities. They say when they do or don't need help. (confident working within a group and choosing resources whilst painting)*			
	Managing feelings and behaviour	**30-50 months** *Begins to accept the needs of others and can take turns and share resources, sometimes with support from others (sharing paint equipment)* **ELG** *Children talk about how they and others show feelings, talk about their own and others' behaviour, and its consequences, and know that some behaviour is unacceptable. They work as part of a group or class, and understand and follow the rules. They adjust their behaviour to different situations, and take changes of routine in their stride. (taking turns and being sensible with paints)*			

Activity guidance

This continuous provision activity inspires children to create their own postcard painting.

Prior to the activity, collect completed postcards from a variety of holiday locations. Prepare the painting equipment and space for several children to paint.

To initiate interest gather engaged children to look at some completed postcards or holiday magazines. What do the holiday places look like? Encourage the children to look for similarities and differences. Draw children's attention to writing and the stamp on the postcard. Ask the children to think about their favourite family holiday or day trip.

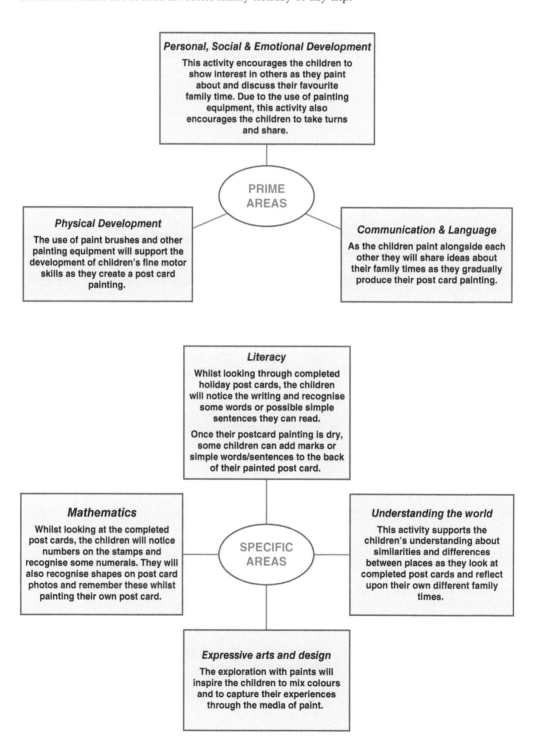

Personal, Social & Emotional Development
This activity encourages the children to show interest in others as they paint about and discuss their favourite family time. Due to the use of painting equipment, this activity also encourages the children to take turns and share.

PRIME AREAS

Physical Development
The use of paint brushes and other painting equipment will support the development of children's fine motor skills as they create a post card painting.

Communication & Language
As the children paint alongside each other they will share ideas about their family times as they gradually produce their post card painting.

Literacy
Whilst looking through completed holiday post cards, the children will notice the writing and recognise some words or possible simple sentences they can read.

Once their postcard painting is dry, some children can add marks or simple words/sentences to the back of their painted post card.

SPECIFIC AREAS

Mathematics
Whilst looking at the completed post cards, the children will notice numbers on the stamps and recognise some numerals. They will also recognise shapes on post card photos and remember these whilst painting their own post card.

Understanding the world
This activity supports the children's understanding about similarities and differences between places as they look at completed post cards and reflect upon their own different family times.

Expressive arts and design
The exploration with paints will inspire the children to mix colours and to capture their experiences through the media of paint.

Possible next steps and opportunities for further development

Snapshot postcards

To continue the idea of sending a postcard, provide opportunities for children to complete a snapshot postcard (provide a small template encouraging children to write a short sentence and/or draw a small picture) that they can send to another person in the class/setting. Alongside this activity, set up a 'postbox' and assign a post person to empty and distribute the post at the end of each day!

The writing for a purpose in this activity will encourage children's engagement. The fun 'posting' of completed postcards and distribution will inspire other children to have a go and be involved.

Computer art

To allow the children to explore postcard creation in digital form, support the children to use a program such as 2Paint a Picture (2simple software) or Tux paint to create and print a digital version of their painted postcard.

Consider how this activity will encourage those children who respond well to technology but less so to creative drawing and painting.

Final thoughts and reflections

Reflect upon how this activity encourages the children to visualise and illustrate their postcard. This illustration then provides a platform for simple writing or mark making as the children write for a purpose inspired by memories and visual illustrations.

Consider the links to real-life mathematics through stamps and the opportunities that can arise. Consider questions and ideas such as: What do numbers on stamps mean? Why are they different? How do stamps relate to money?

Activity 6 Mysteries of the sea

Activity outline and preparation

This sensory activity inspires the children to create their own 'mysteries of the sea' by adding sand, glitter, small shells and other items to a wide-necked bottle that they can shake and observe. Once creating and shaking, children can capture what they see on 'eye recorder' cards.

Resources

- Wide-necked, small, plastic bottles with lids (these will need collecting for several weeks prior to the activity – small, wide-necked smoothie bottles are perfect for this activity)

- Glitter

- Coloured sand (aim for different colours so children can choose a preference or mix)

- Small shells

- Pre-cut strips of green and blue netting

- Small sea toys if possible

- Sea or whale music to play on repeat in the background

- Small plastics scoops (scoops from baby formula feed are perfect), plastic spoons, plastic tweezers, funnels

- Dry-wipe 'eye recorder' cards and dry-wipe pens

- Tuff table-top tray

Preparation

- Gather plastic bottles (with lids) over a number of weeks prior to the activity. Ensure bottles are fully rinsed and air-dried.

- Gather other resources such as coloured sand, small shells, glitter, and netting alongside plastic tweezers, scoops and spoons. Organise all resources in boxes or trays and label.

- Create a WAGOLL ('What A Good One Looks Like') with some of the resources to display that will inspire and guide children.

- Source and set up sea or whale music to play in the background.

- Print and laminate 'eye recorder' cards.

Activity development

ESSENTIAL LITERACY AND MATHEMATICS DEVELOPMENT

PRIME AREAS		Development guidance	SPECIFIC AREAS		Development guidance
COMMUNICATION AND LANGUAGE	Listening and attention	**30-50 months** *Is able to follow directions (if not intently focused on own choice of activity) (following simple ideas about how to add items to the bottle)* **40-60+ months** *Two-channelled attention - can listen and do for short span.* ***ELG*** *Children listen attentively in a range of situations. They listen to stories, accurately anticipating key events and respond to what they hear with relevant comments, questions or actions. They give their attention to what others say and respond appropriately, while engaged in another activity. (able to choose and add items to bottle whilst listening to others also engaged in the activity)*	**LITERACY**	Reading	**30-50 months** *Knows information can be relayed in the form of print (labels on objects/resources)* **40-60+ months** *Can segment the sounds in simple words and blend them together and knows which letters represent some of them* ***ELG*** *Children read and understand simple sentences. They use phonic knowledge to decode regular words and read them aloud accurately. They also read some common irregular words. They demonstrate understanding when talking with others about what they have read. (reading of labels on objects/ resources)*
				Writing	**30-50 months** *Sometimes gives meaning to marks as they draw and paint (illustrations and mark making)* **40-60+ months** *Gives meaning to marks they make as they draw, write and paint (marks and illustrations on eye recorder cards)* ***ELG*** *Children use their phonic knowledge to write words in ways which match their spoken sounds. They also write some irregular common words. They write simple sentences which can be read by themselves and others. Some words are spelt correctly and others are phonetically plausible. (using phonic knowledge to spell out words or simple sentences on eye recorder cards)*
	Under-standing	**30-50 months** *Understands use of objects (use of tweezers, spoons, scoops to add items to the bottle)* **40-60+ months** *Listens and responds to ideas expressed by others in conversation or discussion (while adding items to their bottles)* ***ELG*** *Children follow instructions involving several ideas or actions. They answer 'how' and 'why' questions about their experiences and in response to stories or events. (following simple ideas and completed WAGOLL about what could be added to bottle)*	**MATHEMATICS**	Numbers	**30-50 months** *Uses some number names and number language spontaneously (as choosing and adding to bottle, e.g. 'I'm adding one, two, three shells to the bottle')* **40-60+ months** *Counts up to three or four objects by saying one number name for each item (counting of objects as selected and added to the bottle)*
	Speaking	**30-50 months** *Uses vocabulary focused on objects and people that are of particular importance to them (words related to under the sea or objects used in their bottle)* **40-60+ months** *Uses talk to organise, sequence and clarify thinking, ideas, feelings and events (talk whilst choosing and adding objects to their bottle)*		Shape, space and measure	**30-50 months** *Shows an interest in shape and space by playing with shapes or making arrangements with objects (exploration of objects as added to arrangement in bottle)* **40-60+ months** *Uses familiar objects and common shapes to create and recreate patterns and build models (creation of their own patterns and model within the bottle as they choose and use from available objects/ resources)*

CHARACTERISTICS OF EFFECTIVE LEARNING	Suggested outcomes
Playing and exploring – *engagement*	**Showing continued interest and curiosity while creating their mysteries of the sea bottle**
Active learning – *motivation*	**Being proud of completed mysteries of the sea bottle**
Creating and thinking critically – *thinking*	**Thinking of own ideas for their mysteries of the sea bottle prompted by labelled available resources/objects**

PRIME AREAS		Development guidance	SPECIFIC AREAS		Development guidance
PHYSICAL DEVELOPMENT	Moving and handling	**30-50 months** Uses one-handed tools and equipment *(confident use of tweezers, scoops, spoons and other equipment while adding to bottle)* **40-60+ months** Handles tools, construction objects and malleable materials safely and with increasing control **ELG** Children show good control and co-ordination in large and small movements. They move confidently in a range of ways, safely negotiating space. They handle equipment and tools effectively, including pencils for writing. *(good control and co-ordination of tweezers, scoops, spoons and other equipment whilst adding to bottle)*	UNDERSTANDING THE WORLD	People and communities	
				The world	**30-50 months** Can talk about some of the things they have observed such as natural and found objects *(talk about features of their mysteries of the sea bottle with natural and found objects inside)* **40-60+ months** Looks closely at similarities, differences, patterns and change. **ELG** Children know about similarities and differences in relation to places, objects, materials and living things. They talk about the features of their own immediate environment and how environments might vary from one another. They make observations of animals and plants and explain why some things occur, and talk about changes. *(similarities and differences between objects/ resources chosen and used in bottle)*
				Technology	
	Health and self-care	**30-50 months** Understands that equipment and tools have to be used safely *(safely uses tweezers, scoops, spoons and other equipment while adding to bottle)* **40-60+ months** Practises some appropriate safety measures without direct supervision *(safely and sensibly uses equipment such as tweezers and scoops)*	EXPRESSIVE ARTS AND DESIGN	Exploring and using media and materials	**30-50 months** Realises tools can be used for a purpose *(tools: tweezers for adding small objects to bottle, spoons and scoops for sand)* Explores colour and how colours can be changed *(exploring and mixing coloured sand)* **40-60+ months** Explores what happens when they mix colours Uses simple tools and techniques competently and appropriately **ELG** Children sing songs, make music and dance, and experiment with ways of changing them. They safely use and explore a variety of materials, tools and techniques, experimenting with colour, design, texture, form and function. *(exploring colour, tools and techniques whilst choosing and adding objects to their bottle)*
				Being imaginative	**30-50 months** Captures experiences and responses with a range of media, such as music, dance and paint and other materials or words *(created bottle captures response to children's engagement with materials available and surrounding music)* **40-60+ months** Chooses particular colours to use for a purpose *(choosing from resources for bottle)* Creates simple representations pf events, people and objects *(created bottle - simple representation of under the sea)*
PERSONAL, SOCIAL AND EMOTIONAL DEVELOPMENT	Making relation-ships	**30-50 months** Demonstrates friendly behaviour, initiating conversations and forming good relationships with peers and familiar adults *(sharing ideas for bottles and working well alongside one another)* **40-60+ months** Explains own knowledge and understanding and asks appropriate questions of others *(sharing own knowledge and understanding abut under the sea and what the bottle could look like)*			
	Self-confidence and self-awareness	**30-50 months** Can select and use resources with help *(while selecting from available resources for bottle)* Welcomes and values praise for what they have done *(created mysteries of the sea bottle)* **ELG** Children are confident to try new activities, and say why they like some activities more than others. They are confident to speak in a familiar group, will talk about their ideas, and will choose the resources they need for their chosen activities. They say when they do or don't need help. *(confident working within a group and choosing their own resources for bottle).*			
	Managing feeling and behaviour	**30-50 months** Aware of own feelings and knows that some actions and words can hurt others' feelings *(sharing resources/equipment)* **ELG** Children talk about how they and others show feelings, talk about their own and others' behaviour, and its consequences, and know that some behaviour is unacceptable. They work as part of a group or class, and understand and follow the rules. They adjust their behaviour to different situations, and take changes of routine in their stride. *(taking turns and being sensible with resources/ equipment whilst creating mysteries of the sea bottles)*			

Activity guidance

This continuous provision sensory activity encourages the children to use their imagination to create a snapshot of an underwater world.

Prior to the activity, collect, wash and dry small, wide-necked plastic bottles with lids. Small smoothie bottles are ideal for this activity. To set up the activity, organise resources such as small shells, strips of green and blue netting and small sea toys in labelled boxes or baskets alongside pots of coloured sand, glitter and plastic equipment such as scoops, tweezers and spoons. Display the completed WAGOLL at the activity table so children can be inspired and have a visual guide to follow.

To initiate interest gather interested children to view the WAGOLL mysteries of the sea bottle. Draw attention to the shapes, colours and textures in the bottle. Look at the equipment and discuss how these can be used to add items to the bottle. Encourage the children to choose and add their own sand and other resources and, if they wish to add water at the end, to seek adult support with this.

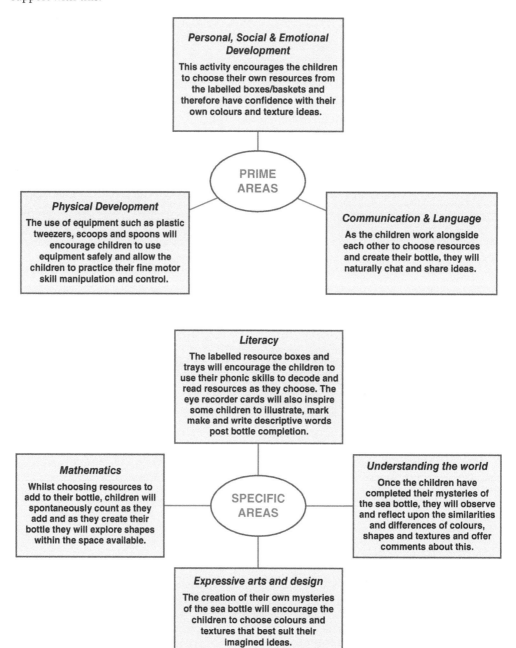

Personal, Social & Emotional Development
This activity encourages the children to choose their own resources from the labelled boxes/baskets and therefore have confidence with their own colours and texture ideas.

PRIME AREAS

Physical Development
The use of equipment such as plastic tweezers, scoops and spoons will encourage children to use equipment safely and allow the children to practice their fine motor skill manipulation and control.

Communication & Language
As the children work alongside each other to choose resources and create their bottle, they will naturally chat and share ideas.

Literacy
The labelled resource boxes and trays will encourage the children to use their phonic skills to decode and read resources as they choose. The eye recorder cards will also inspire some children to illustrate, mark make and write descriptive words post bottle completion.

Mathematics
Whilst choosing resources to add to their bottle, children will spontaneously count as they add and as they create their bottle they will explore shapes within the space available.

SPECIFIC AREAS

Understanding the world
Once the children have completed their mysteries of the sea bottle, they will observe and reflect upon the similarities and differences of colours, shapes and textures and offer comments about this.

Expressive arts and design
The creation of their own mysteries of the sea bottle will encourage the children to choose colours and textures that best suit their imagined ideas.

Possible next steps and opportunities for further development

Mysteries of the sea words

Once bottles are complete, consider creating a display area with the creations. As part of the display, encourage the children to add words that describe the sea. Children could use pencils, paints, chalks or pens to allow exploration with colour and letter shape. Display the words alongside the completed bottles, images and sounds of the sea.

Children will benefit from focusing on writing after they have created and explored colour, shape and texture. The 'visual' clarification and understanding will really help some children to conceptualise and then describe appropriate adjectives.

Mysteries of the sea music

Following the creation of mysteries of the sea bottles make further links with sounds and music. Using their own bottle as inspiration, encourage the children to explore instruments such as triangles, cymbals, chime bars and rain sticks to create their own mysteries of the sea music to accompany their bottle.

As children complete their mysteries of the sea bottles while listening to background sea music or whale sounds they will begin to make links between audio and kinaesthetic actions and this will pave the way for further audio musical exploration.

Final thoughts and reflections

Reflect upon how this activity supports children's sensory development as they explore and create via vision, touch and hearing. Alongside this, it will also inspire imaginative thoughts about under the sea and the creatures that live there.

Consider the foundations this activity lays for future work with mark making and writing. The sensory, creative nature of the activity allows the children to explore colour, texture and shape as well as sound and create confident visual images. Such confident visual images help the children make links with vocabulary and writing.

Resource support: *Photocopiable example eye recorder card*

Look at your bottle...

Draw or write what you can see

_____

_____

CHAPTER 2

LEARNING THREAD SPACE AND SPARKLING STARS

Space and Sparkling Stars

In this chapter

In this chapter, you will find activities related to space. This learning thread links to:

- sensory play and writing exploration through 'cosmic, clever words'

- physical movement and co-ordination via 'astronaut space gym' and 'moonwalking'

- exploration and expression through 'rockets and aliens'

- problem-solving and sensory maths via 'moon maths' and 'planet puzzles' activities.

The activities in this chapter will help you to work towards:

- supporting children's gross motor, physical development through the exploration of movement and co-ordination

- developing children's sensory processing and problem-solving skills through puzzles and challenges

- inspiring children's investigation skills and expression through exploration and discovery.

Activities

	Activity	Page	Provision
1	Rockets and aliens	41	Continuous provision indoors or outdoors
2	Moon maths	47	Continuous provision indoors or outdoors
3	Astronaut space gym	53	Continuous provision outdoors
4	Cosmic, clever words	59	Continuous provision indoors or outdoors
5	Moonwalking	65	Continuous provision indoors (if space) or outdoors
6	Planet puzzles	71	Continuous provision indoors or outdoors

Role-play area links:

- 3D space rocket

- Planetarium tent

- Space lab

- 3D spaceship

Activity 1 Rockets and aliens

Activity outline and preparation

This activity inspires the children to explore shadows via shadow puppets. It will need an enclosed space, preferably a small tent, for the children to explore the puppets with torches. The main aim of the activity is for children to explore and express with the puppets and is less about creating and making a shadow puppet. However, you can easily adjust this activity if a focus on creating a puppet is preferred.

Resources

- Shadow puppet templates related to space, e.g. rockets, aliens, Star Wars characters

- Straws or lolly sticks for puppets

- A selection of books related to space, e.g. non-fiction books about planets and astronauts, space stories, Star Wars magazines or books

- Pencils and crayons

- Torches

- Small tent (if an enclosed area cannot be created) – a small UV protection tent is ideal

- Puppet prompt card to display

Preparation

- Cut out templates and secure a straw or lolly stick so the puppets are ready to be decorated and then used.

- Source and set up a small tent or locate an enclosed area in the setting that can be used. Set up a table next to the tent or enclosed area so the children can decorate their shadow puppets first.

- Organise torches and a box or books and magazines to display on the table next to the tent/enclosed area.

- Print and laminate puppet prompt card to display.

Activity development

ESSENTIAL LITERACY AND MATHEMATICS DEVELOPMENT				
PRIME AREAS	**Development guidance**		**SPECIFIC AREAS**	**Development guidance**
COMMUNICATION AND LANGUAGE	Listening and attention	**30-50 months** *Is able to follow directions (if not intently focused on own choice of activity) (general directions about decorating and exploring shadow puppet with torch)* **40-60+ months** *Two-channelled attention - can listen and do for short span* **ELG** *Children listen attentively in a range of situations. They listen to stories, accurately anticipating key events and respond to what they hear with relevant comments, questions or actions. They give their attention to what others say and respond appropriately, while engaged in another activity. (simultaneous listening to others and exploring of shadow puppets with torches)*	LITERACY	Reading	**30-50 months** *Looks at books independently* *Handles books carefully* *Holds books the correct way up and turns pages (space books and magazines)* **40-60+ months** *Enjoys an increasing range of books* *Knows that information can be retrieved from books and computers (space books and magazines)* **ELG** *Children read and understand simple sentences. They use phonic knowledge to decode regular words and read them aloud accurately. They also read some common irregular words. They demonstrate understanding when talking with others about what they have read. (use of phonic knowledge whilst engaging with space books/magazines and puppet prompt card)*
				Writing	**30-50 months** *Sometimes give meaning to marks as they draw and paint. (words and marks that children use to decorate their shadow puppet)* **40-60+ months** *Gives meaning to marks they make as they draw, write and paint (words and marks that children use to decorate their shadow puppet)* **ELG** *Children use their phonic knowledge to write words in ways which match their spoken sounds. They also write some irregular common words. They write simple sentences which can be read by themselves and others. Some words are spelt correctly and others are phonetically plausible. (using phonic knowledge to sound out and add words to decorated shadow puppet)*
	Understanding	**30-50 months** *Shows understanding of prepositions such as 'under', 'on top', 'behind' by carrying out an action or selecting correct picture. (understanding about how to use a torch to shine on shadow puppet to create shadows. Use of prepositions to direct others with torch)* **40-60+ months** *Responds to instructions involving a two-part sequence. Understands humour e.g. nonsense rhymes, jokes* **ELG** *Children follow instructions involving several ideas or actions. They answer 'how' and 'why' questions about their experiences and in response to stories or events. (responding to general instructions about decorating shadow puppet and then exploring shadow making with torch)*	MATHEMATICS	Numbers	**30-50 months** *Uses some number names and number language spontaneously (spontaneous counting of shadows while exploring alongside others)* **40-60+ months** *Estimates how many objects they can see and checks by counting them (estimation and spontaneous counting of shadows while exploring alongside others)* *Says the number that is one more than a given number (if questioned by an adult during 'seized opportunities')*
	Speaking	**30-50 months** *Builds up vocabulary that reflects the breadth of their experiences (vocabulary related to space)* **40-60+ months** *Uses language to imagine and recreate roles and experiences in play situations (vocabulary related to rockets and aliens)* **ELG** *Children express themselves effectively, showing awareness of listeners' needs. They use past, present and future forms accurately when talking about events that have happened or are to happen in the future. They develop their own narratives and explanations by connecting ideas or events. (talk whilst exploring shadow puppets and improvising with vocabulary and speech)*		Shape, space and measure	**30-50 months** *Shows an interest in shape by playing with shapes or making arrangements with objects (exploration of shadow shapes)* **40-60+ months** *Can describe their relative position such as 'behind' or 'next to'* **ELG** *Children use everyday language to talk about size, weight, capacity, position, distance, time and money to compare quantities and objects and to solve problems. They recognise, create and describe patterns. They explore characteristics of everyday objects and shapes and use mathematical language to describe them. (use of everyday and mathematical language whilst exploring shadow shapes and describing positions)*

CHARACTERISTICS OF EFFECTIVE LEARNING	Suggested outcomes
Playing and exploring – *engagement*	**Acting out ideas with shadow puppets**
Active learning – *motivation*	**Maintaining focus while exploring shadow puppets through open-ended play**
Creating and thinking critically – *thinking*	**Changing strategy when making shadows, e.g. moving torch nearer and further way from puppet**

PRIME AREAS		Development guidance	SPECIFIC AREAS		Development guidance
PHYSICAL DEVELOPMENT	Moving and handling	**30-50 months** Moves freely and with pleasure and confidence in a range of ways, such as slithering, shuffling, rolling, crawling, walking, running, jumping, skipping, sliding and hopping *(moving freely with shadow puppet to create movements)* **40-60+ months** Experiments with different ways of moving *(crawling, walking, shuffling, rolling, jumping, sliding while creating shadows with puppet)* Handles tools, objects, construction and malleable materials safely and with increasing control *(handling shadow puppets and torches)* **ELG** Children show good control and co-ordination in large and small movements. They move confidently in a range of ways, safely negotiating space. They handle equipment and tools effectively, including pencils for writing. *(good control and co-ordination when moving and manipulating shadow puppets)*	**UNDERSTANDING THE WORLD**	People and communities	
				The world	**30-50 months** Talks about why things happen and how things work *(talks about what is happening with shadows)* **40-60+ months** Looks closely at similarities, differences, patterns and change **ELG** Children know about similarities and differences in relation to places, objects, materials and living things. They talk about the features of their own immediate environment and how environments might vary from one another. They make observations of animals and plants and explain why some things occur, and talk about changes. *(exploration of similarities and differences with shadow shapes and sizes)*
				Technology	
	Health and self-care		**EXPRESSIVE ARTS AND DESIGN**	Exploring and using media and materials	
				Being imaginative	**30-50 months** Uses available resources to create props to support role-play *(shadow puppets to support play)* **40-60+ months** Create simple representations of events, people and objects *(role-play with shadow puppets)*
PERSONAL, SOCIAL AND EMOTIONAL DEVELOPMENT	Making relationships	**30-50 months** Keeps play going by responding to what others are saying or doing *(open-ended shadow puppet play)* **40-60+ months** Initiates conversations, attends to and takes account of what others say **ELG** Children play co-operatively, taking turns with others. They take account of one another's ideas about how to organise their activity. They show sensitivity to others' needs and feelings, and form positive relationships with adults and other children. *(conversations children will have whilst exploring shadow puppets. Taking turns to speak and share working space)*			
	Self-confidence and self-awareness	**30-50 months** Can select and use activities and resources with help *(while creating shadows with puppets and torches)* **ELG** Children are confident to try new activities, and say why they like some activities more than others. They are confident to speak in a familiar group, will talk about their ideas, and will choose the resources they need for their chosen activities. They say when they do or don't need help. *(confidence exploring shadows with puppets and torches and sharing ideas)*			
	Managing feelings and behaviour	**30-50 months** Begins to accept the needs of others and can take turns and share resources, sometimes with support from others *(sharing resources and space when creating shadows)* **ELG** Children talk about how they and others show feelings, talk about their own and others' behaviour, and its consequences, and know that some behaviour is unacceptable. They work as part of a group or class, and understand and follow the rules. They adjust their behaviour to different situations, and take changes of routine in their stride. *(working sensibly within shared space creating shadows whilst keeping focused.)*			

Activity guidance

This is a continuous provision activity that aims to encourage the children to explore making and observing shadows alongside role-play.

Organise the enclosed area or assemble a tent to ensure a dark space. Position a table nearby with pencils, crayons, a basket of space books, magazines and shadow puppet templates for the children to work at initially.

To initiate interest gather some children inside the enclosed space or tent to model play with a WAGOLL (completed shadow puppet). Draw the children's attention to the shape and size of shadows as the torch is moved. Ask the children to think about the shadow puppet and to think about adding any words or sounds while making the shadows. Explore suggestions and ideas with the group.

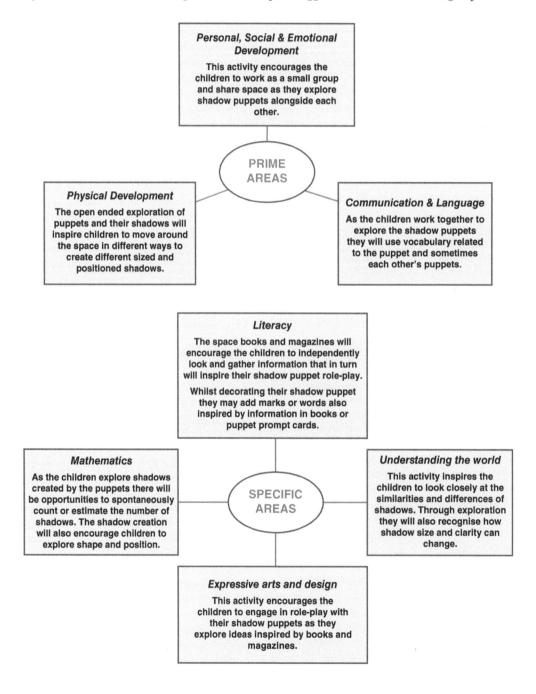

Possible next steps and opportunities for further development

Rocket and alien story pictures

Following on from exploration and initial role-play, encourage the children to record their play or 'story' through illustration. This could be one illustration or a series of two or three ideas like a simple illustrative storyboard.

Children will need adult guidance and direction with this activity as they recall the ideas explored through play and begin to note these through illustration.

Rocket and alien writing exploration

Following on from exploratory role-play with shadow puppets and story illustration/s, children can explore their ideas further through exploratory writing. Through guided direction, encourage children to add marks, words or simple sentences to their story illustrations.

Final thoughts and reflections

Reflect upon the development of the writing process within this activity. First, the children explore marks as they make their puppet inspired by books and the space theme. This then leads to role-play exploration, story illustration and finally simple words and sentences. Consider the impact of a 'journey' through talk and illustration before attempting a focus upon writing.

Consider how this activity lays firm foundations about shadows and their creation. The children will not explore formal teaching and learning about shadows until KS2 but early explorations can lay very firm foundations.

Resource support: *Example puppet prompt card*

Is your puppet...

happy 🙂

sad ☹️

worried 😟

angry 😠

scared 😨

Activity 2 Moon maths

Activity outline and preparation

This sensory problem-solving activity encourages the children to solve mathematics based questions (via differentiated, appropriate subject cards) while exploring through sand (replicating moon sand) to seek 'moon pebbles' with appropriate answers.

Resources

- Moon maths cards – see details below

- Smooth pebbles

- Sand tray or table-top tuff tray

- Sand – normal play sand or coloured sand

- Space ambient music

- Familiar counting apparatus

- Moon maths board – paper, interactive whiteboard or dry-wipe space and appropriate recording tools

Preparation

- Create moon maths card sets – create different sets of question cards that are mindful of differentiation and have the flexibility to relate to current teaching and learning. For example, card sets that relate to addition and subtraction (including some cards with simple words such as 'and' and 'add' as well as symbols), number matching, doubling, halving.

- Smooth pebbles and paint on answers in conjunction with moon maths question cards.

- Organise sand and add sand, pebbles to sand tray or table-top tuff tray.

- Source background space ambient music online or via CD (optional).

- Create a moon maths board (paper, dry-wipe or interactive whiteboard space) for children to add their own maths doodles and marks in relation to puzzles, e.g. simple number sentences or maths symbols.

Activity development

ESSENTIAL LITERACY AND MATHEMATICS DEVELOPMENT				
PRIME AREAS		**Development guidance**	**SPECIFIC AREAS**	**Development guidance**
COMMUNICATION AND LANGUAGE	Listening and attention	**30-50 months** *Listens to others one to one or in small groups when conversation interests them* (while solving maths puzzles and seeking maths pebbles) **40-60+ months** *Two-channelled attention - can listen and do for short span* **ELG** *Children listen attentively in a range of situations. They listen to stories, accurately anticipating key events and respond to what they hear with relevant comments, questions or actions. They give their attention to what others say and respond appropriately, while engaged in another activity.* (simultaneous listening to others whilst solving maths puzzles and seeking maths pebbles)	LITERACY — Reading	**30-50 months** *Recognises familiar words and signs such as own name and advertising logos.* (recognising simple maths words and symbols on moon maths cards) **40-60+ months** *Hears and says initial sound in words* **ELG** *Children read and understand simple sentences. They use phonic knowledge to decode regular words and read them aloud accurately. They also read some common irregular words. They demonstrate understanding when talking with others about what they have read.* (using phonic knowledge to decode and read simple maths words on moon maths cards)
			LITERACY — Writing	**30-50 months** *Sometimes give meaning to marks as they draw and paint* (marks, doodles and symbols on moon maths board). **40-60+ months** *Gives meaning to marks they make as they draw, write and paint* (marks, doodles and symbols on moon maths board) **ELG** *Children use their phonic knowledge to write words in ways which match their spoken sounds. They also write some irregular common words. They write simple sentences which can be read by themselves and others. Some words are spelt correctly and others are phonetically plausible.* (use of phonic knowledge to sound out and add simple maths words to moon maths board)
	Under-standing	**30-50 months** *Shows understanding of prepositions such as 'under', 'on top', 'behind' by carrying out an action or selecting correct picture* (demonstrates understanding through conversation whilst exploring sand and seeking hidden pebbles) **40-60+ months** *Responds to instructions involving a two-part sequence. Understands humour e.g. nonsense rhymes, jokes.* **ELG** *Children follow instructions involving several ideas or actions. They answer 'how' and 'why' questions about their experiences and in response to stories or events.* (following general instructions to solve maths problems and seeking answers among pebbles hidden in sand)	MATHEMATICS — Numbers	**30-50 months** *Uses some number names accurately in play* *Shows an interest in number problems* *Sometimes matches numeral and quantity correctly* (while engaging with problems on moon maths cards) **40-60+ months** *In practical activities and discussion, beginning to use the vocabulary involved in adding and subtracting* (while engaging with addition and subtraction problems on moon maths cards) *Records using marks that they can interpret and explain* (on moon maths board) **ELG** *Children count reliably with numbers from one to 20, place them in order and say which number is one more or one less than a given number. Using quantities and objects, they add and subtract two single-digit numbers and count on or back to find the answer. They solve problems, including doubling, halving and sharing.* (whilst engaging with sequence, addition and subtraction problems on moon maths cards and with familiar apparatus to support)
	Speaking	**30-50 months** *Builds up vocabulary that that reflects the breadth of their experiences* (vocabulary related to mathematics and appropriate moon maths cards, e.g. related to number names (matching) or doubling, halving) **40-60+ months** *Uses talk to organise, sequence and clarify thinking, ideas, feelings and events.* (whilst solving maths problems) **ELG** *Children express themselves effectively, showing awareness of listeners' needs. They use past, present and future forms accurately when talking about events that have happened or are to happen in the future. They develop their own narratives and explanations by connecting ideas or events.* (children express themselves whilst solving maths problems)	MATHEMATICS — Shape, space and measure	**30-50 months** *Uses positional language* (while seeking and locating pebbles) **40-60+ months** *Can describe their relative position such as 'behind' or 'next to'* (use of positional words while seeking and locating pebbles)

CHARACTERISTICS OF EFFECTIVE LEARNING	Suggested outcomes
Playing and exploring – *engagement*	**Engaging in open-ended maths problem-solving**
Active learning – *motivation*	**Bouncing back after difficulties with questions on moon maths cards**
Creating and thinking critically – *thinking*	**Seeking ways to solve problems on moon maths cards**

PRIME AREAS		Development guidance	SPECIFIC AREAS		Development guidance
PHYSICAL DEVELOPMENT	Moving and handling	**30-50 months** *Holds pencil between thumb and two fingers, no longer using whole-hand grasp (while mark making on moon maths board)* **40-60+ months** *Begins to form recognisable letters* *Uses a pencil and holds it effectively to form recognisable letters, most of which are correctly formed* **ELG** *Children show good control and co-ordination in large and small movements. They move confidently in a range of ways, safely negotiating space. They handle equipment and tools effectively, including pencils for writing. (good control and co-ordination whilst mark making or recording simple words and symbols on moon maths board)*	UNDERSTANDING THE WORLD	People and communities	
				The world	
				Technology	**30-50 months** *Knows how to operate simple equipment (CD player, laptop for space ambient music or interactive whiteboard if to be used for moon maths board)* **ELG** *Children recognise that a range of technology is used in places such as homes and schools* *They select and use technology for particular purposes (recognising purpose of, selecting and using CD player, laptop for space ambient music or interactive whiteboard if to be used for moon maths board)*
	Health and self-care	**30-50 months** *Understands that equipment and tools have to be used safely (sensible with sand, e.g. no blowing in eyes)* **40-60+ months** *Practises some appropriate safety measures without direct supervision (sensible and safe with sand)*	EXPRESSIVE ARTS AND DESIGN	Exploring and using media and materials	**30-50 months** *Imitates movement in response to music (in response to space ambient music in background)*
				Being imaginative	
PERSONAL, SOCIAL AND EMOTIONAL DEVELOPMENT	Making relationships	**30-50 months** *Demonstrates friendly behaviour, initiating conversations and forming good relationships with peers and familiar adults (initiating conversations while problem-solving)* **40-60+ months** *Explains own knowledge and understanding and asks appropriate questions of others (own knowledge and understanding in relation to maths problems)* **ELG** *Children play co-operatively, taking turns with others. They take account of one another's ideas about how to organise their activity. They show sensitivity to others' needs and feelings, and form positive relationships with adults and other children. (co-operating and taking turns with moon maths cards and pebbles)*			
	Self-confidence and self-awareness	**30-50 months** *Shows confidence in asking adults for help (if help required solving maths problems)* **ELG** *Children are confident to try new activities, and say why they like some activities more than others. They are confident to speak in a familiar group, will talk about their ideas, and will choose the resources they need for their chosen activities. They say when they do or don't need help. (confidence engaging with maths problems and choosing familiar counting apparatus)*			
	Managing feelings and behaviour	**30-50 months** *Begins to accept the needs and can take turns and share resources, sometimes with support from others (sharing moon maths cards, pebbles, moon maths board)* **40-60+ months** *Aware of boundaries set and of behavioural expectations in the setting* **ELG** *Children talk about how they and others show feelings, talk about their own and others' behaviour, and its consequences, and know that some behaviour is unacceptable. They work as part of a group or class, and understand and follow the rules. They adjust their behaviour to different situations, and take changes of routine in their stride. (sharing resources such as moon maths cards, pebbles, moon maths board)*			

Activity guidance

This is a continuous provision sensory activity that challenges the children to problem-solve and use mathematical skills.

Organise the sand tray and consider adding a dark backdrop to replicate the darkness of the moon. Add and bury moon pebbles (with pre-painted answers displayed). Choose appropriate moon maths card sets and display next to sand tray for children to choose from. Set up space ambient music to play in the background.

To initiate interest encourage some children to come along and visit the moon and listen to the space ambient music. Model to the group of children interested in the activity how to choose a moon maths card, solve the problem using counting apparatus, and seek and find the moon pebble with the appropriate answer.

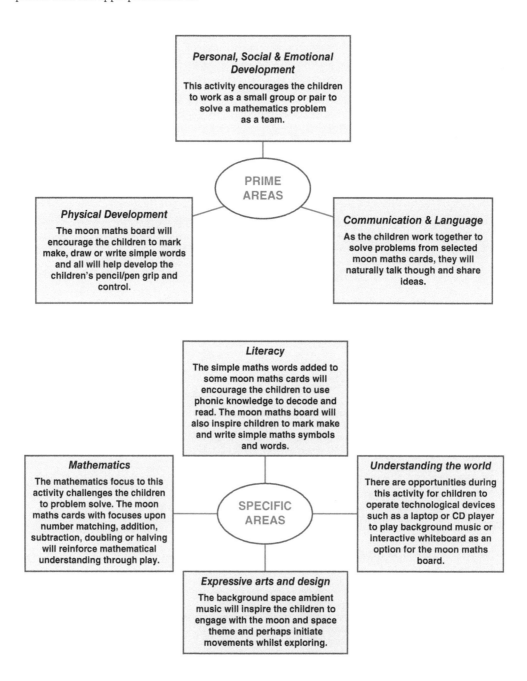

Possible next steps and opportunities for further development

Sorting and sharing

Using pebbles, introduce sorting, classifying and sharing. Paint the pebbles to group them in 'sets', e.g. colour set, pattern set. This can lead to modelling and exploration with sorting and then sharing.

The development of sorting and classification skills is built upon observation. Therefore it is important to make the pebbles as visual and bright as possible to help the children look closely and observe the colours and patterns.

Estimation

Use pebbles to develop the children's understanding about estimation. Add pebbles to a closed box or bag and encourage children to feel inside and estimate before opening and counting.

Some children will struggle with estimating or predicting as they feel that an incorrect estimation or prediction is 'wrong'. Children need to learn that estimating and predicting are part of learning. With this in mind, it is important that children have repeated opportunities to explore estimation and prediction properly.

Final thoughts and reflections

Consider the combination of sensory exploration and mathematics within this activity. Reflect upon the impact that touch, sight and sound have upon this activity and how this helps the children to process while inspiring them to problem-solve.

This activity introduces the children to simple problem-solving linked to the learning thread of 'space and sparkling stars'. Reflect upon the impact of relating problem-solving to a learning thread or theme.

Resource support: *Example moon maths cards (addition)*

4 + 2 =

8 + 3 =

9 + 4 =

6 add 2 =

8 plus 4 =

2 more than 5 =

Activity 3 Astronaut space gym

Activity outline and preparation

This energetic, physical activity is best suited to the outside due to the space required. The activity challenges the children to reach physical goals and targets through movements such as skips, jumps and steps. It also reminds the children about the importance of keeping our bodies healthy through fitness, which should be a constant for everyone, even for astronauts on the space station!

Resources

- Skipping ropes, plastic hula hoops, balls, steppers – use toddler steps/foot stools

- Astronaut space gym prompt cards

- Rocket image

- Astronaut personal best board

- Space station fitness clip via YouTube or other online source

Preparation

- Gather equipment and plan where to set up each gym challenge.

- Print and laminate Astronaut space gym prompt cards and rocket image.

- Download a space station fitness clip via YouTube or other online source.

- Create large-scale **Astronaut personal best boards** for each gym challenge – see the example below.

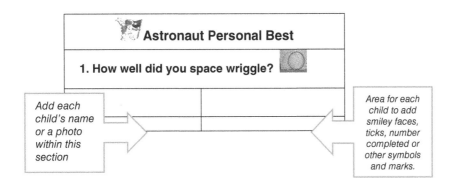

Activity development

ESSENTIAL LITERACY AND MATHEMATICS DEVELOPMENT				
PRIME AREAS		**Development guidance**	**SPECIFIC AREAS**	**Development guidance**
COMMUNICATION AND LANGUAGE	Listening and attention	**30-50 months** *Is able to follow directions (if not intently focused on own choice of activity) (general directions of space gym challenges)* **40-60+ months** *Two-channelled attention - can listen and do for short span* ***ELG** Children listen attentively in a range of situations. They listen to stories, accurately anticipating key events and respond to what they hear with relevant comments, questions or actions. They give their attention to what others say and respond appropriately, while engaged in another activity. (simultaneous actions and listening to others while working through space gym challenges)*	**LITERACY** — Reading	**30-50 months** *Recognises familiar words and signs such as own name and advertising logos (recognising words, signs, symbols and name on astronaut personal best boards)* **40-60+ months** *Begins to read words and simple sentences* ***ELG** Children read and understand simple sentences. They use phonic knowledge to decode regular words and read them aloud accurately. They also read some common irregular words. They demonstrate understanding when talking with others about what they have read. (using phonic knowledge to read words on space gym prompt cards and astronaut personal best boards)*
			Writing	**30-50 months** *Sometimes give meaning to marks as they draw and paint (marks on astronaut personal best boards)* *Ascribes meanings to marks that they see in different places (marks on astronaut personal best boards)* **40-60+ months** *Gives meaning to marks they make as they draw, write and paint (marks and drawings on astronaut personal best boards)*
	Under-standing	**30-50 months** *Understands use of objects (use of equipment, e.g. skipping ropes, hula hoops)* **40-60+ months** *Responds to instructions involving a two-part sequence. Understands humour e.g. nonsense rhymes, jokes.* ***ELG** Children follow instructions involving several ideas or actions. They answer 'how' and 'why' questions about their experiences and in response to stories or events. (responding to general instructions about each space gym challenge)*	**MATHEMATICS** — Numbers	**30-50 months** *Uses some number names accurately in play* *Realises not only objects but anything can be counted, including steps, claps or jumps (counting steps, jumps etc. while completing space gym challenges)* **40-60+ months** *Counts actions or objects which cannot be moved (counting steps, jumps, etc. while completing space gym challenges)* *Records, using marks that they can interpret and explain (on astronaut personal best boards)*
	Speaking	**30-50 months** *Uses vocabulary focused on objects and people that are of particular importance to them (using vocabulary related to space and astronauts while completing space gym challenges)* **40-60+ months** *Uses language to imagine and recreate roles and experiences in play situations (using relevant language and vocabulary to recreate the astronaut role)*	Shape, space and measure	**30-50 months** *Uses positional language (while completing space gym challenges)* **40-60+ months** *Can describe their relative position such as 'behind' or 'next to' (use of positional words while completing space gym challenges)*

CHARACTERISTICS OF EFFECTIVE LEARNING	Suggested outcomes
Playing and exploring – *engagement*	**Engaging with the role of astronaut while completing space gym challenges**
Active learning – *motivation*	**Showing high levels of energy and seeking physical challenges**
Creating and thinking critically – *thinking*	**Thinking about how to reach space gym challenge goals**

PRIME AREAS		Development guidance	SPECIFIC AREAS		Development guidance
PHYSICAL DEVELOPMENT	Moving and handling	**30-50 months** Moves freely and with pleasure and confidence in a range of ways, such as slithering, shuffling, rolling, crawling, walking, running, jumping, skipping, sliding and hopping Mounts stairs, steps or climbing equipment using alternate feet Can catch a large ball *(while completing space gym challenges)* **40-60+ months** Shows increasing control over an object in pushing, patting, throwing, catching or kicking it **ELG** Children show good control and co-ordination in large and small movements. They move confidently in a range of ways, safely negotiating space. They handle equipment and tools effectively, including pencils or writing. *(while completing space gym challenges and astronaut personal best boards)*	**UNDERSTANDING THE WORLD**	People and communities	
				The world	
				Technology	**30-50 months** Knows that information can be retrieved from computers *(retrieval of online space station fitness clip)* **ELG** Children recognise that a range of technology is used in places such as homes and schools. They select and use technology for particular purposes. *(recognising purpose of using the internet for information – retrieval of online space station fitness clip)*
	Health and self-care	**30-50 months** Observes the effects of activity on their bodies *(while engaging with space gym challenges)* **40-60+ months** Shows some understanding that good practices with regard to exercise, eating, sleeping and hygiene can contribute to good health **ELG** Children know the importance for good health of physical exercise, and a healthy diet, and talk about ways to keep healthy and safe. They manage their own basic hygiene and personal needs successfully, including dressing and going to the toilet independently. *(understanding the purpose of space gym challenges and their connection to real-life astronauts and their requirements to keep fit and healthy.)*	**EXPRESSIVE ARTS AND DESIGN**	Exploring and using media and materials	
				Being imaginative	**30-50 months** Notices what adults do, imitating what is observed and then doing it spontaneously when the adult is not there *(imitating observed actions from online space station fitness clip)*. **40-60+ months** Plays alongside other children who are engaged in the same theme *(astronauts and space gym theme)*
PERSONAL, SOCIAL AND EMOTIONAL DEVELOPMENT	Making relationships	**30-50 months** Imitates play, offering cues to peers to join them *(encouraging other children to join in space gym challenges)* **40-60+ months** Initiates conversations, attends to and takes account of what others say *(conversations as working through space gym challenges alongside others)* **ELG** Children talk about how they and others show feelings, talk about their own and others' behaviour, and its consequences, and know that some behaviour is unacceptable. They work as part of a group or class, and understand and follow the rules. They adjust their behaviour to different situations, and take changes of routine in their stride. *(working as part of a group to explore space gym challenges and following challenge rules).*			
	Self-confidence and self-awareness	**30-50 months** Can select and use activities and resources with help *(use of space gym equipment and seeking help if needed)* **ELG** Children are confident to try new activities and say why they like some activities more than others. They are confident to speak in a familiar group, will talk about their ideas and will choose the resources they need for the chosen activities. They say when they do or don't need help. *(confidence with each space gym challenge and seeking help if needed)*			
	Managing feelings and behaviour	**30-50 months** Begins to accept the needs and can take turns and share resources, sometimes with support from others *(sharing space gym challenge equipment)* **40-60+ months** Beginning to be able to negotiate and solve problems without aggression *(solving equipment-sharing problems)*			

Activity guidance

This is a continuous provision physical activity that encourages the children to be active within the role of a space astronaut.

Organise and set up the equipment for each space gym challenge with the associated space gym prompt and astronaut personal best board displayed:

1. Can you space wriggle 5 times? *(with hula hoops)*

2. Can you jump and hit the rocket target 8 times? *(hit rocket image)*

3. Can moon step 6 times? *(with toddler step/foot stool)*

4. Can you star skip 10 times? *(with skipping rope)*

5. Can you throw and catch the cosmic ball 4 times? *(with large-sized ball)*

To initiate interest encourage a small group of children to gather and watch a short internet video of astronauts exercising on the space station. Ask the children to consider why we need to exercise and why astronauts still need to do this in space (to keep their bodies healthy and stop muscle wastage). Model a couple of the space gym challenges and draw attention to the astronaut personal best boards.

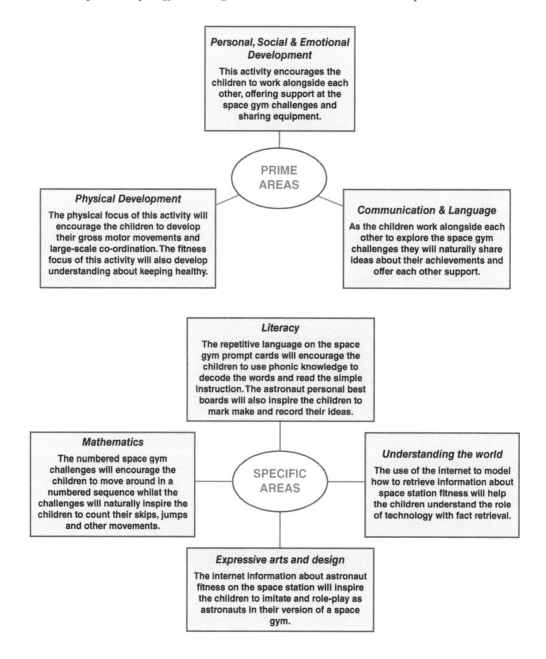

Personal, Social & Emotional Development

This activity encourages the children to work alongside each other, offering support at the space gym challenges and sharing equipment.

PRIME AREAS

Physical Development

The physical focus of this activity will encourage the children to develop their gross motor movements and large-scale co-ordination. The fitness focus of this activity will also develop understanding about keeping healthy.

Communication & Language

As the children work alongside each other to explore the space gym challenges they will naturally share ideas about their achievements and offer each other support.

Literacy

The repetitive language on the space gym prompt cards will encourage the children to use phonic knowledge to decode the words and read the simple instruction. The astronaut personal best boards will also inspire the children to mark make and record their ideas.

Mathematics

The numbered space gym challenges will encourage the children to move around in a numbered sequence whilst the challenges will naturally inspire the children to count their skips, jumps and other movements.

SPECIFIC AREAS

Understanding the world

The use of the internet to model how to retrieve information about space station fitness will help the children understand the role of technology with fact retrieval.

Expressive arts and design

The internet information about astronaut fitness on the space station will inspire the children to imitate and role-play as astronauts in their version of a space gym.

Possible next steps and opportunities for further development

Space moves and dance

After exploring skips, steps and jumps during space gym challenges, guide the children to plan a sequence of moves and create a simple space dance. This could be with or without music.

Some children will struggle with planning a 'sequence' of moves so encourage these children to consider two moves that connect together to simplify the process.

Obstacle track

To develop physical skills further, encourage the children to engage with an obstacle track with resources such as hula hoops, skipping ropes and balancing bean bags to challenge different physical skills within one activity.

Final thoughts and reflections

Consider how this activity develops the children's ability to move with controlled confidence within their space.

Reflect upon how relating physical play to the idea of an astronaut gym helps the children make sense of their world. In this case, it helps the children to understand how astronauts need to keep fit while away from earth.

Resource support: *Example astronaut space gym prompt cards*

Can you space wriggle **5** times?

Can you jump and hit the rocket **8** times?

Activity 4 Cosmic, clever words

Activity outline and preparation

This sensory activity encourages the children to draw, mark make or write simple words within a tray of glitter or sparkly stars or on illuminated writing boards.

Displayed images, books and adult discussion should provide ideas and prompts as the children explore and play.

Resources

- Shallow trays

- Glitter or small metallic stars

- Illuminated mark making boards (if you do not have these, then the activity can run with another tray instead)

- Space-related coloured images, e.g. planets, rockets, stars, astronauts – add numbers to the images to support mathematical development and help children differentiate between images

- Cosmic, ambient music

- Selection of non-fiction books related to the space learning thread

Preparation

- Gather and fill shallow trays with glitter or metallic stars.

- Charge illuminated mark making boards (if used).

- Print images to display of rockets, astronauts, planets, stars – add numbers to the images.

- Organise non-fiction books related to space, astronauts, rockets and planets and display with the activity.

- Source cosmic, ambient music to play in the background.

Activity development

ESSENTIAL LITERACY AND MATHEMATICS DEVELOPMENT				
PRIME AREAS	**Development guidance**	**SPECIFIC AREAS**		**Development guidance**
COMMUNICATION AND LANGUAGE — Listening and attention	**30-50 months** Listens to others one to one or in small groups, when conversation interests them *(listening to others ideas about space related words)* **40-60+ months** *Two-channelled attention - can listen and do for short span* **ELG** *Children listen attentively in a range of situations. They listen to stories, accurately anticipating key events and respond to what they hear with relevant comments, questions or actions. They give their attention to what others say and respond appropriately, while engaged in another activity. (simultaneous listening to others and creation of drawings, mark makings or words)*	**LITERACY**	Reading	**30-50 months** *Shows interest in illustrations and print in books and print in the environment* *Looks at books independently* *Handles books carefully* *Holds books the correct way up and turns pages (handling and looking at non-fiction books related to space, planets, etc.)* **40-60+ months** *Enjoys an increasing range of books* **ELG** *Children read and understand simple sentences. They use phonic knowledge to decode regular words and read them aloud accurately. They also read some common irregular words. They demonstrate understanding when talking with others about what they have read. (reading of simple sentences in space non-fiction books)*
			Writing	**30-50 months** *Sometimes give meaning to marks as they draw and paint (tracing in glitter, drawing and mark making simple space words or symbols in trays or illuminated boards)* **40-60+ months** *Gives meaning to marks they make as they draw, write and paint.* *Can segment the sounds in simple words and blend them together* **ELG** *Children use their phonic knowledge to write words in ways that match their spoken sounds. They also write some irregular common words. They write simple sentences which can be read by themselves and others. Some words are spelt correctly and others are phonetically plausible. (tracing in glitter, drawing, mark making and writing simple space words or symbols in trays)*
Understanding	**30-50 months** *Understands use of objects (use of glitter trays and illuminated mark making boards)* **40-60+ months** *Listens and responds to ideas expressed by others in conversation or discussion (responding to others' ideas while creating own drawings, marks or words)*	**MATHEMATICS**	Numbers	**30-50 months** *Shows curiosity about numbers by offering comments or asking questions (numbers displayed among inspiring space images)* **40-60+ months** *Recognises numerals 1 to 5 (numbers displayed on inspiring space images)* *Says number that is one more or than a given number (if questioned by an adult)*
Speaking	**30-50 months** *Builds up vocabulary that reflects the breadth of their experiences (vocabulary related to space, rockets, astronauts, planets)* **40-60+ months** *Extends vocabulary, especially by grouping and naming, exploring the meaning and sounds of new words (vocabulary familiar and new related to space rockets, astronauts and planets)*		Shape, space and measure	**30-50 months** *Beginning to talk about the shapes of everyday objects, e.g. 'round' and 'tall' (while looking through space related books)* **40-60+ months** *Beginning to use mathematical names for 'solid' 3D shapes and 'flat' 2D shapes and mathematical terms to describe shapes (while looking at the different shapes in space related books)*

CHARACTERISTICS OF EFFECTIVE LEARNING	Suggested outcomes
Playing and exploring – *engagement*	**Engaging in an open-ended mark making and word creating activity**
Active learning – *motivation*	**Maintaining focus when exploring mark making and word creation**
Creating and thinking critically – *thinking*	**Thinking of cosmic, clever words inspired by images, books and background music.**

PRIME AREAS		Development guidance	SPECIFIC AREAS		Development guidance
PHYSICAL DEVELOPMENT	Moving and handling	**30-50 months** *Holds pencil between thumb and two fingers, no longer using whole-hand grasp (while exploring illuminated mark making boards and pens)* **40-60+ months** *Shows a preference for a dominant hand* *Begins to form recognisable letters* **ELG** *Children show good control and co-ordination in large and small movements. They move confidently in a range of ways, safely negotiating space. They handle equipment and tools effectively, including pencils for writing. (exploring glitter trays and illuminated mark making boards)*	UNDERSTANDING THE WORLD	People and communities	
				The world	
				Technology	**30-50 months** *Knows how to operate simple equipment (operating illuminated mark making boards and CD player/laptop for cosmic music)* **ELG** *Children recognise that a range of technology is used in places such as homes and schools* *They select and use technology for particular purposes (selecting and using illuminated mark making boards and/or CD player/laptop for cosmic music)*
	Health and self-care	**30-50 months** *Understands that equipment and tools have to be used safely (sensible with glitter, e.g. no blowing in eyes)* **40-60+ months** *Practises some appropriate safety measures without direct supervision (sensible and safe with glitter)*	EXPRESSIVE ARTS AND DESIGN	Exploring and using media and materials	
				Being imaginative	**30-50 months** *Captures experiences and responses with a range of media such as music, dance and paint and other materials or words (drawing, mark making, writing)* **40-60+ months** *Creates simple representations of events, people and objects (space representations through words, marks and drawings in trays and on boards)*
PERSONAL, SOCIAL AND EMOTIONAL DEVELOPMENT	Making relationships	**30-50 months** *Imitates play, offering cues to peers to join them (encouraging other children to join in exploring trays or boards)* **40-60+ months** *Explains own knowledge and understanding and asks appropriate questions of others (discusses and shares own knowledge and understanding about space)* **ELG** *Children play co-operatively, taking turns with others. They take account of one another's ideas about how to organise their activity. They show sensitivity to others' needs and feelings, and form positive relationships with adults and other children. (taking turns and playing co-operatively with mark making boards and trays)*			
	Self-confidence and self-awareness	**30-50 months** *Enjoys the responsibility of carrying out small tasks (creating own space-inspired drawings, marks and words)* **40-60+ months** *Confident to speak to others about own needs, wants, interests and opinions.* **ELG** *Children are confident to try new activities, and say why they like some activities more than others. They are confident to speak in a familiar group, will talk about their ideas, and will choose the resources they need for their chosen activities. They say when they do or don't need help. (confidence trying the space words activity and sharing own ideas)*			
	Managing feelings and behaviour	**30-50 months** *Begins to accept the needs and can take turns and share resources, sometimes with support from others (sharing trays, boards and books)* **40-60+ months** *Aware of boundaries set and of behavioural expectations in the setting (being sensible with glitter and star trays)*			

Activity guidance

This is a continuous provision sensory activity that inspires the children to visualise space and planets before drawing, mark making or word-writing with sensory resources.

Organise and display space-related images, e.g. rockets, planets, astronauts, and gather space-related non-fiction books to arrange nearby. Set up cosmic music via a CD player or laptop within the same area and organise the glitter and star trays. If you plan to use the illuminated mark making boards as well, ensure they are fully charged and removed from their docking station.

To initiate interest encourage a small group of children to explore the glitter, star trays and illuminated boards if using these too. Draw children's attention to the music playing, the space-related inspirational images and the non-fiction books on display. As children explore further, return to the group and ask if any children can think of a space symbol, word or picture they could capture in the trays or on a board.

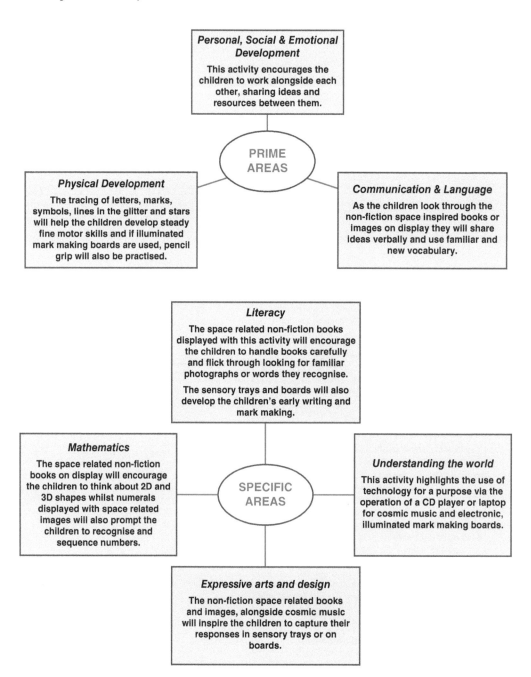

Possible next steps and opportunities for further development

Display cosmic, clever words

Building upon marks and words created during the initial activity, encourage the children to re-create their marks or words this time with pastels, paints, chalks or pens. Display the collection of colourful and creative words.

The free rein regarding colour, media and style will inspire children to mark make and write. For those children who are still struggling with consistent grip, encourage painting or chalk marks with fingers instead.

Chatty sentences

Using previous work on cosmic, clever words as a foundation encourage the children to think of a short cosmic, clever sentence to structure and record via video or other recording medium.

Switching back to 'talk' and oral recording for this activity is important as it will be this talk that will help to slowly build understanding before future work on sentence writing.

Final thoughts and reflections

Consider the impact of letter and word tracing in glitter and other sensory trays for this activity. The tactile, sensory approach will encourage children to literally 'feel' the shapes of the letters as they form them.

Reflect again upon writing becoming a product of other experiences. In this activity, the children will listen to cosmic music, observe inspiring images and absorb book information before tracing letters in glitter and other resources. All this stimulation will inspire thinking before children produce simple marks or words with sensory resources.

Activity 5 Moonwalking

Activity outline and preparation

This physical activity encourages the children to move and dance in response to music. It will need sufficient space to allow the children to move freely without causing disruption to other children and activities.

Resources

- Space music, e.g. Gustav Holst, *The Planets*, or *Symphonies of the Planets* – both can be accessed via CD or YouTube

- Dance record cards and dry-wipe pens

- Movement prompt cards

Preparation

- Create a space for the activity that will allow the children to move freely without restriction.

- Source and organise space music.

- Create dance record cards – laminate for multiple use.

- Display movement prompts, e.g.

  o *Can you moon walk?*

  o *Can you turn like a planet?*

  o *Can you twinkle like a star?*

  o *Can you move like a shooting star?*

  o *Can you jump like a rocket?*

Add images to the prompt cards to support understanding.

Activity development

ESSENTIAL LITERACY AND MATHEMATICS DEVELOPMENT				
PRIME AREAS	**Development guidance**		**SPECIFIC AREAS**	**Development guidance**
COMMUNICATION AND LANGUAGE	Listening and attention	**30-50 months** *Is able to follow directions (if not intently focused on own choice of activity) (following general directions about moving to the music and creating own dance sequence)* **40-60+ months** *Two-channelled attention - can listen and do for short span (ability to listen to music while co-ordinating movements)*	**LITERACY** — Reading	**30-50 months** *Knows information can be relayed in the form of print (information on movement prompt cards)* **40-60+ months** *Begins to read words and simple sentences* ***ELG** Children read and understand simple sentences. They use phonic knowledge to decode regular words and read them aloud accurately (reading of words and simple sentences on movement prompt cards)*
			Writing	**30-50 months** *Sometimes give meaning to marks as they draw and paint (mark making and symbol-drawing on dance record cards)* **40-60+ months** *Gives meaning to marks they make as they draw, write and paint.* *Uses some clearly identifiable letters to communicate meaning, representing some sounds correctly and in sequence* ***ELG** Children use their phonic knowledge to write words in ways which match their spoken sounds. They also write some irregular common words. They write simple sentences which can be read by themselves and others. Some words are spelt correctly and others are phonetically plausible. (mark making, symbols and writing simple words on dance record cards)*
	Understanding	**30-50 months** *Responds to simple instructions e.g. to get or put away an object (simple guidance and instructions about creating movements in response to music)* **40-60+ months** *Responds to instructions involving a two-part sequence. Understands humour e.g. nonsense rhymes, jokes (simple instructions about listening to music, creating movements and recording some ideas on dance record cards)*	**MATHEMATICS** — Numbers	**30-50 months** *Realises not only objects but anything can be counted, including steps, claps, jumps (counting of movements while responding to music)* **40-60+ months** *Counts actions or objects which cannot be moved (counting of movements while responding to music)*
	Speaking	**30-50 months** *Uses talk to connect ideas, explain what is happening and anticipate what might happen next, recall and relive past experiences (using talk to connect ideas about music and movements)* **40-60+ months** *Uses talk to organise, sequence and clarify thinking, ideas, feelings and events (using talk to connect music, movements and sequence thoughts and actions)* ***ELG** Children read and understand simple sentences. They use phonic knowledge to decode regular words and read them aloud accurately. They also read some common irregular words. They demonstrate understanding when talking with others about what they have read. (reading of words and simple sentences on movement prompt cards)*	Shape, space and measure	**30-50 months** *Uses positional language (while co-ordinating movements to music)* **40-60+ months** *Can describe their relative position such as 'behind' or 'next to' (while co-ordinating movements to music)*

CHARACTERISTICS OF EFFECTIVE LEARNING	Suggested outcomes
Playing and exploring – *engagement*	**Representing their ideas about space and planets through movement and dance**
Active learning – *motivation*	**Being proud of their own movements to music**
Creating and thinking critically – *thinking*	**Thinking of their own movements in response to music**

PRIME AREAS		Development guidance	SPECIFIC AREAS		Development guidance
PHYSICAL DEVELOPMENT	Moving and handling	**30-50 months** Moves freely and with pleasure and confidence in a range of ways, such as slithering, shuffling, rolling, crawling, walking, running, jumping, skipping, sliding and hopping (variety of movements in response to music) **40-60+ months** Experiments with different ways of moving **ELG** Children show good control and co-ordination in large and small movements. They move confidently in a range of ways, safely negotiating space. They handle equipment and tools effectively, including pencils for writing. (variety of movements in response to music, safely negotiating space)	UNDERSTANDING THE WORLD	People and communities	
				The world	
				Technology	**30-50 months** Knows how to operate simple equipment e.g. turns on CD player and uses remote control (operating CD player/laptop for space music) **ELG** Children recognise that a range of technology is used in places such as homes and schools They select and use technology for particular purposes (selecting and using CD player/laptop for space music)
	Health and self-care	**30-50 months** Observes the effects of activity on their bodies (while moving and dancing) **40-60+ months** Shows some understanding that good practices with regard to exercise contribute to good health (understanding movement and dance is a form of exercise that keeps us healthy) **ELG** Shows some understanding that good practices with regard to exercise, eating, sleeping and hygiene can contribute to good health (understanding movement and dance is a form of exercise that keeps us healthy)	EXPRESSIVE ARTS AND DESIGN	Exploring and using media and materials	**30-50 months** Beginning to move rhythmically Imitates movement in response to music (movements in response to space music) **ELG** Children sing songs, make music and dance, and experiment with ways of changing them. They safely use and explore a variety of materials, tools and techniques, experimenting with colour, design, texture, form and function. (responding to space music with dance movements and sequences)
				Being imaginative	**30-50 months** Uses movement to express feelings Creates movement in response to music (different movements in response to space music) **40-60+ months** Initiates new combinations of movement and gesture in order to express and respond to feelings, ideas and experiences. **ELG** Children use what they have learnt about media and materials in original ways, thinking about uses and purposes. They represent their own ideas, thoughts and feelings through design and technology, art, music, dance, role-play and stories. (exploration of own dance movements in response to space music)
PERSONAL, SOCIAL AND EMOTIONAL DEVELOPMENT	Making relation-ships	**30-50 months** Imitates play, offering cues to peers to join them (encouraging other children to join in with movement to music) **40-60+ months** Takes steps to resolve conflicts with other children e.g. finding a compromise (resolves possible conflicts regarding movement space or copying of each other's dance moves)			
	Self-confidence and self-awareness	**30-50 months** Enjoys the responsibility of carrying out small tasks (creating own movements in response to music) **40-60+ months** Can describe self in positive terms and talk about abilities (positive views about own dance and ability to move to music) **ELG** Children are confident to try new activities, and say why they like some activities more than others. They are confident to speak in a familiar group, will talk about their ideas, and will choose the resources they need for their chosen activities. They say when they do or don't need help. (confidence responding to music and creating own dance movements)			
	Managing feelings and behaviour	**30-50 months** Can usually adapt behaviour to different events, social situations and changes in routine (adapting behaviour to free space and open movements) **40-60+ months** Aware of boundaries set and of behavioural expectations in the setting (sensible in response to music)			

Activity guidance

This is a continuous provision physical activity that encourages the children to listen to music and respond with movement. It also prompts the children to begin linking simple movements and actions in sequence.

Organise an open space where children are able to move freely and set up music via a CD player or laptop. Display movement prompt cards around the area and set up dance record cards with dry-wipe pens on a table nearby.

To initiate interest encourage children to listen to the space music and respond as they feel. After a while, return to the activity area and gather children to observe movements and discuss sequencing. For those children who are sequencing several actions, model how to record dance movements with illustrations, symbols or words on the dance record card.

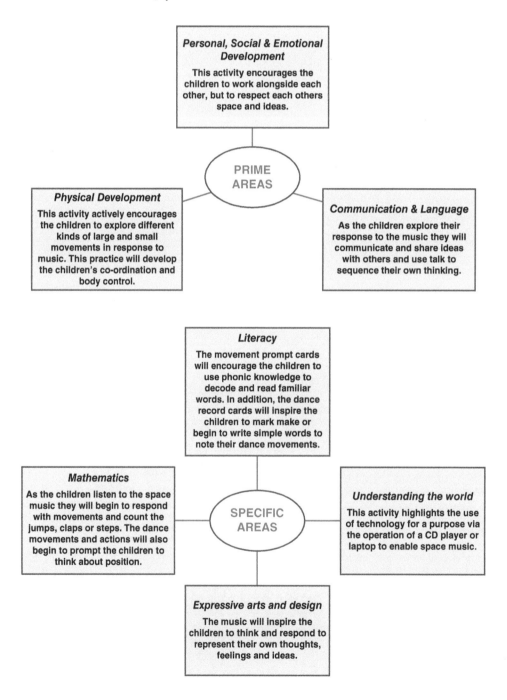

Personal, Social & Emotional Development

This activity encourages the children to work alongside each other, but to respect each others space and ideas.

PRIME AREAS

Physical Development

This activity actively encourages the children to explore different kinds of large and small movements in response to music. This practice will develop the children's co-ordination and body control.

Communication & Language

As the children explore their response to the music they will communicate and share ideas with others and use talk to sequence their own thinking.

Literacy

The movement prompt cards will encourage the children to use phonic knowledge to decode and read familiar words. In addition, the dance record cards will inspire the children to mark make or begin to write simple words to note their dance movements.

Mathematics

As the children listen to the space music they will begin to respond with movements and count the jumps, claps or steps. The dance movements and actions will also begin to prompt the children to think about position.

SPECIFIC AREAS

Understanding the world

This activity highlights the use of technology for a purpose via the operation of a CD player or laptop to enable space music.

Expressive arts and design

The music will inspire the children to think and respond to represent their own thoughts, feelings and ideas.

Possible next steps and opportunities for further development

Perfect performance

Building upon the recordings from dance record cards, encourage the children to perform their own short dance sequences for others.

The informal sharing of their own short dance sequences may provide opportunity for others to peer evaluate. Consider asking the children to share two things that were brilliant about the dance and suggestion to add or change.

Musical mood drawing

Encourage the children to listen to other space-related music and draw ideas and pictures in response.

While completing this activity, encourage the children to close their eyes and properly listen first. This will help them to visualise ideas and make the link between sound and illustration.

Final thoughts and reflections

Consider the impact of dance and movement as a form of open expression to convey thoughts and ideas about a subject, in this case space and planets.

Reflect upon the importance of children taking the time to 'listen' to music and the instrument sounds involved. Consider the impact of developed listening, attention and concentration skills in the early years.

Resource support: *Example dance recorder card*

Name_____

My moonwalking dance

Activity 6 Planet puzzles

Activity outline and preparation

This activity encourages the children to problem solve and think in stages as they follow oral directions (via recordable buttons) to solve problems using literacy and mathematical knowledge and understanding.

Resources

- 3D versions of the eight planets – painted different sized balls, papier-mâché planets or a purchased resource. If you make the planets, be aware that planets should not be the same size. The inflatable solar system is the best resource available for purchase

- Velcro labels

- Recordable buttons – the 'Talking-point recordable buttons' that can be purchased online work very well. You can use individual iPads instead if you do not have recordable buttons

- Paper and pencils, crayons

- Planet order card – ensure the images used on this card match the planets created for the activity. An easy way to do this is to take quick photos of the 3D planets you will be using and add these to the planet order card

Preparation

- Organise or create planets for the activity: Mercury, Venus, Earth, Mars, Jupiter, Saturn, Uranus and Neptune. Add name labels to each planet.

- Create number labels (1–8) and add Velcro squares so they can easily be attached and unattached to the planets.

- Print planet order card.

- Record puzzle questions on individual recordable buttons. If you do not have recordable buttons, record individual puzzle questions on separate iPads via video so the children can access them this way instead. Suggested planet puzzle questions:

  o *How many planets can you count?*

  o *Can you sound out and read any planet names?*

  o *Can you place a number on each of the planets?*

  o *Look at the planet order. Can you place the planets in the correct order?*

  o *Can you choose a planet to draw and write its name?*

Activity development

ESSENTIAL LITERACY AND MATHEMATICS DEVELOPMENT				
PRIME AREAS		Development guidance	SPECIFIC AREAS		Development guidance

PRIME AREAS		Development guidance	SPECIFIC AREAS		Development guidance
COMMUNICATION AND LANGUAGE	Listening and attention	**30-50 months** *Is able to follow directions (if not intently focused on own choice of activity) (following general directions via recordable buttons/ iPads to solve planet puzzles)* **40-60+ months** *Two-channelled attention - can listen and do for short span (ability to listen to directions via recordable buttons/iPads and complete planet puzzles)*	**LITERACY**	Reading	**30-50 months** *Knows information can be relayed in the form of print (planet name labels and planet order card)* **40-60+ months** *Hears and says the initial sound in words* *Can segment the sounds in simple words and blend them together, and knows which letters represent some of them* ***ELG** Children read and understand simple sentences. They use phonic knowledge to decode regular words and read them aloud accurately. They also read some common irregular words. They demonstrate understanding when talking with others about what they have read. (using phonic knowledge to decode and read planet name labels and order card)*
				Writing	**30-50 months** *Sometimes give meaning to marks as they draw and paint (completion of one of the planet puzzles that requires drawing of planet and mark making for planet name)* **40-60+ months** *Gives meaning to marks they make as they draw, write and paint.* *Uses some clearly identifiable letters to communicate meaning, representing some sounds correctly and in sequence* ***ELG** Children use their phonic knowledge to write words in ways which match their spoken sounds. They also write some irregular common words. They write simple sentences which can be read by themselves and others. Some words are spelt correctly and others are phonetically plausible. (completion of one of the planet puzzles that requires drawing of planet and mark making or using phonic knowledge to write planet name)*
	Understanding	**30-50 months** *Beginning to understand 'why' and 'how' questions (responding to and understanding questions via recordable buttons/iPads)* **40-60+ months** *Responds to instructions involving a two-part sequence* ***ELG** Children follow instructions involving several ideas or actions. They answer 'how' and 'why' questions about their experiences and in response to stories or events. (responding to simple planet puzzle instructions via recordable buttons/iPads)*	**MATHEMATICS**	Numbers	**30-50 months** *Uses some number names accurately in play.* *Recites numbers in order to 10 (competition of the planet puzzles that focus upon number and sequencing)* **40-60+ months** *Recognises numerals 1 to 5* *Selects the correct numeral to represent 1 to 5, then 1 to 10 objects* ***ELG** Children count reliably with numbers from one to 20, place them in order and say which number is one more or one less than a given number. Using quantities and objects, they add and subtract two single-digit numbers and count on or back to find the answer. They solve problems, including doubling, halving and sharing. (completion of planet puzzles that focus upon recognition, counting and sequencing numbers from one to 20)*
	Speaking	**30-50 months** *Uses vocabulary focused on objects and people that are of particular importance to them (simple vocabulary related to planets and space)* **40-60+ months** *Links statements and sticks to a main theme or intention (statements linked to planet puzzles and main theme of space and planets)*		Shape, space and measure	**30-50 months** *Shows an interest in shape and space by playing with shapes or making arrangements with shapes* *Uses positional language (completion of planet puzzles that focus upon moving and ordering planets)* **40-60+ months** *Beginning to use mathematical names for 'solid' 3D shapes and mathematical terms to describe shapes (while completing planet puzzles, moving and ordering planets)*

CHARACTERISTICS OF EFFECTIVE LEARNING	Suggested outcomes
Playing and exploring – *engagement*	**Showing curiosity about planets and space**
Active learning – *motivation*	**Persisting with planet puzzles and the challenges they pose**
Creating and thinking critically – *thinking*	**Thinking of ideas to solve planet puzzles**

PRIME AREAS		Development guidance	SPECIFIC AREAS		Development guidance
PHYSICAL DEVELOPMENT	Moving and handling	**30-50 months** *Holds pencil near point between first two fingers, no longer using whole-hand grasp.* *Holds pencil near point between first two fingers and thumb and uses it with good control (completion of planet puzzle that focuses upon drawing a planet and mark making or writing the planet's name)* **40-60+ months** *Begins to form recognisable letters* **ELG** *Children show good control and co-ordination in large and small movements. They move confidently in a range of ways, safely negotiating space.* *They handle equipment and tools effectively, including pencils for writing. (completion of planet puzzle that focuses upon drawing a planet and mark making or writing the planet's name)*	**UNDERSTANDING THE WORLD**	People and communities	
				The world	**30-50 months** *Comments and asks questions about aspects of their familiar world such as the place where they live or the natural world (comments and asks questions about planets and space)* **40-60+ months** *Looks closely at similarities, differences, patterns and change.* **ELG** *Children know about similarities and differences in relation to places, objects, materials and living things. They talk about the features of their own immediate environment and how environments might vary from one another. They make observations of animals and plants and explain why some things occur, and talk about changes. (looking closely at simple similarities and differences in relation to planets)*
				Technology	**30-50 months** *Knows how to operate simple equipment e.g. turns on CD player and uses remote control (recordable buttons or iPads)* **ELG** *Children recognise that a range of technology is used in places such as homes and schools. They select and use technology for particular purposes (selecting and using recordable buttons or iPads)*
	Health and self-care	**30-50 months** *Holds pencil near point between first two fingers, no longer using whole-hand grasp.* *Holds pencil near point between first two fingers and thumb and uses it with good control (completion of planet puzzle that focuses upon drawing a planet and mark making or writing the planet name)* **40-60+ months** *Begins to form recognisable letters* **ELG** *Children show good control and co-ordination in large and small movements. They move confidently in a range of ways, safely negotiating space. They handle equipment and tools effectively, including pencils for writing. (completion of planet puzzle that focuses upon drawing a planet and mark making or writing the planet name)*	**EXPRESSIVE ARTS AND DESIGN**	Exploring and using media and materials	
				Being imaginative	
PERSONAL, SOCIAL AND EMOTIONAL DEVELOPMENT	Making relationships	**30-50 months** *Imitates play, offering cues to peers to join them (encouraging other children to join in with solving planet puzzles)* **40-60+ months** *Explains own knowledge and understanding, and asks appropriate questions of others (discussing own knowledge and understanding about planets)*			
	Self-confidence and self-awareness	**30-50 months** *Can select and use activities and resources with help (engaging with some planet puzzles and asking for help if needed)* **40-60+ months** *Confident to speak to others about own needs, wants, interests and opinions* **ELG** *Children are confident to try new activities, and say why they like some activities more than others. They are confident to speak in a familiar group, will talk about their ideas, and will choose the resources they need for their chosen activities. They say when they do or don't need help. (confidence sharing ideas about planets and choosing resources to complete planet puzzles)*			
	Managing feelings and behaviour	**30-50 months** *Begins to accept the needs of others and can take turns and share resources, sometimes with support from others (sharing of recordable buttons/iPads and planets, labels)* **40-60+ months** *Understands that own actions affect other people, for example becomes upset or tries to comfort another child when they realise they have upset them (understands sharing of resources, e.g. planets and the impact if they do not do this)*			

Activity guidance

This is a continuous provision activity that challenges the children to engage with puzzles and solve problems using mathematical and reading knowledge and understanding.

Display the labelled planets on a table area or on the floor. Place the recordable buttons or iPads (with pre-recorded planet puzzle questions) on a nearby table. Organise Velcro number labels in a box or basket within the same area and display the planet order card.

To initiate interest gather an engaged group of children around the planets and generate interest about the planets, asking children to share information they may already know. Model how to use the recordable button or iPad for this activity and work through one puzzle together.

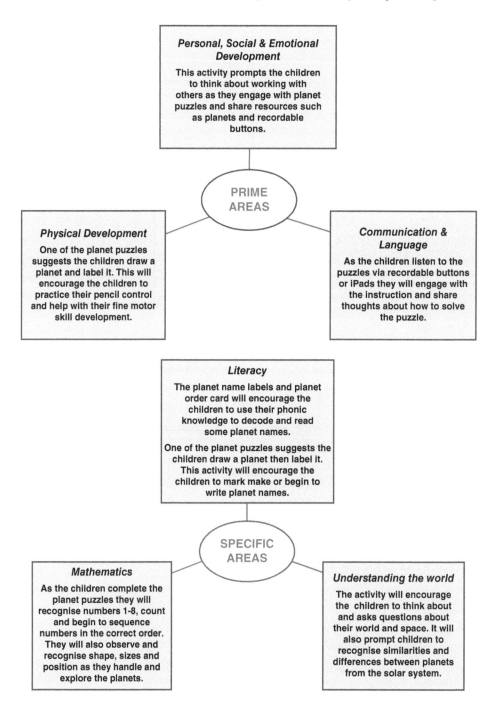

Personal, Social & Emotional Development

This activity prompts the children to think about working with others as they engage with planet puzzles and share resources such as planets and recordable buttons.

PRIME AREAS

Physical Development

One of the planet puzzles suggests the children draw a planet and label it. This will encourage the children to practice their pencil control and help with their fine motor skill development.

Communication & Language

As the children listen to the puzzles via recordable buttons or iPads they will engage with the instruction and share thoughts about how to solve the puzzle.

Literacy

The planet name labels and planet order card will encourage the children to use their phonic knowledge to decode and read some planet names.

One of the planet puzzles suggests the children draw a planet then label it. This activity will encourage the children to mark make or begin to write planet names.

SPECIFIC AREAS

Mathematics

As the children complete the planet puzzles they will recognise numbers 1-8, count and begin to sequence numbers in the correct order. They will also observe and recognise shape, sizes and position as they handle and explore the planets.

Understanding the world

The activity will encourage the children to think about and asks questions about their world and space. It will also prompt children to recognise similarities and differences between planets from the solar system.

Possible next steps and opportunities for further development

Planets, planets, planets

Following the focus upon planet names and order during the original activity, encourage the children to find out some simple facts about the planets. This can be organised via QR codes. First select simple websites or create your own basic information sheets for individual planets, generate QR codes, print and display the codes and encourage children to explore using iPads/tablets with a QR code reader installed.

The use of QR codes for this activity will allow the children to explore small amounts of information about planets in a safe and easy way.

Planet music

Encourage the children to think about planets and space from a musical perspective. Listen to a piece of music such as an extract from Gustav Holst, *The Planets* and ask the children to think about instrument sounds, speed and volume. Then encourage children to explore a box of instruments and create planet sounds.

While children are listening to a piece of music, encourage them to close their eyes (wear eye masks if possible) and listen very carefully to the different sounds and instruments. Some children may be able to identify an instrument with a familiar sound and then replicate this afterwards, e.g. drum or twinkling triangle.

Final thoughts and reflections

Consider the impact of exploratory play and the foundations this lays. This activity encourages children to absorb planet names and other small pieces of indirect information. When children experience formal science teaching about space and planets in upper KS2, these foundations can easily be built upon.

Reflect upon the use of recorded voice to direct the children in this activity. It is important the children have lots of practice with 'listening' carefully to directions and instructions so they can logically compute them. The recordable buttons are excellent for this because the children can simply play, replay and listen several times.

Resource support: *Example planet order card*

Our Planets

1	Mercury	
2	Venus	
3	Earth	
4	Mars	
5	Jupiter	
6	Saturn	
7	Uranus	
8	Neptune	

CHAPTER 3

LEARNING THREAD
DANGEROUS DINOSAURS

Dangerous Dinosaurs

In this chapter

In this chapter, you will find activities related to 'dinosaurs'. This learning thread links to:

- exploration and discovery, through activities such as 'Dino dig' alongside 'Hide and seek dinosaurs'

- estimation and logic, through activities such as 'Bones, bones, bones!', 'Big feet!' and 'Shape shifting dinosaurs'

- word writing inspired by drama and interaction, through 'Roar and growl!'

The activities in this chapter will help you to work towards:

- developing children's wider knowledge about dinosaurs and excavation through curiosity and discovery

- encouraging children's estimation and logic skills through large-scale floor discovery

- developing children's initial writing through talk and drama.

Activities

	Activity	Page	Provision
1	Roar and growl!	79	Interactive display/continuous provision indoors
2	Bones, bones, bones!	85	Continuous provision indoors or outdoors
3	Dino dig	91	Continuous provision indoors or outdoors
4	Shape shifting dinosaur	97	Continuous provision indoors or outdoors
5	Hide and seek dinosaurs	103	Continuous provision indoors or outdoors
6	Big feet!	109	Continuous provision indoors or outdoors

Role-play area links:

- Rainforest or jungle area

- Volcano or cave

- Dinosaur museum (with fossils and magnifiers, information posters, booklets) with ticket admission

Activity 1 Roar and growl!

Activity outline and preparation

This activity encourages the children to engage with several micro activities such as listening to dinosaur sounds or songs, observing fossils, building with Duplo, engaging with dinosaur books or photos and creating dinosaur speech bubbles, and works well presented as an interactive display. It aims to develop the children's interest through interaction and talk which in turn will inspire word mark making and writing.

To encourage quality interaction with this display and micro activities, consider outlaying for resources that will develop different skills in various ways with the children. For example:

Resources

- *Visual* – dinosaur books, laminated photos (dinosaurs, fossils, bones) magnifiers, posters, dinosaur number line

- *Auditory* – dinosaur sounds or songs, through a player and headphones or out loud if possible

- *Kinaesthetic* – Duplo (for dinosaur building), fossils (for observing and handling), magnifiers

Plus:

- Roaring dinosaur image (plenty of images online suitable for printing)

- Speech bubbles (laminated to use with dry-wipe pens) and Blu-tack or Velcro tabs

Preparation

- In preparation for the activity, clear a small area in the setting, ideally a tabled area against a back wall or board as this allows more space for display. Within this area, display examples of visual, auditory and kinaesthetic resources as suggested above.

- On the back wall or board, display a large roaring dinosaur image. Around the image, create space for children to add completed speech bubbles.

- In front of the roaring image, organise baskets or boxes with speech bubbles, Blu-tack or Velcro tabs, dry-wipe pens and dry-wipe erasers.

Activity development

ESSENTIAL LITERACY AND MATHEMATICS DEVELOPMENT				
PRIME AREAS		**Development guidance**	**SPECIFIC AREAS**	**Development guidance**
COMMUNICATION AND LANGUAGE	Listening and attention	**30-50 months** *Focusing attention - still listen or do but can shift own attention (while engaging with interactive display)* **40-60+ months** *Two-channelled attention - can listen and do for short span* ***ELG** Children listen attentively in a range of situations. They listen to stories, accurately anticipating key events and respond to what they hear with relevant comments, questions or actions. They give their attention to what others say and respond appropriately, while engaged in another activity. (simultaneous listening to dinosaur sounds, looking at visuals or exploring practical resources within display)*	LITERACY — Reading	**30-50 months** *Shows interest in illustrations and print in books and print in the environment (interest in dinosaur books on display)* **40-60+ months** *Enjoys an increasing range of books* *Knows information can be retrieved from books* ***ELG** Children read and understand simple sentences. They use phonic knowledge to decode regular words and read them aloud accurately. They also read some common irregular words. They demonstrate understanding when talking with others about what they have read. (using phonic knowledge to understand simple words and sentences in dinosaur books)*
			LITERACY — Writing	**30-50 months** *Sometimes gives meaning to marks as they draw and paint (dinosaur speech bubbles)* **40-60+ months** *Hears and says initial sounds in words* *Can segment sounds in simple words and blend them together* *Uses some clearly identifiable letters to communicate meaning, representing some sounds correctly and in sequence* ***ELG** Children use their phonic knowledge to write words in ways which match their spoken sounds. They also write some irregular common words. They write simple sentences which can be read by themselves and others. Some words are spelt correctly and others are phonetically plausible. (independently sounding out and spelling words whilst completing dinosaur speech bubbles)*
	Understanding	**30-50 months** *Understands use of objects (within interactive display, e.g. magnifiers with visuals, Duplo for building)* **40-60+ months** *Listens and responds to ideas expressed by others in conversation or discussion (using interactive experiences to develop word writing)* ***ELG** Children follow instructions involving several ideas or actions. They answer 'how' and 'why' questions about their experiences and in response to stories or events. (children follow ideas and instructions about how to access interactive display resources)*	MATHEMATICS — Numbers	**30-50 months** *Shows an interest in representing numbers (recognition of some numbers on displayed dinosaur number line)* ***ELG** Children count reliably with numbers from one to 20, place them in order and say which number is one more or one less than a given number. Using quantities and objects, they add and subtract two single-digit numbers and count on or back to find the answer. They solve problems, including doubling, halving and sharing. (interaction with numbers one to 20 on displayed dinosaur number line)*
	Speaking	**30-50 months** *Uses vocabulary focused on objects and people that are of particular importance to them (vocabulary inspired by and related to dinosaurs)* **40-60+ months** *Uses talk to organise, sequence and clarify thinking, ideas, feelings and events (inspired by interactive resources on display, using language related to dinosaurs)*	MATHEMATICS — Shape, space and measure	**30-50 months** *Shows an interest in shape and space by playing with shapes and making arrangements with objects (Duplo dinosaur building)* **40-60+ months** *Uses familiar objects and common shapes to create and recreate patterns and build models* ***ELG** Children use everyday language to talk about size, weight, capacity, position, distance, time and money to compare quantities and objects and to solve problems. They recognise, create and describe patterns. They explore characteristics of everyday objects and shapes and use mathematical language to describe them. (exploring characteristics of shapes whilst Duplo dinosaur building)*

CHARACTERISTICS OF EFFECTIVE LEARNING	Suggested outcomes
Playing and exploring – *engagement*	Engaging in open-ended activities within the interactive display
Active learning – *motivation*	Being proud of achievements, e.g. dinosaur word writing and mark making
Creating and thinking critically – *thinking*	Thinking and planning how to approach activities within the interactive display - choosing and pursuing

PRIME AREAS		Development guidance	SPECIFIC AREAS		Development guidance
PHYSICAL DEVELOPMENT	Moving and handling	**30-50 months** *Holds pencil between thumb and two fingers, no longer using whole-hand grasp (while mark making on dinosaur speech bubbles)* **40-60+ months** *Shows a preference for dominant hand* *Begins to form recognisable letters* **ELG** *Children show good control and co-ordination in large and small movements. They move confidently in a range of ways, safely negotiating space. They handle equipment and tools effectively, including pencils for writing. (good pencil control and co-ordination whilst creating dinosaur speech bubble)*	UNDERSTANDING THE WORLD	People and communities	
				The world	**30-50 months** *Comments on and asks questions about aspects of their familiar world such as the place where they live or the natural world* *Can talk about some things they have observed such as plants, animals, natural and found objects (interaction with displayed resources - books, fossils)* **ELG** *Children know about similarities and differences in relation to places, objects, materials and living things. They talk about the features of their own immediate environment and how environments might vary from one another. They make observations of animals and plants and explain why some things occur, and talk about changes. (making observations and noticing similarities and differences whilst interacting with display books, fossils and other resources)*
				Technology	
	Health and self-care		EXPRESSIVE ARTS AND DESIGN	Exploring and using media and materials	**30-50 months** *Uses various construction materials (Duplo dinosaur building)* **40-60+ months** *Constructs with a purpose in mind, using a variety of resources (whilst engaging in Duplo dinosaur building)*
				Being imaginative	
PERSONAL, SOCIAL AND EMOTIONAL DEVELOPMENT	Making relationships	**30-50 months** *Keeps play going by responding to what others are saying or doing (while exploring interactive display)* *Explains own knowledge and understanding and asks appropriate questions of others* **ELG** *Children play co-operatively, taking turns with others. They take account of one another's ideas about how to organise their activity. They show sensitivity to others' needs and feelings, and form positive relationships with adults and other children. (playing co-operatively and taking turns whilst exploring activities as part of interactive display).*			
	Self-confidence and self-awareness	**30-50 months** *Enjoys responsibility of carrying out small tasks (interactive display activities)* **ELG** *Children are confident to try new activities, and say why they like some activities more than others. They are confident to speak in a familiar group, will talk about their ideas, and will choose the resources they need for their chosen activities. They say when they do or don't need help. (confidence choosing activities and selecting resources from interactive display)*			
	Managing feelings and behaviour	**30-50 months** *Begins to accept the needs of others and can take turns and share resources, sometimes with support from others (taking turns and sharing whilst exploring activities as part of interactive display)* **40-60+ months** *Beginning to be able to negotiate and solve problems without aggression* **ELG** *Children talk about how they and others show feelings, talk about their own and others' behaviour, and its consequences, and know that some behaviour is unacceptable. They work as part of a group or class, and understand and follow the rules. They adjust their behaviour to different situations, and take changes of routine in their stride. (exploring interactive display sensibly alongside other children)*			

Activity guidance

This is a continuous provision interactive display that aims to develop independent discovery and inspire early writing.

Set up the interactive display area following the ideas listed within resources and preparation.

To initiate interest ask the children what they know about dinosaurs. Ask them to think about the shapes of dinosaurs and the sounds they may have made. Encourage the children to explore the interactive resources to discover further.

Children may need some guidance when completing speech bubbles. It is a good idea to model some examples on display to guide and inspire children.

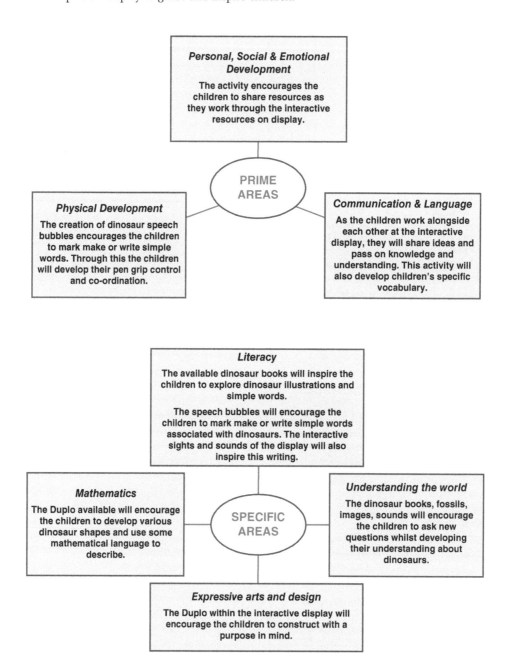

Personal, Social & Emotional Development

The activity encourages the children to share resources as they work through the interactive resources on display.

PRIME AREAS

Physical Development

The creation of dinosaur speech bubbles encourages the children to mark make or write simple words. Through this the children will develop their pen grip control and co-ordination.

Communication & Language

As the children work alongside each other at the interactive display, they will share ideas and pass on knowledge and understanding. This activity will also develop children's specific vocabulary.

Literacy

The available dinosaur books will inspire the children to explore dinosaur illustrations and simple words.

The speech bubbles will encourage the children to mark make or write simple words associated with dinosaurs. The interactive sights and sounds of the display will also inspire this writing.

Mathematics

The Duplo available will encourage the children to develop various dinosaur shapes and use some mathematical language to describe.

SPECIFIC AREAS

Understanding the world

The dinosaur books, fossils, images, sounds will encourage the children to ask new questions whilst developing their understanding about dinosaurs.

Expressive arts and design

The Duplo within the interactive display will encourage the children to construct with a purpose in mind.

Possible next steps and opportunities for further development

Dinosaur discovery book

Collect photos of dinosaur Duplo building, fossil handling and copies of completed speech bubbles to create a discovery book that can be displayed within the setting.

Some children will be reluctant to mark make or write so the examples of completed speech bubbles will inspire those children retrospectively. The main purpose of the discovery book is to celebrate achievements and inspire others.

Dinosaur sounds

Some children will really enjoy listening to the dinosaur sounds or songs as part of the interactive display. These children would also then enjoy exploring making dinosaur sounds with instruments.

The use of instruments to create 'dinosaur sounds' will inspire some children with their vocabulary and early writing. As they create loud or spiky sounds, the children can be encouraged to describe those sounds with a word, which encourages association between thinking and written description.

Final thoughts and reflections

These early explorations with audio, visual and kinaesthetic resources will help different children develop understanding about dinosaurs through various approaches.

Reflect upon the impact of practical activities and the development of children's vocabulary and written recordings. Experience, questioning and talk helps children visualise ideas before the stage of mark making or writing.

Resource support: Example speech bubbles

Activity 2 Bones, bones, bones!

Activity outline and preparation

This activity involves a large-scale dinosaur outline and encourages the children to think about organising and arranging 'bones' inside a dinosaur body using art straws. Engaging with dinosaur books forms part of the activity so children can observe dinosaur illustrations and relate observations of skeletons to the activity. It works best as a large-scale floor activity but if you are short on space it may be better suited outdoors.

Resources

- Large-scale dinosaur outline – either drawn on a large sheet of paper or chalked along the floor outside

- Art straws

- Scissors

- Laminated name labels

- Dinosaur books

Preparation

- In preparation for the activity, create a large-scale floor dinosaur outline either on paper or chalked on the floor.

- Display dinosaur books nearby.

- Provide a basket of art straws and a box of scissors by the activity.

- Print and laminate templates for dinosaur name labels.

ESSENTIAL LITERACY AND MATHEMATICS DEVELOPMENT				
PRIME AREAS		**Development guidance**	**SPECIFIC AREAS**	**Development guidance**
COMMUNICATION AND LANGUAGE	Listening and attention	**30-50 months** *Listens to others one to one or in small groups when conversation interests them (while engaging with bones activity)* **40-60+ months** *Two-channelled attention – can listen and do for short span* **ELG** *Children listen attentively in a range of situations. They listen to stories, accurately anticipating key events and respond to what they hear with relevant comments, questions or actions. They give their attention to what others say and respond appropriately, while engaged in another activity. (simultaneous listening to others stories and ideas and conversations while engaging with bones activity)*	**LITERACY** — Reading	**30-50 months** *Shows an interest in illustrations and print in books and print in the environment (illustrations and print in dinosaur books alongside the activity)* **40-60+ months** *Enjoys an increasing range of books* *Knows information can be retrieved from books and computers.* **ELG** *Children read and understand simple sentences. They use phonic knowledge to decode regular words and read them aloud accurately. They also read some common irregular words. They demonstrate understanding when talking with others about what they have read. (reading and understanding simple words and sentences whilst engaging with dinosaur books alongside the activity)*
			Writing	**30-50 months** *Sometimes give meaning to marks as they draw and paint.* *Ascribe meaning to marks that they see in different places (dinosaur name labels)* **40-60+ months** *Hears and says initial sounds in words* *Can segment sounds in simple words and blend them together* *Uses some clearly identifiable letters to communicate meaning, representing some sounds correctly and in sequence* **ELG** *Children use their phonic knowledge to write words in ways which match their spoken sounds. They also write some irregular common words. They write simple sentences which can be read by themselves and others. Some words are spelt correctly and others are phonetically plausible. (using phonic knowledge to sound out and write dinosaur names labels)*
	Understanding	**30-50 months** *Shows understanding of prepositions such as 'under', 'on top', 'behind' by carrying out an action or selecting correct picture (while arranging bones 'inside' the outline)* **40-60+ months** *Listens and responds to ideas expressed by others in conversation or discussion (listens to others' ideas while arranging bones)*	**MATHEMATICS** — Numbers	**30-50 months** *Shows an interest in representing numbers* *Recites numbers in order to ten (spontaneous counting while constructing bones)* **ELG** *Children count reliably with numbers from one to 20, place them in order and say which number is one more or one less than a given number. Using quantities and objects, they add and subtract two single-digit numbers and count on or back to find the answer. They solve problems, including doubling, halving and sharing. (spontaneous counting with numbers to 20 whilst selecting and constructing with bones)*
	Speaking	**30-50 months** *Uses vocabulary focused on objects and people that are of particular importance to them (vocabulary inspired by and related to dinosaurs)* **40-60+ months** *Extends vocabulary, especially by grouping and naming, exploring the meaning and sounds of new words* **ELG** *Children express themselves effectively, showing awareness of listeners' needs. They use past, present and future forms accurately when talking about events that have happened or are to happen in the future. They develop their own narratives and explanations by connecting ideas or events. (developing vocabulary associated with dinosaurs inspired by books and activity)*	Shape, space and measure	**30-50 months** *Shows interest in shape by sustained construction activity or by talking about shapes or arrangements (interest and discussion whilst arranging bones within large-scale dinosaur outline)* **40-60+ months** *Can describe their relative position such as 'behind' or 'next to'* **ELG** *Children use everyday language to talk about size, weight, capacity, position, distance, time and money to compare quantities and objects and to solve problems. They recognise, create and describe patterns. They explore characteristics of everyday objects and shapes and use mathematical language to describe them. (use of everyday and mathematical language whilst arranging bones within large-scale dinosaur outline)*

CHARACTERISTICS OF EFFECTIVE LEARNING	Suggested outcomes
Playing and exploring – *engagement*	**Showing an interest in dinosaurs**
Active learning – *motivation*	**Paying attention to ideas and detail while constructing dinosaur 'bones'**
Creating and thinking critically – *thinking*	**Making links between activity and dinosaur bones in books**

PRIME AREAS		Development guidance		SPECIFIC AREAS		Development guidance
PHYSICAL DEVELOPMENT	Moving and handling	**30-50 months** *Uses one-handed tools and equipment (snips of straws while assembling)* **40-60+ months** *Handles tools, objects, construction and malleable materials safely and with increasing control (while using art straws for bones)* **ELG** *Children show good control and co-ordination in large and small movements. They move confidently in a range of ways, safely negotiating space. They handle equipment and tools effectively, including pencils for writing. (handling of art straws, scissors with good control and co-ordination with pens when adding dinosaur names)*	UNDERSTANDING THE WORLD	People and communities		
				The world	**30-50 months** *Can talk about some of the things they have observed such as plants, animals, natural and found objects (talk about observed information from dinosaur books)* **ELG** *Children know about similarities and differences in relation to places, objects, materials and living things. They talk about the features of their own immediate environment and how environments might vary from one another. They make observations of animals and plants and explain why some things occur, and talk about changes. (they make observations whist exploring dinosaur books and share some ideas about how dinosaur bones could be arranged)*
					Technology	
	Health and self-care	**30-50 months** *Understands that equipment and tools have to be used safely (use of scissors when snipping art straws)* **40-60+ months** *Practises some appropriate safety measures without direct supervision (use of scissors when snipping art straws)*	EXPRESSIVE ARTS AND DESIGN	Exploring and using media and materials	**30-50 months** *Joins construction pieces together to build and balance (use of art straws to construct, arrange and join 'bones')* **40-60+ months** *Constructs with a purpose in mind, using a variety of resources.* *Selects tools and techniques needed to shape, assemble and join materials they are using (uses art straws to construct 'bones' and selects tools such as scissors to shape and assemble)*
					Being imaginative	
PERSONAL, SOCIAL AND EMOTIONAL DEVELOPMENT	Making relationships	**30-50 months** *Initiates play, offering cues to peers to join them (encouraging others to join group floor activity)* *Children play co-operatively, taking turns with others. They take account of one another's ideas about how to organise their activity. They show sensitivity to others' needs and feelings, and form positive relationships with adults and other children. (taking turns, working co-operatively about how the dinosaur should look/where bones should go)*				
	Self-confidence and self-awareness	**30-50 months** *Enjoys responsibility of carrying out small tasks (involvement in open-ended task)* **ELG** *Children are confident to try new activities, and say why they like some activities more than others. They are confident to speak in a familiar group, will talk about their ideas, and will choose the resources they need for their chosen activities. They say when they do or don't need help. (confidence selecting and arranging straws to represent bones without help but checking if they become stuck)*				
	Managing feelings and behaviour	**30-50 months** *Begins to accept the needs of others and can take turns and share resources, sometimes with support from others (taking turns and sharing resources whilst involved in open-ended task of 'bone' arranging)* **ELG** *Children talk about how they and others show feelings, talk about their own and others' behaviour, and its consequences, and know that some behaviour is unacceptable. They work as part of a group or class, and understand and follow the rules. They adjust their behaviour to different situations, and take changes of routine in their stride. (working within the group to keep on task and negotiate how the dinosaur should look/ where the 'bones' should go)*				

Activity guidance

This is a continuous provision activity that aims to develop shape and space awareness.

Create a large-scale floor dinosaur outline either on paper or on the floor. Set up supporting resources such as art straws, scissors and dinosaur books nearby.

To initiate interest ask the children what they know about dinosaurs. Ask them to think about dinosaur bones that have been discovered (show examples from books). What would those bones have looked like inside dinosaur bodies?

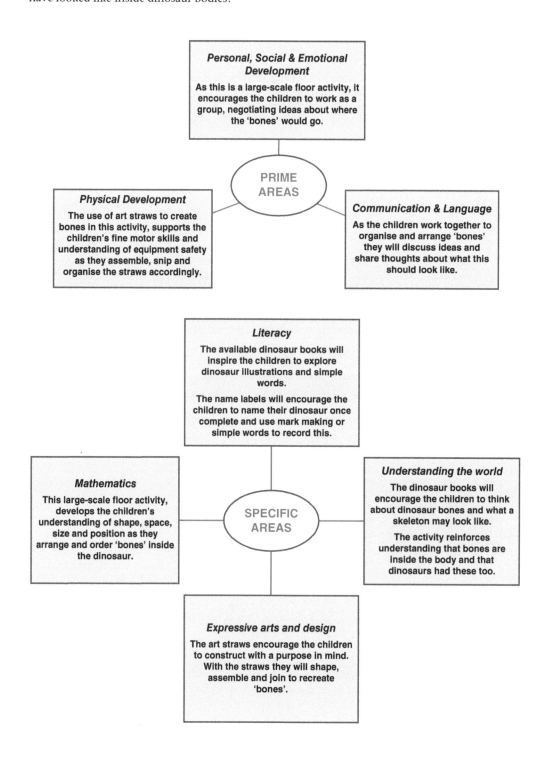

Personal, Social & Emotional Development

As this is a large-scale floor activity, it encourages the children to work as a group, negotiating ideas about where the 'bones' would go.

PRIME AREAS

Physical Development

The use of art straws to create bones in this activity, supports the children's fine motor skills and understanding of equipment safety as they assemble, snip and organise the straws accordingly.

Communication & Language

As the children work together to organise and arrange 'bones' they will discuss ideas and share thoughts about what this should look like.

Literacy

The available dinosaur books will inspire the children to explore dinosaur illustrations and simple words.

The name labels will encourage the children to name their dinosaur once complete and use mark making or simple words to record this.

Mathematics

This large-scale floor activity, develops the children's understanding of shape, space, size and position as they arrange and order 'bones' inside the dinosaur.

SPECIFIC AREAS

Understanding the world

The dinosaur books will encourage the children to think about dinosaur bones and what a skeleton may look like.

The activity reinforces understanding that bones are inside the body and that dinosaurs had these too.

Expressive arts and design

The art straws encourage the children to construct with a purpose in mind. With the straws they will shape, assemble and join to recreate 'bones'.

Possible next steps and opportunities for further development

X-rays

Explore further work on bones through X-rays. Look at human and animal X-rays so children can observe different skeletons.

For some children this will ignite real interest in bones inside our bodies. Others will be less interested but curious about some X-ray images.

Palaeontologists!

Explore what science detectives (palaeontologists) do and how they discover clues from the past. Look at developing understanding through role-play.

Some children will be curious about the role of a science detective and will be interested in activities related to this. For these children consider more input with fossils so they can observe closely and notice similarities and differences with shapes.

Final thoughts and reflections

Consider the impact of early exploration and the foundation it lays. Through this activity, children will begin to recognise bones as collective, linear structures. Future teaching and learning will build upon this in more detail but the initial interest begins with early exploration.

Reflect upon the impact of large-scale floor activities. This approach encourages team working, confidence building and group sharing of thoughts.

Resource support: *Example dinosaur name labels*

This dinosaur's name is

This dinosaur is called

Activity 3 Dino dig

Activity outline and preparation

This activity encourages the children to role-play as a science detective (palaeontologist) and dig through sand to locate and collect dinosaur bones.

It will need a sand tray or pit so the children have sufficient space to dig freely. A sand tray will work inside but an outdoor sand pit area would be ideal.

Resources

- Plastic set of bones (can be bought online) or printed and laminated set of bones – laminated bones can also include labels such as 'skull', 'leg bone', 'rib'

- Sand tray or outside sand pit

- Trowels, scoops, different sized paint brushes

- Scribble sheet to display – include a question such as 'Can you draw and label any bones you have found?'

- Sheet to lay out discovered bones

Preparation

- Print and laminate bones (if you choose to use these, as opposed to plastic bones) and ensure all bones are labelled.

- Organise the sand tray or sand pit with fresh sand. If you add a small amount of water, it will help.

- Gather tools such as trowels, scoops, brushes to use.

- Find a short video online about palaeontologists and the job they do.

- Prepare a 'scribble sheet' for children to record their findings. This can be displayed on a wall or on the floor.

Activity development

ESSENTIAL LITERACY AND MATHEMATICS DEVELOPMENT				
PRIME AREAS	Development guidance	SPECIFIC AREAS		Development guidance
COMMUNICATION AND LANGUAGE — Listening and attention	**30-50 months** *Listens to stories with increasing attention and recall (while listening to short video about palaeontologist)* **ELG** *Children listen attentively in a range of situations. They listen to stories, accurately anticipating key events and respond to what they hear with relevant comments, questions or actions. They give their attention to what others say and respond appropriately, while engaged in another activity. (listens to a short video about palaeontologist and their job)*	**LITERACY**	Reading	**30-50 months** *Knows information can be relayed in the form of print (bone labels)* **40-60+ months** *Hears and says initial sounds in words* *Can segment the sounds in simple words and blend them together and knows which letters represent some of them* **ELG** *Children read and understand simple sentences. They use phonic knowledge to decode regular words and read them aloud accurately. They also read some common irregular words. They demonstrate understanding when talking with others about what they have read. (using phonic knowledge to decode and read bone labels)*
			Writing	**30-50 months** *Sometimes give meaning to marks as they draw and paint (illustrations, marks on scribble sheet)* **40-60+ months** *Uses some clearly identifiable letters to communicate meaning, representing some sounds correctly and in sequence* **ELG** *Children use their phonic knowledge to write words in ways which match their spoken sounds. They also write some irregular common words. They write simple sentences which can be read by themselves and others. Some words are spelt correctly and others are phonetically plausible. (using their phonic knowledge to make marks, write words or simple sentences on scribble sheet)*
Understanding	**30-50 months** *Shows understanding of prepositions such as 'under', 'on top', 'behind' by carrying out an action or selecting correct picture (while digging through sand)* **40-60+ months** *Listens and responds to ideas expressed by others in conversation or discussion (listens to others' ideas while digging)*	**MATHEMATICS**	Numbers	**30-50 months** *Uses some number names and number language spontaneously (spontaneous counting while finding and collecting bones)* **40-60+ months** *Estimates how many objects they can see and checks by counting them (estimation as digging for bones)* **ELG** *Children count reliably with numbers from one to 20, place them in order and say which number is one more or one less than a given number. Using quantities and objects, they add and subtract two single-digit numbers and count on or back to find the answer. They solve problems, including doubling, halving and sharing. (spontaneous counting of numbers up to 20 whilst finding and collecting bones)*
Speaking	**30-50 months** *Uses vocabulary focused on objects and people that are of particular importance to them (vocabulary inspired by and related to dinosaurs)* **40-60+ months** *Uses language to imagine and recreate roles and experiences in play situations (as palaeontologist)* **ELG** *Children express themselves effectively, showing awareness of listeners' needs. They use past, present and future forms accurately when talking about events that have happened or are to happen in the future. They develop their own narratives and explanations by connecting ideas or events. (expressing themselves and sharing ideas whilst digging.)*		Shape, space and measure	**30-50 months** *Uses positional language (while digging for bones)* **40-60+ months** *Can describe their relative position such as 'behind' or 'next to'* **ELG** *Children use everyday language to talk about size, weight, capacity, position, distance, time and money to compare quantities and objects and to solve problems. They recognise, create and describe patterns. They explore characteristics of everyday objects and shapes and use mathematical language to describe them. (use of everyday and mathematical language whilst digging, locating and comparing bones)*

CHARACTERISTICS OF EFFECTIVE LEARNING	Suggested outcomes
Playing and exploring – *engagement*	**Meeting challenge to seek and find within sand**
Active learning – *motivation*	**High levels of enthusiasm and fascination while digging**
Creating and thinking critically – *thinking*	**Changing strategies as progress, i.e. choosing best/preferred tools**

PRIME AREAS		Development guidance	SPECIFIC AREAS		Development guidance
PHYSICAL DEVELOPMENT	Moving and handling	**30-50 months** *Uses one-handed tools and equipment (tools while digging)* **40-60+ months** *Handles tools, objects, construction and malleable materials safely and with increasing control (handling of tools while digging)* **ELG** *Children show good control and co-ordination in large and small movements. They move confidently in a range of ways, safely negotiating space. They handle equipment and tools effectively, including pencils for writing. (good co-ordination and handling of tools as well as pencils whilst recording on scribble sheet)*	UNDERSTANDING THE WORLD	People and communities	**30-50 months** *Shows interest in different occupations and ways of life (Interest in palaeontologist in video)*
				The world	**30-50 months** *Can talk about some of the things they have observed such as plants, animals, natural and found objects (talk about natural, found bones)* **40-60+ months** *Looks closely at similarities, differences, patterns and change* **ELG** *Children know about similarities and differences in relation to places, objects, materials and living things. They talk about the features of their own immediate environment and how environments might vary from one another. They make observations of animals and plants and explain why some things occur, and talk about changes. (talking about observations, similarities and differences with discovered bones)*
				Technology	**30-50 months** *Knows information can be retrieved from computers (internet - video of palaeontologist)* **ELG** *Children recognise that a range of technology is used in places such as homes and schools. They select and use technology for particular purposes. (understanding select and use of the internet – video of palaeontologist)*
	Health and self-care	**30-50 months** *Understands that equipment and tools have to be used safely (use of trowels and other digging equipment safely)* **40-60+ months** *Practises some appropriate safety measures without direct supervision (safely using trowels and other digging equipment)*	EXPRESSIVE ARTS AND DESIGN	Exploring and using media and materials	**30-50 months** *Realises tools can be used for a purpose (tools for digging and discovering)* **40-60+ months** *Uses tools and techniques competently and appropriately* **ELG** *Children sing songs, make music and dance, and experiment with ways of changing them. They safely use and explore a variety of materials, tools and techniques, experimenting with colour, design, texture, form and function. (safely explore and look for bones with tools and techniques)*
				Being imaginative	
PERSONAL, SOCIAL AND EMOTIONAL DEVELOPMENT	Making relationships	**30-50 months** *Can play in a group, extending and elaborating play ideas (role-play palaeontologist)* **40-60+ months** *Explains own knowledge and understanding and asks appropriate questions of others (whilst digging and discovering)* **ELG** *Children play co-operatively, taking turns with others. They take account of one another's ideas about how to organise their activity. They show sensitivity to others' needs and feelings, and form positive relationships with adults and other children. (playing co-operatively and taking turns with tools and digging space)*			
	Self-confidence and self-awareness	**30-50 months** *Enjoys responsibility of carrying out small tasks (while digging and exploring - enjoying the responsibility of discovering for themselves)* **ELG** *Children are confident to try new activities, and say why they like some activities more than others. They are confident to speak in a familiar group, will talk about their ideas, and will choose the resources they need for their chosen activities. They say when they do or don't need help. (confidence selecting tools without help and digging).*			
	Managing feelings and behaviour	**30-50 months** *Begins to accept the needs of others and can take turns and share resources, sometimes with support from others (sharing tools whilst digging, sometimes with encouragement)* **ELG** *Children talk about how they and others show feelings, talk about their own and others' behaviour, and its consequences, and know that some behaviour is unacceptable. They work as part of a group or class, and understand and follow the rules. They adjust their behaviour to different situations, and take changes of routine in their stride. (digging co-operatively as a group and sensible with sand)*			

Activity guidance

This is a continuous provision activity that will probe curiosity and encourage the children to role-play and develop learning though discovery.

Set up the sand pit or tray with buried bones and arrange tools and a scribble sheet nearby.

To initiate interest locate a short video about science detectives (palaeontologists) online and share with the children. What do science detectives (palaeontologists) do? How do they do it? What tools do they use to make discoveries? Can we dig and make discoveries like science detectives?

Once children have been digging and exploring for some time, return to the activity and encourage children to record their findings via illustrations, marks or words on the scribble sheet.

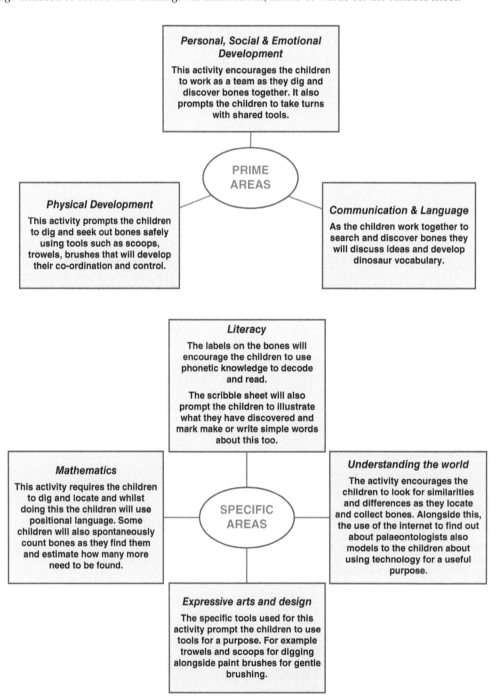

Personal, Social & Emotional Development

This activity encourages the children to work as a team as they dig and discover bones together. It also prompts the children to take turns with shared tools.

PRIME AREAS

Physical Development

This activity prompts the children to dig and seek out bones safely using tools such as scoops, trowels, brushes that will develop their co-ordination and control.

Communication & Language

As the children work together to search and discover bones they will discuss ideas and develop dinosaur vocabulary.

Literacy

The labels on the bones will encourage the children to use phonetic knowledge to decode and read.

The scribble sheet will also prompt the children to illustrate what they have discovered and mark make or write simple words about this too.

Mathematics

This activity requires the children to dig and locate and whilst doing this the children will use positional language. Some children will also spontaneously count bones as they find them and estimate how many more need to be found.

SPECIFIC AREAS

Understanding the world

The activity encourages the children to look for similarities and differences as they locate and collect bones. Alongside this, the use of the internet to find out about palaeontologists also models to the children about using technology for a useful purpose.

Expressive arts and design

The specific tools used for this activity prompt the children to use tools for a purpose. For example trowels and scoops for digging alongside paint brushes for gentle brushing.

Possible next steps and opportunities for further development

Fossils

Introduce the children to fossils and discuss how bones can often be fossilised. Let the children explore the texture and shapes of the fossils and ask them to talk about what they can see.

This activity will encourage those children who like to touch and feel objects. It is also good for developing speaking and listening and helping children talk about their simple observations.

Illustrating dinosaurs

Children will often enjoy illustrating pictures of dinosaurs. As a follow-on from discovering bones, children can develop their visual thinking skills by drawing a picture of the dinosaur they think the bones may belong to.

Consider grouping the children to complete this activity with a large-scale sheet of paper. While working though this activity as a group, the children will often stimulate each other's ideas and show greater confidence as a result.

Final thoughts and reflections

The links between the activity and real life via watching videos about palaeontologists will help the children make connections about the purpose of the activity.

Consider the confidence that an activity like this develops as children emulate the role of a palaeontologist and choose their approach, e.g. the preferred tool for different stages of digging and finding.

Activity 4 Shape shifting dinosaur

Activity outline and preparation

This activity inspires the children to work in pairs or small groups to create their representation of large-scale dinosaurs from shapes provided. It works best as a large-scale floor activity but can also be set up on a table or magnetic board if magnetic shapes are used.

Resources

- Printed, laminated shapes - triangles, squares, oblongs, diamonds, circles, semicircles, kites (approx. 15-20 of each shape). If you wish to use a magnetic board as opposed to the floor or a table for this activity then attach pieces of magnetic tape on the back of the shapes

- Labelled boxes for each shape

- Camera

- Printed dinosaur images

Preparation

- Print and laminate the different shapes (see above for types and quantity) and add to labelled baskets or boxes for children to choose from.

- Create a 'Dino gallery' space in the activity area for children to display photos. Begin with some example photos (alongside matching dinosaur images) that adults have assembled to give the children an idea of the shapes dinosaurs could have had.

Activity development

ESSENTIAL LITERACY AND MATHEMATICS DEVELOPMENT				
PRIME AREAS		**Development guidance**	**SPECIFIC AREAS**	**Development guidance**
COMMUNICATION AND LANGUAGE	Listening and attention	**30-50 months** Focusing attention - still listen or do, but can shift own attention *(while exploring shapes in group)* **40-60+ months** Two-channelled attention - can listen and do for short span. **ELG** *Children listen attentively in a range of situations. They listen to stories, accurately anticipating key events and respond to what they hear with relevant comments, questions or actions. They give their attention to what others say and respond appropriately, while engaged in another activity. (listening to others' ideas while exploring the shapes)*	LITERACY — Reading	**30-50 months** Recognises familiar words and signs such as own name and advertising logo *(recognises some shape name labels)* **40-60+ months** Begins to read words and simple sentences Hears and says initial sounds in words. Can segment the sounds in simple words and blend them together and knows which letters represent some of them. **ELG** *Children read and understand simple sentences. They use phonic knowledge to decode regular words and read them aloud accurately. They also read some common irregular words. They demonstrate understanding when talking with others about what they have read. (using phonic knowledge to decode and read shape labels)*
			LITERACY — Writing	**30-50 months** Sometimes give meaning to marks as they draw and paint *(mark making alongside photos in dinosaur gallery)* **40-60+ months** Gives meaning to marks they make as they draw, write and paint Uses some clearly identifiable letters to communicate meaning, representing some sounds correctly and in sequence **ELG** *Children use their phonic knowledge to write words in ways which match their spoken sounds. They also write some irregular common words. They write simple sentences which can be read by themselves and others. Some words are spelt correctly and others are phonetically plausible. (mark making and simple word writing alongside photos in dinosaur gallery)*
	Understanding	**30-50 months** Shows understanding of prepositions such as 'under', 'on top', 'behind' by carrying out an action or selecting correct picture *(while exploring shapes and creating a dinosaur)* **40-60+ months** Listens and responds to ideas expressed by others in conversation or discussion *(listens to others' ideas while constructing a dinosaur in a group)*	MATHEMATICS — Numbers	**30-50 months** Realises not only objects, but anything can be counted, including steps, claps or jumps *(counting of shapes whilst exploring and creating dinosaur)* **40-60+ months** Estimates how many objects they can see and checks by counting them *(estimation of amount of shapes needed while creating large-scale dinosaur)*
	Speaking	**30-50 months** Uses vocabulary focused on objects and people that are of particular importance to them. **40-60+ months** Extends vocabulary, especially by grouping and naming, exploring the meaning and sounds of new words *(extending vocabulary with dinosaur names and words)* **ELG** *Children express themselves effectively, showing awareness of listeners' needs. They use past, present and future forms accurately when talking about events that have happened or are to happen in the future. They develop their own narratives and explanations by connecting ideas or events. (developing own narratives and ideas whilst creating dinosaur with shapes)*	MATHEMATICS — Shape, space and measure	**30-50 months** Shows an interest in shape and space by playing with shapes or making arrangements with objects. Shows interest in shape by sustained construction activity or by talking about shapes or arrangements Uses shapes appropriately for tasks *(while exploring different shapes and creating dinosaur)* **40-60+ months** Beginning to use mathematical names for flat 2D shapes, and mathematical terms to describe shapes Selects a particular named shape Can describe their relative position such as 'behind' or 'next to' **ELG** *Children use everyday language to talk about size, weight, capacity, position, distance, time and money to compare quantities and objects and to solve problems. They recognise, create and describe patterns. They explore characteristics of everyday objects and shapes and use mathematical language to describe them. (use of everyday and mathematical language whilst selecting and exploring different, quantities, positions and shapes to create a dinosaur)*

CHARACTERISTICS OF EFFECTIVE LEARNING	Suggested outcomes
Playing and exploring – *engagement*	**Showing interest and curiosity in dinosaurs and their body shapes**
Active learning – *motivation*	**Paying attention to detail while selecting shapes**
Creating and thinking critically – *thinking*	**Making links and noticing patterns with dinosaur shapes**

PRIME AREAS		Development guidance		SPECIFIC AREAS		Development guidance
PHYSICAL DEVELOPMENT	Moving and handling	**30-50 months** *Holds pencil between thumb and two fingers, no longer using whole-hand grasp (while mark making in dino gallery.)* **40-60+ months** *Begins to form recognisable letters* *Uses a pencil and holds it effectively to form recognisable letters, most of which are correctly formed* **ELG** *Children show good control and co-ordination in large and small movements. They move confidently in a range of ways, safely negotiating space. They handle equipment and tools effectively, including pencils for writing. (whilst mark making and writing recognisable words in dino. gallery)*	UNDERSTANDING THE WORLD	People and communities		
					The world	**30-50 months** *Can talk about some of the things they have observed such as plants, animals, natural and found objects (talk about observations of dinosaur images)* **ELG** *Children know about similarities and differences in relation to places, objects, materials and living things. They talk about the features of their own immediate environment and how environments might vary from one another. They make observations of animals and plants and explain why some things occur, and talk about changes. (noticing simple similarities and differences whilst observing dinosaur images)*
					Technology	**30-50 months** *Knows how to operate simple equipment (camera to catch completed dinosaur image)* **ELG** *Children recognise that a range of technology is used in places such as homes and schools. They select and use technology for particular purposes. (operating a camera with help to catch completed dinosaur image)*
	Health and self-care		EXPRESSIVE ARTS AND DESIGN	Exploring and using media and materials		**30-50 months** *Understands that they can use lines to enclose a space and then begin to use these shapes to represent objects (while exploring shapes to create dinosaur)* **40-60+ months** *Constructs with purpose in mind, using a variety of resources (inspired by dinosaur image, recreating dinosaur with shapes)*
				Being imaginative		
PERSONAL, SOCIAL AND EMOTIONAL DEVELOPMENT	Making relationships	**30-50 months** *Can play in a group, extending and elaborating play ideas (inspired by activity, initiate and extend play, e.g. dinosaur sounds and movements)* **40-60+ months** *Explains own knowledge and understanding and asks appropriate questions of others (whilst creating shape dinosaur)* **ELG** *Children play co-operatively, taking turns with others. They take account of one another's ideas about how to organise their activity. They show sensitivity to others' needs and feelings, and form positive relationships with adults and other children. (taking turns to choose shapes and make decisions whilst creating dinosaur)*				
	Self-confidence and self-awareness	**30-50 months** *Confident to talk to other children when playing and will communicate freely about own home and community (confident talking and sharing ideas whilst creating dinosaur)* **ELG** *Children are confident to try new activities, and say why they like some activities more than others. They are confident to speak in a familiar group, will talk about their ideas, and will choose the resources they need for their chosen activities. They say when they do or don't need help. (confidence to make decisions whilst choosing shapes to create dinosaur)*				
	Managing feelings and behaviour	**30-50 months** *Begins to accept the needs of others and can take turns and share resources, sometimes with support from others.* *Can usually tolerate delay when needs are not immediately met, and understands wishes may not always be met (whilst sharing shapes, making decisions and creating dinosaur as a group)* **ELG** *Children talk about how they and others show feelings, talk about their own and others' behaviour, and its consequences, and know that some behaviour is unacceptable. They work as part of a group or class, and understand and follow the rules. They adjust their behaviour to different situations, and take changes of routine in their stride. (working co-operatively as part of a group, sharing shapes and creating dinosaur)*				

Activity guidance

This is a continuous provision activity that aims to develop shape and space awareness.

Set up all the shapes in separate labelled boxes or baskets.

Display printed dinosaur images to inspire the children with ideas about long or tall dinosaurs. Also display a WAGOLL (What A Good One Looks Like) photo/s of previously created dinosaur shapes to add visual stimulus.

To initiate interest ask the children what they know about dinosaurs. Ask them to think about the different dinosaurs and their shapes. For example, a Brontosaurus is long, a Tyrannosaurus rex is tall and a Stegosaurus has shaped plates all along its back. Draw their attention to the photo/s of the WAGOLL and discuss the shapes and how they have been used.

Once children have explored and worked to create a dinosaur shape, return to the activity to help children take photos of their creations and print these out.

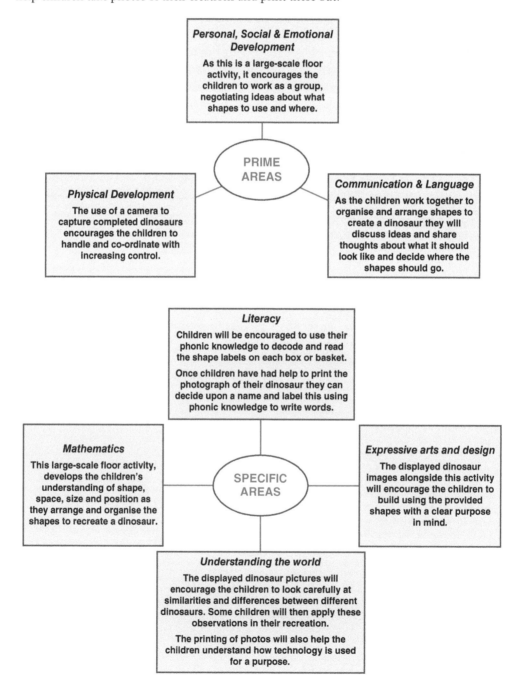

Possible next steps and opportunities for further development

3D shape building

To develop the children's understanding of shape further, introduce 3D shapes (cubes, cuboids, spheres, pyramids, cylinders) for the children to explore and build with. Encourage the children to consider building a 3D dinosaur with the shapes.

Some children may struggle with the transition from flat 2D to solid 3D shapes. If so, encourage these children to play with the 3D shapes without any intention to build a specific model. These children will also benefit from observing others who are more confident.

Creative collage

Children will enjoy exploring dinosaur shapes further through creative activities such as collage. This will build upon the children's understanding about shapes and encourage the children to create a dinosaur within a full picture.

Some children will need pre-cut shapes for this activity yet others may wish to create some of their own. If children want to cut out their own shapes, consider providing some plastic shapes for them to draw around first.

Final thoughts and reflections

The focus upon shapes for this activity will encourage the children to look closely at images of dinosaurs to identify the shapes of bodies, legs and tails. This in turn will help develop their observational skills.

Consider how this activity will help the children to develop spatial awareness. Spatial awareness is a complex, cognitive skill that should develop naturally among children but some will have difficulties with this.

Resource support: *Example image of shape-shifting dinosaur*

Activity 5 Hide and seek dinosaurs

Activity outline and preparation

This sensory activity is good for messy play as children dig and delve through set jelly to retrieve little plastic dinosaurs. Once located the children can observe closely and aim to match the dinosaur to an illustrated image. There are also opportunities to mark make and handwrite if they wish. The activity works well inside or outside within a table-top tuff tray.

Resources

- Small, plastic dinosaurs

- Transparent bowls

- Jelly – yellow, lime green or orange work well

- Play-Doh tools (for digging and retrieving dinosaurs) or children can attempt this activity with hands instead of tools but it will be messy!

- Magnifying glasses

- Laminated dinosaur images with name labels (*that match plastic dinosaurs*) and space to trace or rewrite the dinosaur name underneath the image

- Dry-wipe pens

Preparation

- Create laminated images of dinosaurs with name labels and space to trace or rewrite the names.

- In one big bowl or several smaller transparent bowls/other containers, add several plastic dinosaurs. Mix up jelly as per packet instructions and add to the bowls. Leave in a fridge for the jelly to set.

- Gather and organise tools for digging through the jelly.

Activity development

ESSENTIAL LITERACY AND MATHEMATICS DEVELOPMENT				
PRIME AREAS		**Development guidance**	**SPECIFIC AREAS**	**Development guidance**
COMMUNICATION AND LANGUAGE	Listening and attention	**30-50 months** Listen to others one to one or in small groups when conversation interests them *(while working alongside others exploring jelly)* **40-60+ months** Two-channelled attention - can listen and do for short span. **ELG** *Children listen attentively in a range of situations. They listen to stories, accurately anticipating key events and respond to what they hear with relevant comments, questions or actions. They give their attention to what others say and respond appropriately, while engaged in another activity. (listening to others whilst working alongside others exploring jelly)*	LITERACY — Reading	**30-50 months** Knows information can be relayed in the form of print *(dinosaur names on laminated image/name labels)* **40-60+ months** Begins to read words and simple sentences. Hears and says initial sounds in words Can segment the sounds in simple words and blend them together and knows which letters represent some of them. **ELG** *Children read and understand simple sentences. They use phonic knowledge to decode regular words and read them aloud accurately. They also read some common irregular words. They demonstrate understanding when talking with others about what they have read. (using phonic knowledge to decode and read on dinosaur image/name labels)*
			LITERACY — Writing	**30-50 months** Sometimes give meaning to marks as they draw and paint *(mark making and/or tracing on dinosaur image/name labels)* **40-60+ months** Gives meaning to marks they make as they draw, write and paint. Hears and says the initial sound in words Uses some clearly identifiable letters to communicate meaning, representing some sounds correctly and in sequence **ELG** *Children use their phonic knowledge to write words in ways which match their spoken sounds. They also write some irregular common words. They write simple sentences which can be read by themselves and others. Some words are spelt correctly and others are phonetically plausible. (use of phonic knowledge to mark make, trace or write on dinosaur image/name labels)*
	Understanding	**30-50 months** Understand use of objects *(while using tools to explore jelly)* **40-60+ months** Listens and responds to ideas expressed by others in conversation or discussion *(listens to others ideas while exploring jelly)*	MATHEMATICS — Numbers	**30-50 months** Uses some number names and number language spontaneously *(spontaneous counting of dinosaurs once retrieved from jelly)* **40-60+ months** Counts objects to 10, and begins counting beyond 10 Estimates how many objects they can see and checks by counting them *(counting and estimation of dinosaurs in jelly)*
	Speaking	**30-50 months** Questions why things happen and gives explanations. Asks e.g. who, what, when, how *(questioning and explanations whilst exploring jelly)* **40-60+ months** Extends vocabulary, especially by grouping and naming, exploring the meaning and sounds of new words *(extending vocabulary with dinosaur names and words)* **ELG** *Children express themselves effectively, showing awareness of listeners' needs. They use past, present and future forms accurately when talking about events that have happened or are to happen in the future. They develop their own narratives and explanations by connecting ideas or events. (developing their own narratives and explanations whilst exploring jelly and locating dinosaurs)*	MATHEMATICS — Shape, space and measure	**30-50 months** Beginning to talk about the shapes of everyday objects *(dinosaur shapes)* **40-60+ months** Can describe their relative position such as 'behind' or 'next to' *(while locating dinosaurs in jelly)* **ELG** *Children use everyday language to talk about size, weight, capacity, position, distance, time and money to compare quantities and objects and to solve problems. They recognise, create and describe patterns. They explore characteristics of everyday objects and shapes and use mathematical language to describe them. (use of everyday and mathematical language whilst exploring and describing of dinosaur shapes)*

CHARACTERISTICS OF EFFECTIVE LEARNING	Suggested outcomes
Playing and exploring – *engagement*	**Using senses to explore and seek dinosaurs in jelly**
Active learning – *motivation*	**Persistence while seeking out dinosaurs**
Creating and thinking critically – *thinking*	**Changing strategies to seek and locate dinosaurs**

PRIME AREAS		Development guidance		SPECIFIC AREAS	Development guidance
PHYSICAL DEVELOPMENT	Moving and handling	**30-50 months** Uses one-handed tools and equipment (tools for digging out dinosaurs) **40-60+ months** Uses simple tools to effect changes to materials (uses tools for digging out dinosaurs) Begins to form recognisable letters Uses a pencil and holds it effectively to form recognisable letters, most of which are correctly formed (mark making, tracing and/or writing dinosaur name labels) **ELG** Children show good control and co-ordination in large and small movements. They move confidently in a range of ways, safely negotiating space. They handle equipment and tools effectively, including pencils for writing. (good control and co-ordination with tools whilst digging through jelly alongside control of writing tools whilst completing dinosaur name labels)	**UNDERSTANDING THE WORLD**	People and communities	
				The world	**30-50 months** Can talk about some of the things they have observed such as plants, animals, natural and found objects and found objects (whilst observing discovered dinosaurs) **40-60+ months** Looks closely at similarities, differences, patterns and change **ELG** Children know about similarities and differences in relation to places, objects, materials and living things. They talk about the features of their own immediate environment and how environments might vary from one another. They make observations of animals and plants and explain why some things occur, and talk about changes. (knowing about some similarities and differences whilst observing discovered dinosaurs)
				Technology	
	Health and self-care	**30-50 months** Understands that equipment and tools have to be used safely (use jelly digging equipment safely) **40-60+ months** Practises some appropriate safety measures without direct supervision (safely using jelly digging equipment)	**EXPRESSIVE ARTS AND DESIGN**	Exploring and using media and materials	**30-50 months** Beginning to be interested in and describe the texture of things Realises tools can be used for a purpose (while exploring jelly) **40-60+ months** Uses simple tools and techniques competently and appropriately **ELG** Children sing songs, make music and dance, and experiment with ways of changing them. They safely use and explore a variety of materials, tools and techniques, experimenting with colour, design, texture, form and function. (safely using and exploring tools/equipment whilst exploring jelly. Exploring texture and form whilst locating dinosaurs in jelly)
				Being imaginative	
PERSONAL, SOCIAL AND EMOTIONAL DEVELOPMENT	Making relationships	**30-50 months** Initiates play, offering cues to peers to join them Keeps play going by responding to what others are saying or doing (continues exploration alongside others) **40-60+ months** Explains own knowledge and understanding and asks appropriate questions of others (asking appropriate questions whilst exploring jelly) **ELG** Children play co-operatively, taking turns with others. They take account of one another's ideas about how to organise their activity. They show sensitivity to others' needs and feelings, and form positive relationships with adults and other children. (playing co-operatively and taking turns with tools whilst exploring jelly)			
	Self-confidence and self-awareness	**30-50 months** Can select and use activities and resources with help (while exploring jelly) **40-60+ months** Confident to speak to others about own needs, wants, interests and opinions. **ELG** Children are confident to try new activities, and say why they like some activities more than others. They are confident to speak in a familiar group, will talk about their ideas, and will choose the resources they need for their chosen activities. They say when they do or don't need help. (confidence exploring the jelly during the activity and choosing tools)			
	Managing feelings and behaviour	**30-50 months** Begins to accept the needs of others and can take turns and share resources, sometimes with support from others. Can usually tolerate delay when needs are not immediately met (whilst sharing tools) **40-60+ months** Beginning to be able to negotiate and solve problems without aggression **ELG** Children talk about how they and others show feelings, talk about their own and others' behaviour, and its consequences, and know that some behaviour is unacceptable. They work as part of a group or class, and understand and follow the rules. They adjust their behaviour to different situations, and take changes of routine in their stride. (sensible whilst exploring messy jelly and understand behaviour expectations with activity.)			

Activity guidance

This is a continuous provision activity that aims to develop sensory skills alongside knowledge and understanding.

Once the jelly has set, arrange the bowls or pop out the set jelly into a table-top tuff tray with tools and magnifiers.

Display laminated dinosaur images with name labels and dry-wipe pens alongside the activity.

To initiate interest ask the children what they know about dinosaurs. Can you think of any dinosaur names and describe what they look like? Ask the children if they could solve a problem: some dinosaurs fell into the jelly before it set. Could you find, rescue and name them?

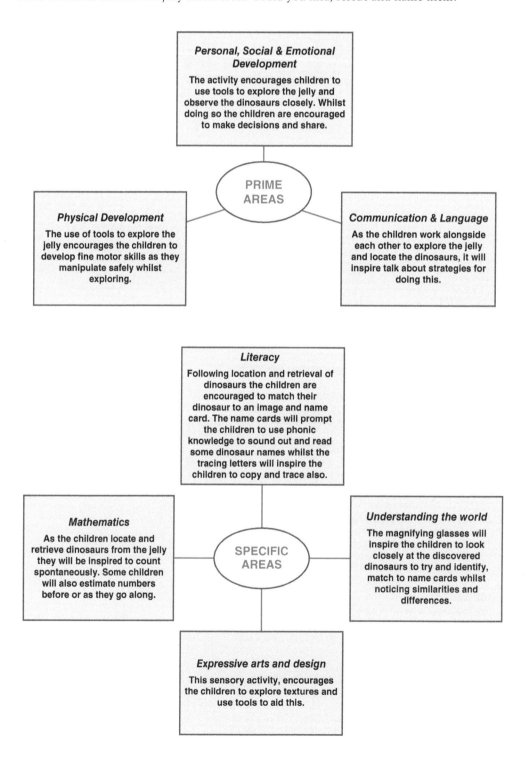

Personal, Social & Emotional Development

The activity encourages children to use tools to explore the jelly and observe the dinosaurs closely. Whilst doing so the children are encouraged to make decisions and share.

PRIME AREAS

Physical Development

The use of tools to explore the jelly encourages the children to develop fine motor skills as they manipulate safely whilst exploring.

Communication & Language

As the children work alongside each other to explore the jelly and locate the dinosaurs, it will inspire talk about strategies for doing this.

Literacy

Following location and retrieval of dinosaurs the children are encouraged to match their dinosaur to an image and name card. The name cards will prompt the children to use phonic knowledge to sound out and read some dinosaur names whilst the tracing letters will inspire the children to copy and trace also.

Mathematics

As the children locate and retrieve dinosaurs from the jelly they will be inspired to count spontaneously. Some children will also estimate numbers before or as they go along.

SPECIFIC AREAS

Understanding the world

The magnifying glasses will inspire the children to look closely at the discovered dinosaurs to try and identify, match to name cards whilst noticing similarities and differences.

Expressive arts and design

This sensory activity, encourages the children to explore textures and use tools to aid this.

Possible next steps and opportunities for further development

Hide and seek in different materials

To consolidate knowledge and understanding about dinosaurs consider repeating the activity through further sensory exploration. Try hiding the dinosaurs in custard, foam or dry materials such as flour or rice.

The repetition of the activity will help to reinforces subject knowledge about dinosaur names and key features. Some children will develop this knowledge faster than others and for these children introduce new dinosaurs to the activity.

Dinosaur textures

To develop children's understanding of textures, consider an exploration activity that encourages the children to think about what dinosaur skins may have felt like. Use pieces of fabric and other materials such as bubble wrap, foil and corrugated cardboard for the children to feel. Concealing the materials in a box or bag for the children to feel as opposed to observe makes this activity more successful.

Some children will be able to visualise better than others during this activity. For these children consider more sensory activities to encourage the connection between textures and other ideas.

Final thoughts and reflections

Dinosaur names are tricky to read but some children will recognise the initial phonemes and associate this with an illustration. This is why the dinosaur name labels are an important part of this activity.

Consider the impact of sensory play and researched connections to brain development alongside other aspects such as language and motor skill improvement.

Resource support: *Example dinosaur name label*

Stegosaurus

Stegosaurus

Activity 6 Big feet!

Activity outline and preparation

This activity encourages the children to observe and begin to 'measure' dinosaur footprints in damp sand using familiar apparatus and to record these measurements if they wish. It works well inside or outside using damp, smooth sand in large or small trays. Ideally, the more space available for the activity the better.

Resources

- Sand

- Large or small trays

- Familiar counting apparatus such as lolly sticks, bead strings, multilink towers, straws

- Magnifiers

- Laminated recorder cards

- Dry-wipe pens

Preparation

- In preparation for the activity, add damp sand to a large or several small trays. Smooth this sand so it is completely flat.

- Once the sand is ready, use the pointed end of a paint brush to trace a dinosaur footprint (or several footprints if using a large tray) in the smooth sand.

- Organise familiar counting apparatus and magnifiers in different trays or baskets.

- Create laminated recorder cards.

- Locate a short video clip online about discovering dinosaur footprints.

Activity development

ESSENTIAL LITERACY AND MATHEMATICS DEVELOPMENT				
PRIME AREAS	**Development guidance**	**SPECIFIC AREAS**		**Development guidance**
COMMUNICATION AND LANGUAGE	Listening and attention	**30-50 months** *Listens to stories with increasing attention and recall* (listening to online stories associated with palaeontologists and dinosaur footprints) *Listens to others one to one or in small groups when conversation interests them* (while investigating footprints) **40-60+ months** *Two-channelled attention - can listen and do for short span* **ELG** *Children listen attentively in a range of situations. They listen to stories, accurately anticipating key events and respond to what they hear with relevant comments, questions or actions. They give their attention to what others say and respond appropriately, while engaged in another activity.* (listening to online stories associated with palaeontologists and dinosaur footprints. Two-channelled attention whilst investigating footprints)	**LITERACY**	Reading	**30-50 months** *Knows information can be relayed in the form of print* (words on recorder cards) **40-60+ months** *Begins to read words and simple sentences* **ELG** *Children read and understand simple sentences. They use phonic knowledge to decode regular words and read them aloud accurately. They also read some common irregular words. They demonstrate understanding when talking with others about what they have read.* (using phonic knowledge to decode and read words on recorder cards)
				Writing	**30-50 months** *Ascribe meanings to marks that they see in different places* (marks on recorder cards) **40-60+ months** *Uses some clearly identifiable letters to communicate meaning, representing some sounds correctly and in sequence* **ELG** *Children use their phonic knowledge to write words in ways which match their spoken sounds. They also write some irregular common words. They write simple sentences which can be read by themselves and others. Some words are spelt correctly and others are phonetically plausible.* (using phonic knowledge to add marks or simple words and sentences on recorder cards)
	Under-standing	**30-50 months** *Understands use of objects* (familiar apparatus for measuring) **40-60+ months** *Listens and responds to ideas expressed by others in conversation or discussion* (while investigating footprints) **ELG** *Children follow instructions involving several ideas or actions. They answer 'how' and 'why' questions about their experiences and in response to stories or events.* (asking and answering how and why questions whilst investigating footprints inspired by online stories associated with palaeontologists)	**MATHEMATICS**	Numbers	**30-50 months** *Sometimes matches numerals and quantity correctly* (attempting to measure and record with familiar counting apparatus) **40-60+ months** *Selects the correct numeral to represent 1 to 5, then 1 to 10 objects* *Estimates how many objects they can see and checks by counting them* *Records using marks that they can interpret and explain* (estimating, counting and recording while attempting measuring with apparatus)
	Speaking	**30-50 months** *Builds up vocabulary that reflects the breadth of their experiences* (vocabulary inspired by and related to dinosaurs) **40-60+ months** *Uses language to imagine and recreate roles and experiences in play situations* *Uses talk to organise, sequence and clarify thinking, ideas, feelings and events* (language and talk inspired by online stories associated with palaeontologists)		Shape, space and measure	**30-50 months** *Uses shapes appropriately for tasks* (use of familiar apparatus while exploring measuring) **ELG** *Children use everyday language to talk about size, weight, capacity, position, distance, time and money to compare quantities and objects and to solve problems. They recognise, create and describe patterns. They explore characteristics of everyday objects and shapes and use mathematical language to describe them.* (use of everyday and mathematical language whilst exploring the size, shape and measurement of footprints with familiar apparatus)

CHARACTERISTICS OF EFFECTIVE LEARNING	**Suggested outcomes**
Playing and exploring – *engagement*	**Engaged by challenge of investigating dinosaur footprints**
Active learning – *motivation*	**Persisting with attempting to measure footprints**
Creating and thinking critically – *thinking*	**Using counting apparatus to solve problems**

PRIME AREAS		Development guidance	SPECIFIC AREAS		Development guidance
PHYSICAL DEVELOPMENT	Moving and handling	**30-50 months** *Uses one-handed tools and equipment (familiar apparatus while attempting measuring)* **40-60+ months** *Handles tools, objects, construction and malleable materials safely and with increasing control* **ELG** *Children show good control and co-ordination in large and small movements. They move confidently in a range of ways, safely negotiating space. They handle equipment and tools effectively, including pencils for writing. (good control and co-ordination when recording with pens and handling familiar apparatus whilst attempting to measure)*	UNDERSTANDING THE WORLD	People and communities	**30-50 months** *Shows interest in different occupations and ways of life (online videos of science detectives (palaeontologists)*
				The world	**30-50 months** *Can talk about some of the things they have observed such as plants, animals, natural and found objects (talk about observed, found dinosaur footprints)* **40-60+ months** *Looks closely at similarities, differences, patterns and change* **ELG** *Children know about similarities and differences in relation to places, objects, materials and living things. They talk about the features of their own immediate environment and how environments might vary from one another. They make observations of animals and plants and explain why some things occur, and talk about changes. (observing similarities and differences with footprint sizes and shapes)*
				Technology	**30-50 months** *Knows that information can be retrieved from computers* **ELG** *Children recognise that a range of technology is used in places such as homes and schools. They select and use technology for particular purposes. (adult to lead online search for children to watch palaeontologist/dinosaur footprint clips and demonstrate use and purpose of the internet)*
	Health and self-care		EXPRESSIVE ARTS AND DESIGN	Exploring and using media and materials	
				Being imaginative	**30-50 months** *Uses available resources to create props to support role-play (exploring footprints 'as' science detectives/palaeontologists)* **40-60+ months** *Create simple representations of people and objects (exploring footprints 'as' science detectives/palaeontologists)*
PERSONAL, SOCIAL AND EMOTIONAL DEVELOPMENT	Making relationships	**30-50 months** *Initiates play, offering cues to peers to join them (encouraging others to work in pairs or small groups to attempt to measure)* **40-60+ months** *Explains own knowledge and understanding and asks appropriate questions of others* **ELG** *Children play co-operatively, taking turns with others. They take account of one another's ideas about how to organise their activity. They show sensitivity to others' needs and feelings, and form positive relationships with adults and other children. (playing co-operatively, taking turns with others and sharing measuring apparatus)*			
	Self-confidence and self-awareness	**30-50 months** *Can select and use activities and resources with help (choose and use familiar counting apparatus and asking for help if needed)* **ELG** *Children are confident to try new activities, and say why they like some activities more than others. They are confident to speak in a familiar group, will talk about their ideas, and will choose the resources they need for their chosen activities. They say when they do or don't need help. (confidence attempting to use measuring apparatus and asking for help if needed)*			
	Managing feelings and behaviour	**30-50 months** *Can usually tolerate delay when needs are not immediately met, and understands wishes may not always be met (tolerating delay whilst attempting to 'measure' with familiar apparatus)* **ELG** *Children talk about how they and others show feelings, talk about their own and others' behaviour, and its consequences, and know that some behaviour is unacceptable. They work as part of a group or class, and understand and follow the rules. They adjust their behaviour to different situations, and take changes of routine in their stride. (keeping focused and working as pair or small group to attempt to measure)*			

Activity guidance

This is a continuous provision activity that aims to develop children's early mathematics and fine motor skills.

Once the sand and footprint outlines have been added to trays, set up baskets or boxes of familiar counting apparatus nearby. Display laminated recorder cards and dry-wipe pens in the same area.

To initiate interest show the children a short clip about locating dinosaur footprints (there are some good examples on YouTube) to inspire the children's curiosity. Introduce or re-introduce the role of science detectives (palaeontologists) and their mission to examine and measure any footprints they find.

Could you be a science detective? Show children the footprints and model how the familiar counting apparatus, e.g. lolly sticks, multilink, bead strings, can be used to measure the footprint 'across' or 'up and down'.

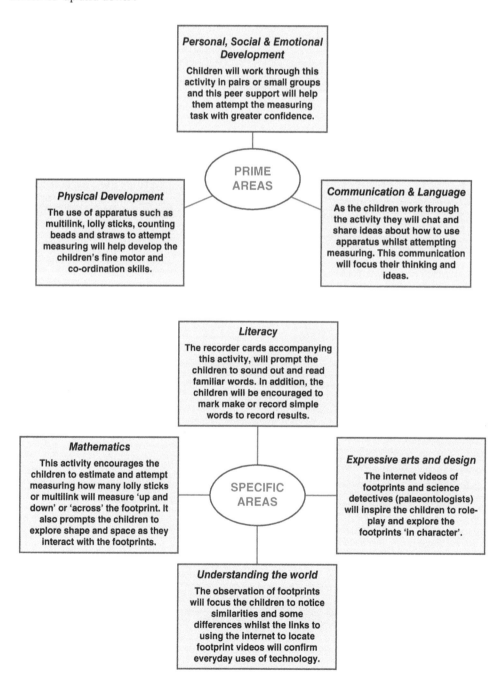

Possible next steps and opportunities for further development

Fossils

The children can consolidate their work estimating and measuring yet this time with fossils. Add fossil imprints to damp sand or other materials such as Play-Doh or clay for the children to continue measuring.

Some children will take longer to grasp the concept of measuring 'edge to edge'. These children will need some group guidance or help when they next attempt this activity. Small stickers on two places of the imprint can help to focus these children to use lolly sticks, multilink, etc. and measure from one sticker to the other.

Measuring at home

To further consolidate ideas about measuring, send home a list of familiar objects to locate (e.g. a book, a remote control, a food tin, a juice bottle) and measure with household objects such as Lego, straws, dry spaghetti.

Final thoughts and reflections

Consider the benefit of linking this activity to real life through science detectives (palaeontologists) and videos online. This link opens the children's thinking about the world around them and helps add real-life purpose to the activity.

Consider how this activity begins to introduce the children to the idea of measuring. Children will interpret this activity in different ways and this exploration of interpretation is important for later learning.

Resource support: *Example recorder card*

multilink

How many multilink?

Draw or write in here

CHAPTER 4

LEARNING THREAD
WACKY AND WONDERFUL WEATHER

Wacky and Wonderful Weather

In this chapter

In this chapter, you will find activities related to 'weather' and 'seasons'. This learning thread links to:

- exploration and discovery, through activities such as 'Outdoor detectives' and 'Fruit of the season'

- reflection upon experiences from their world with 'What should I wear?', 'Bee-Bot seasons' and 'Rain or shine today?'

- musical expression through 'Sunny or stormy music'.

The activities in this chapter will help you to work towards:

- encouraging children to reflect upon experiences from the world around them and express this through actions and role-play

- developing children's prediction and observational skills through curiosity and discovery

- inspiring children's musical expression through imitation and exploration.

Activities

Activity		Page	Provision
1	*What should I wear?*	117	Continuous provision indoors or outdoors
2	*Sunny or stormy music*	123	Continuous provision indoors or outdoors
3	*Sunshine or showery fruits*	129	Continuous provision indoors or outdoors
4	*Rain or shine today?*	135	Continuous provision indoors or outdoors
5	*Bee-Bot seasons*	141	Continuous provision indoors or outdoors
6	*Outdoor detectives*	147	Continuous provision outdoors

Role-play area links:

- Weather station (scientists' prediction desk)

- Seasonal area, e.g. for 'spring', trays of flowers, leaves and blossom to observe, cameras, spring images on the walls, photographs to sort though

- Weather observation lookout – sited close to a window with a step and clear lookout, with binoculars, cameras and charts for recording weather throughout the day

Activity 1 What should I wear?

Activity outline and preparation

This activity inspires the children to choose and wear items such as wellies, sun hats and gloves while others capture photographs against the appropriate weather backdrop. This activity will need to be organised against a changeable backdrop area so consider preparing different backdrops the children can alter, i.e. simple poster sheets or via the interactive whiteboard. The backdrops should focus on one type of weather and display images and adjectives that match.

Resources

- Large-scale backdrops: rain, sun, cloud, snow, ice. The backdrops should show an image or images of the weather alongside displayed adjectives, for example for rain: raindrops, plops, splash, splish, puddle

- Box or boxes of mixed items to use/wear, for example: umbrella, wellies, raincoat, waterproof trousers, sandals, sunglasses, cap, sun hat, scarf, wool hat, gloves, winter coat

- iPads or cameras

- Pencils and crayons

Preparation

- In preparation for the activity, create several backdrops via poster paper or interactive whiteboard. Each backdrop should include images and adjectives for the particular type of weather.

- Organise resources for the children to choose and present these in boxes or baskets. This activity works best when all resources are mixed together so the children have to sort through and discuss each item.

- Organise and charge cameras or iPads ready for children to capture images.

- Provide pencils and crayons nearby so children can mark make or write words on the backdrops.

Activity development

ESSENTIAL LITERACY AND MATHEMATICS DEVELOPMENT				
PRIME AREAS	**Development guidance**		**SPECIFIC AREAS**	**Development guidance**
COMMUNICATION AND LANGUAGE — Listening and attention	**30-50 months** Is able to follow directions (if not intently focused on own choice of activity) (able to follow directions from adults or other children whilst exploring clothes and backdrops) **40-60+ months** Two-channelled attention - can listen and do for short span **ELG** Children listen attentively in a range of situations. They listen to stories, accurately anticipating key events and respond to what they hear with relevant comments, questions or actions. They give their attention to what others say and respond appropriately, while engaged in another activity. (simultaneous listening and doing whilst working with others to choose and use resources for photos)	**LITERACY**	Reading	**30-50 months** Knows information can be relayed in the form of print (adjectives on backdrop) **40-60+ months** Can segment sounds in simple words and blend them together and knows which letters represent some of them Begins to read words and simple sentences **ELG** Children read and understand simple sentences. They use phonic knowledge to decode regular words and read them aloud accurately. They also read some common irregular words. They demonstrate understanding when talking with others about what they have read. (using phonic knowledge to decode and read weather adjectives on backdrop)
			Writing	**30-50 months** Sometimes give meaning to marks as they draw and paint (marks and drawings added to weather backdrop) **40-60+ months** Uses some clearly identifiable letters to communicate meaning, representing some sounds correctly and in sequence **ELG** Children use their phonic knowledge to write words in ways which match their spoken sounds. They also write some irregular common words. They write simple sentences which can be read by themselves and others. Some words are spelt correctly and others are phonetically plausible. (children use phonic knowledge to sound out and write simple weather adjectives on backdrop)
Understanding	**30-50 months** Understands use of objects. Shows understanding of prepositions such as 'under', 'on top', 'behind', by carrying out an action or selecting correct picture (choosing and using correct resources and following others' guidance about how to wear) **40-60+ months** Responds to instructions involving a two-part sequence. Understands humour e.g. nonsense rhymes, jokes **ELG** Children follow instructions involving several ideas or actions. They answer 'how' and 'why' questions about their experiences and in response to stories or events. (following guidance about selecting seasonal clothes to take simple photos)	**MATHEMATICS**	Numbers	**30-50 months** Knows that numbers identify how many objects are in a set (resources for photos) **40-60+ months** Estimates how many objects they can see and checks by counting them (estimation and spontaneous counting of resources while exploring)
Speaking	**30-50 months** Beginning to use more complex sentences to link thoughts (whilst working with others and directing each other for photographs) **40-60+ months** Extends vocabulary, especially by grouping and naming, exploring the meaning and sounds of new words (adjectives on backdrop) **ELG** Children express themselves effectively, showing awareness of listeners' needs. They use past, present and future forms accurately when talking about events that have happened or are to happen in the future. They develop their own narratives and explanations by connecting ideas or events. (children express themselves effectively whilst exploring seasonal clothes)		Shape, space and measure	**30-50 months** Uses positional language (while taking photos) **40-60+ months** Can describe their relative position such as 'behind' or 'next to' **ELG** Children use everyday language to talk about size, weight, capacity, position, distance, time and money to compare quantities and objects and to solve problems. They recognise, create and describe patterns. They explore characteristics of everyday objects and shapes and use mathematical language to describe them. (use of positional language whilst taking photos)

CHARACTERISTICS OF EFFECTIVE LEARNING	Suggested outcomes
Playing and exploring – engagement	**Representing ideas through resources (props)**
Active learning – motivation	**Showing good levels of energy and interest while exploring resources**
Creating and thinking critically – thinking	**Group thinking while exploring resources and making decisions**

PRIME AREAS		Development guidance	SPECIFIC AREAS		Development guidance
PHYSICAL DEVELOPMENT	Moving and handling	**30-50 months** *Holds pencil near point between first two fingers and thumb and uses it with good control (while adding marks or words to backdrop)* **ELG** *Children show good control and co-ordination in large and small movements. They move confidently in a range of ways, safely negotiating space. They handle equipment and tools effectively, including pencils for writing. (good pen control and co-ordination whilst adding marks, words or illustrations to backdrop)*	UNDERSTANDING THE WORLD	People and communities	
				The world	**30-50 months** *Comments on and asks questions about aspects of their familiar location such as the place where they live or the natural world (weather from their natural world)* **ELG** *Children know about similarities and differences in relation to places, objects, materials and living things. They talk about the features of their own immediate environment and how environments might vary from one another. They make observations of animals and plants and explain why some things occur, and talk about changes. (children talk about similarities and differences in clothes/ accessories that match the weather)*
				Technology	**30-50 months** *Knows how to operate simple equipment (cameras or iPads)* **ELG** *Children recognise that a range of technology is used in places such as homes and schools. They select and use technology for particular purposes. (selecting and using iPads or simple cameras to capture photos. Asking for help if needed)*
	Health and self-care	**30-50 months** *Dresses with help, e.g. puts arms into open-fronted coat or shirt when held up, pulls up own trousers, and pulls up zipper once it is fastened at the bottom (adding accessories, clothes for photos, seeking help with zips and boots)* **ELG** *Children know the importance for good health of physical exercise, and a healthy diet, and talk about ways to keep healthy and safe. They manage their own basic hygiene and personal needs successfully, including dressing and going to the toilet independently. (adding accessories, clothes for photos; zipping up coats, putting boots on/taking off independently)*	EXPRESSIVE ARTS AND DESIGN	Exploring and using media and materials	
				Being imaginative	**30-50 months** *Uses available resources to create props to support role-play (use of clothes/ accessories to role-play walking in rain or sunbathing for photos)* **40-60+ months** *Create simple representations of events, people and objects (use of resources to role-play walking in rain or sunbathing while exploring resources)*
PERSONAL, SOCIAL AND EMOTIONAL DEVELOPMENT	Making relationships	**30-50 months** *Initiates play, offering cues to peers to join them (encouraging others to join in taking photos)* **ELG** *Children play co-operatively, taking turns with others. They take account of one another's ideas about how to organise their activity. They show sensitivity to others' needs and feelings, and form positive relationships with adults and other children. (taking turns with clothes and accessories, sharing ideas and suggestions)*			
	Self-confidence and self-awareness	**30-50 months** *Can select and use resources with help (asking for help if needed with dressing)* **ELG** *Children are confident to try new activities, and say why they like some activities more than others. They are confident to speak in a familiar group, will talk about their ideas, and will choose the resources they need for their chosen activities. They say when they do or don't need help. (confidence selecting appropriate accessories and clothes without help)*			
	Managing feelings and behaviour	**30-50 months** *Can usually tolerate delay when needs are not immediately met and understands wishes may not always be met (while sharing resources and cameras/iPads)* **ELG** *Children talk about how they and others show feelings, talk about their own and others' behaviour, and its consequences, and know that some behaviour is unacceptable. They work as part of a group or class, and understand and follow the rules. They adjust their behaviour to different situations, and take changes of routine in their stride. (working within a group keeping focused on choosing accessories/ clothes for activity and sharing resources)*			

Activity guidance

This is a continuous provision activity that aims to develop reflection upon experiences from the surrounding world.

Organise the backdrops for this activity and resources for the children to sort through and choose. Ensure the cameras or iPads are charged and displayed nearby.

To initiate interest ask the children to think about different types of weather. Do we wear the same clothes in all types of weather? Would we wear a woolly hat in the summer or sandals in the snow? Model how the resources can match the weather on the backdrop once tried on. Remind the children how to capture images with the camera.

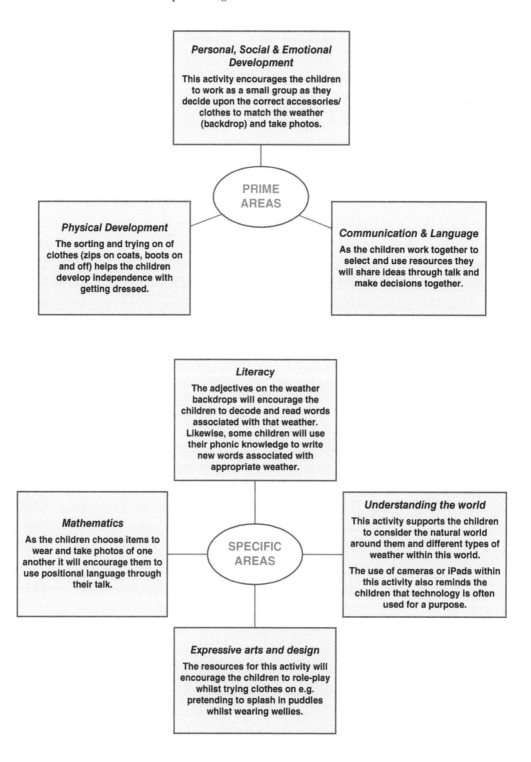

PRIME AREAS

Personal, Social & Emotional Development

This activity encourages the children to work as a small group as they decide upon the correct accessories/clothes to match the weather (backdrop) and take photos.

Physical Development

The sorting and trying on of clothes (zips on coats, boots on and off) helps the children develop independence with getting dressed.

Communication & Language

As the children work together to select and use resources they will share ideas through talk and make decisions together.

SPECIFIC AREAS

Literacy

The adjectives on the weather backdrops will encourage the children to decode and read words associated with that weather. Likewise, some children will use their phonic knowledge to write new words associated with appropriate weather.

Mathematics

As the children choose items to wear and take photos of one another it will encourage them to use positional language through their talk.

Understanding the world

This activity supports the children to consider the natural world around them and different types of weather within this world.

The use of cameras or iPads within this activity also reminds the children that technology is often used for a purpose.

Expressive arts and design

The resources for this activity will encourage the children to role-play whilst trying clothes on e.g. pretending to splash in puddles whilst wearing wellies.

Possible next steps and opportunities for further development

Seasonal clothes

The children can explore the idea of clothes and weather further at home. Children can send in photos of themselves and family out in the rain or sunbathing in the sun. Photos can be added to an interactive display about weather and seasons.

Weather explorations

Focus upon one type of weather further, e.g. rain, and ask the children to bring in their own rain clothes (coats, wellies, umbrellas, hats) for the next rainy day so children can explore outside and splash about in their own rainy clothes.

This activity provides great opportunity to encourage and develop children's vocabulary and language too and can often be linked to speaking and listening or writing activities.

Final thoughts and reflections

Consider the importance of making links with the world around us. Young children will all naturally experience the weather and changing seasons as they progress though life. Making links with familiar themes that all children can access adds security and helps build confidence.

This activity encourages the children to reflect as they think about different weather and their memories associated with snow, rain, sun.

Resource support: *Example backdrop image*

Activity 2 Sunny or stormy music

Activity outline and preparation

This activity encourages children to explore instruments to make sounds inspired by different weather and words associated with that weather. Some children can also begin to note their created sounds/music using symbols and pictures if they wish.

As this activity is about musical expression with lots of noise, consider the best location beforehand. It will need a good selection of musical instruments (see below) as the children should be free to choose from a range of instruments.

As preparation or for further inspiration, the children would benefit from some adult focus via seized opportunities. An idea for this is to share extracts of Vivaldi's *The Four Seasons* with a focus upon Spring or Summer alongside Autumn or Winter so the children can listen to music associated with sunshine or storms and the cold.

Resources

- Instruments: try to include triangle/s, tambourine/s, jingle sticks, maracas, xylophone/s, bells, sand blocks, egg shakers, drums

- Download Vivaldi's *The Four Seasons*

- Dry-wipe music sheets and pens

- Season and weather cards

Preparation

- Organise musical instruments in different baskets or trays. If possible, label these baskets/trays so the children can see the names of instruments displayed.

- Create season and weather cards to inspire the children about the types of weather associated with the seasons.

- Create dry-wipe music cards (cards with boxes or lines for children's note marks) so children can add their own symbols to express the music they have created.

ESSENTIAL LITERACY AND MATHEMATICS DEVELOPMENT				
PRIME AREAS		**Development guidance**	**SPECIFIC AREAS**	**Development guidance**
COMMUNICATION AND LANGUAGE	Listening and attention	**30-50 months** *Is able to follow directions (from adults prior to the activity)* **40-60+ months** *Maintains attention, concentrates and sits quietly during appropriate activity* ***ELG** Children listen attentively in a range of situations. They listen to stories, accurately anticipating key events and respond to what they hear with relevant comments, questions or actions. They give their attention to what others say and respond appropriately, while engaged in another activity. (listening to adult led Vivaldi music, then simultaneously listening and doing whilst playing with others exploring instruments)*	LITERACY — Reading	**30-50 months** *Knows information can be relayed in the form of print (words on season and weather cards/instrument basket labels)* **40-60+ months** *Can segment sounds in simple words and blend them together and knows which letters represent some of them.* *Begins to read words and simple sentences.* ***ELG** Children read and understand simple sentences. They use phonic knowledge to decode regular words and read them aloud accurately. They also read some common irregular words. They demonstrate understanding when talking with others about what they have read. (using phonic knowledge to decode and read words on season and weather cards/instrument basket labels)*
			Writing	**30-50 months** *Sometimes give meaning to marks as they draw and paint (marks and symbols children add to music writing cards)* **40-60+ months** *Gives meaning to marks they make as they draw, write and paint (marks and symbols children add to music writing cards)*
	Understanding	**30-50 months** *Understands use of objects (instruments as objects to create music)* ***ELG** Children follow instructions involving several ideas or actions. They answer 'how' and 'why' questions about their experiences and in response to stories or events. (following guidance about creating music with instruments)*	MATHEMATICS — Numbers	**30-50 months** *Realises not only objects but anything can be counted, including steps, claps and jumps (counting sounds while exploring instruments)* **40-60+ months** *Counts actions or objects which cannot be moved (counting sounds while exploring instruments)*
	Speaking	**30-50 months** *Uses vocabulary focused on objects and people that are of particular importance to them (using vocabulary related to instruments and sounds they make)* **40-60+ months** *Uses language to imagine and recreate roles and experiences in play situations (relating vocabulary associated with weather seasons to instrument exploration)* ***ELG** Children express themselves effectively, showing awareness of listeners' needs. They use past, present and future forms accurately when talking about events that have happened or are to happen in the future. They develop their own narratives and explanations by connecting ideas or events. (expressing themselves effectively whilst exploring instruments with others)*	Shape, space and measure	**30-50 months** *Shows an interest in shape and space by playing with shapes or making arrangements with objects (representation of own music with shapes and symbols on music cards)* **40-60+ months** *Uses familiar objects and common shapes to create and recreate patterns and build models (representation of own music with shapes and symbols on music cards)* ***ELG** Children use everyday language to talk about size, weight, capacity, position, distance, time and money to compare quantities and objects and to solve problems. They recognise, create and describe patterns. They explore characteristics of everyday objects and shapes and use mathematical language to describe them. (creation and representation of own music patterns with shapes and symbols on music cards)*

CHARACTERISTICS OF EFFECTIVE LEARNING	Suggested outcomes
Playing and exploring – *engagement*	**Representing their experiences of weather in music and sounds**
Active learning – *motivation*	**Being proud of accomplished music matched to a type of weather**
Creating and thinking critically – *thinking*	**Making links and noticing patterns with sounds**

PRIME AREAS		Development guidance	SPECIFIC AREAS		Development guidance
PHYSICAL DEVELOPMENT	Moving and handling	**30-50 months** *Holds pencil near point between first two fingers and thumb and uses it with good control (while creating marks and symbols on music card)* **40-60+ months** *Handles tools, objects, construction and malleable materials safely and with increasing control.* **ELG** *Children show good control and co-ordination in large and small movements. They move confidently in a range of ways, safely negotiating space. They handle equipment and tools effectively, including pencils for writing. (confident handling of musical instruments and pens for completing music cards)*	**UNDERSTANDING THE WORLD**	People and communities	**30-50 months** *Shows interest in different occupations and ways of life (Vivaldi as a musical composer)*
				The world	**30-50 months** *Talks about why things happen and how things work (musical instruments and the sounds they make)* **40-60+ months** *Looks closely at similarities, differences, patterns and change* **ELG** *Children know about similarities and differences in relation to places, objects, materials and living things. They talk about the features of their own immediate environment and how environments might vary from one another. They make observations of animals and plants and explain why some things occur, and talk about changes. (exploring and talking about the similarities and differences musical instruments/ sounds make)*
				Technology	
	Health and self-care		**EXPRESSIVE ARTS AND DESIGN**	Exploring and using media and materials	**30-50 months** *Imitates movement in response to music* *Taps out simple repeated rhythms* *Explores and learns how sounds can be changed (while exploring musical instruments and sounds)* **40-60+ months** *Explores different sounds of instruments* **ELG** *Children sing songs, make music and dance, and experiment with ways of changing them. They safely use and explore a variety of materials, tools and techniques, experimenting with colour, design, texture, form and function. (whilst exploring musical instruments and sounds, experimenting with changes)*
				Being imaginative	**30-50 months** *Makes up rhythms (while exploring musical instruments and sounds)* **40-60+ months** *Create simple representations of events, people and objects* **ELG** *Children use what they have learnt about media and materials in original ways, thinking about uses and purposes. They represent their own ideas, thoughts and feelings through design and technology, art, music, dance, role-play and stories. (exploration of instruments to represent their weather sounds and music)*
PERSONAL, SOCIAL AND EMOTIONAL DEVELOPMENT	Making relation-ships	**30-50 months** *Keeps play going by responding to what others are saying or doing. (inspiring each other while making sounds and music)* **ELG** *Children play co-operatively, taking turns with others. They take account of one another's ideas about how to organise their activity. They show sensitivity to others' needs and feelings, and form positive relationships with adults and other children. (playing co-operatively and taking turns with instruments and sharing ideas)*			
	Self-confidence and self-awareness	**30-50 months** *Can select and use resources with help (choosing instruments and asking for help if needed)* *Enjoys responsibility of carrying out small tasks (making own music)* **40-60+ months** *Confident to speak to others about own needs, wants, interests and opinions* **ELG** *Children are confident to try new activities, and say why they like some activities more than others. They are confident to speak in a familiar group, will talk about their ideas, and will choose the resources they need for their chosen activities. They say when they do or don't need help. (confidence whilst exploring instruments and creating music)*			
	Managing feelings and behaviour	**30-50 months** *Aware of own feelings and knows that some actions and words can hurt feelings (sharing of instruments)* **40-60+ months** **ELG** *Children talk about how they and others show feelings, talk about their own and others' behaviour, and its consequences, and know that some behaviour is unacceptable. They work as part of a group or class, and understand and follow the rules. They adjust their behaviour to different situations, and take changes of routine in their stride. (understands real use of instruments and exploring sensibly)*			

Activity guidance

This is a continuous provision activity that aims to develop musical expression through rhythm and sound.

Arrange different musical instruments in labelled boxes or baskets. Display season/weather and music cards nearby with dry-wipe pens.

To initiate interest explore some extracts of Vivaldi's *The Four Seasons* and encourage the children to close their eyes and think about what types of weather 'Summer' or 'Autumn' makes them think of. What kind of weather do we have in summer? In autumn? What instrument sounds make us think of sunshine, wind or rain?

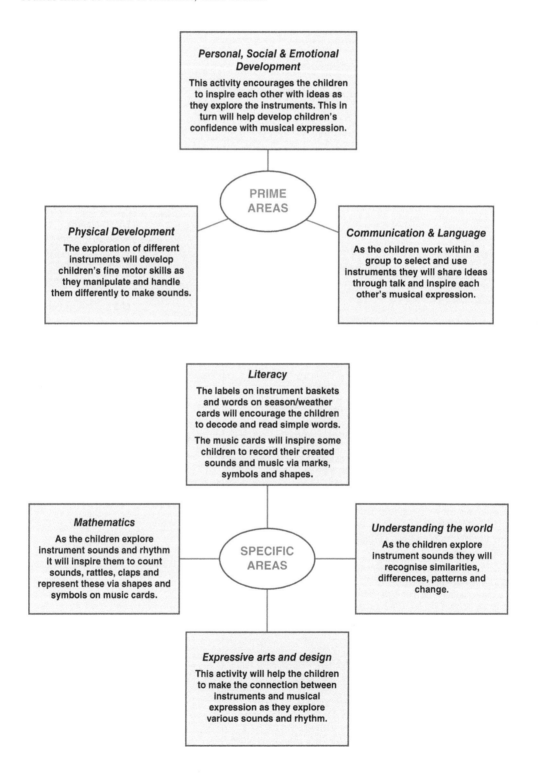

Personal, Social & Emotional Development

This activity encourages the children to inspire each other with ideas as they explore the instruments. This in turn will help develop children's confidence with musical expression.

PRIME AREAS

Physical Development

The exploration of different instruments will develop children's fine motor skills as they manipulate and handle them differently to make sounds.

Communication & Language

As the children work within a group to select and use instruments they will share ideas through talk and inspire each other's musical expression.

Literacy

The labels on instrument baskets and words on season/weather cards will encourage the children to decode and read simple words.

The music cards will inspire some children to record their created sounds and music via marks, symbols and shapes.

Mathematics

As the children explore instrument sounds and rhythm it will inspire them to count sounds, rattles, claps and represent these via shapes and symbols on music cards.

SPECIFIC AREAS

Understanding the world

As the children explore instrument sounds they will recognise similarities, differences, patterns and change.

Expressive arts and design

This activity will help the children to make the connection between instruments and musical expression as they explore various sounds and rhythm.

Possible next steps and opportunities for further development

Music writing

Not all children will create their own music card during this activity but it is important that children make this link. The children will need further experience of recording signs, symbols, marks and patterns to note their musical creations.

Musical performance

As children explore instruments and create their own musical representations it is also important that there are opportunities for performance. A performance afternoon with invited family members provides this opportunity.

This activity does not need to be 'individual' performances. Many children will enjoy performing in groups or with friends who have created similar musical expressions. Performances can be in various places around the setting to make this activity more informal and a real celebration of the children's musical expression.

Final thoughts and reflections

Reflect upon the importance of musical exploration with young children. Many children will be unsure about different instruments and the sounds they make and need to discover this for themselves.

This activity also encourages the children to think about rhythm and movement. Consider the potential links with dance and gross motor skill development.

Summer sunshine

hot

shiny

bright

sparkly

light

Activity 3 Sunshine or showery fruits

Activity outline and preparation

We are lucky to have access to most fruits all year long but fruits are naturally linked with the seasons due to the associated weather. With this in mind, this observational drawing activity teaches the children about fruits with links to the natural season and weather that occurs at that time.

Focus upon one season or more (and the associated weather) and choose fruits for the children to draw or paint. This will encourage the children to observe selected fruit and copy the colours and patterns they see.

As this activity encourages the children to draw or paint the fruit, consider which approach would work well, i.e. painting with easels or drawing and colouring (with pastels, crayons or chalks) in sketchbooks or large-scale paper.

Here are some ideas of good fruits to draw associated with the seasons.

Sunny summer:	Showery spring:
Berries (blueberries, blackberries, raspberries, strawberries)	Apricots
Cherries	Cherries
Figs	Kumquats
Watermelons	Lychees
Dragon fruit	Pineapples
Pineapples	Peaches
Peaches	**Warm and windy autumn:**
Icy winter:	Apples
Tangerines	Berries (blackberries, raspberries, strawberries)
Blood oranges	Clementines
Kumquats	Cranberries
Pomegranates	Guava
Kiwi fruit	Pomegranates
Guava	Plums

Resources

- Fruits – follow the list above and label the fruits clearly

- Sketch pads, paper with easels or large-scale table paper

- Paints, wax crayons, chalks or pastels – aim to choose one media rather than allowing children to use several

- Aprons if using paint, chalks or pastels

- Magnifiers to look closely at the fruit

Preparation

- Display all fruits with a clear label.

- Organise sketchpads, paper on easels or large-scale table paper along with the chosen media and aprons.

- Sort out a box of magnifiers to encourage the children to observe closely.

ESSENTIAL LITERACY AND MATHEMATICS DEVELOPMENT				
PRIME AREAS	Development guidance	SPECIFIC AREAS		Development guidance
COMMUNICATION AND LANGUAGE	Listening and attention	**30-50 months** *Focusing attention - still listen or do, but can shift own attention (while exploring fruit)* **40-60+ months** *Two-channelled attention - can listen and do for a short span (while exploring fruit)* **ELG** *Children listen attentively in a range of situations. They listen to stories, accurately anticipating key events and respond to what they hear with relevant comments, questions or actions. They give their attention to what others say and respond appropriately, while engaged in another activity. (listening to others whilst observing and drawing/painting an image of their chosen fruit)*	LITERACY	Reading	**30-50 months** *Knows that print carries meaning and, in English, is read from left to right and top to bottom (recognition and reading of fruit labels)* **40-60+ months** *Can segment sounds in simple words and blend them together and knows which letters represent some of them.* *Begins to read words and simple sentences.* **ELG** *Children read and understand simple sentences. They use phonic knowledge to decode regular words and read them aloud accurately. They also read some common irregular words. They demonstrate understanding when talking with others about what they have read. (using phonic knowledge to decode and read fruit labels)*
				Writing	**30-50 months** *Sometimes give meaning to marks as they draw and paint (marks on fruit drawing or painting)* **40-60+ months** *Uses some clearly identifiable letters to communicate meaning, representing some sounds correctly and in sequence* *Gives meaning to marks they make as they draw, write and paint (marks and words added to fruit drawings or paintings)*
	Under-standing	**30-50 months** *Shows understanding of prepositions such as 'under', 'on top', 'behind' by carrying out an action or selecting correct picture (while exploring fruit)* **40-60+ months** *Listens and responds to ideas expressed by others in conversation or discussion (while exploring fruits alongside each other)*	MATHEMATICS	Numbers	**30-50 months** *Uses some number names and number language spontaneously (while exploring fruit)* **40-60+ months** *Finds the total number of items in two groups by counting all of them (spontaneous counting while exploring fruit)*
	Speaking	**30-50 months** *Builds up vocabulary that reflects the breadth of their experiences (vocabulary related to chosen fruits)* **40-60+ months** *Extends vocabulary, especially by grouping and naming, exploring the meaning and sounds of new words (relating vocabulary associated with fruit)*		Shape, space and measure	**30-50 months** *Shows an interest in shape and space by playing with shapes or making arrangements with objects (while exploring fruit)* **40-60+ months** *Selects a particularly named shape (links fruits to known shapes, i.e. passion fruit and sphere)* **ELG** *Children use everyday language to talk about size, weight, capacity, position, distance, time and money to compare quantities and objects and to solve problems. They recognise, create and describe patterns. They explore characteristics of everyday objects and shapes and use mathematical language to describe them. (children use everyday and mathematical language whilst describing fruit shapes and sizes)*

CHARACTERISTICS OF EFFECTIVE LEARNING	Suggested outcomes
Playing and exploring – *engagement*	**Using senses of sight, smell and touch to explore fruits**
Active learning – *motivation*	**Showing good levels of fascination with fruits**
Creating and thinking critically – *thinking*	**Making links and noticing patterns with fruits**

PRIME AREAS		Development guidance	SPECIFIC AREAS		Development guidance
PHYSICAL DEVELOPMENT	Moving and handling	**30-50 months** *Holds pencil near point between first two fingers and thumb and uses it with good control (while drawing with pastels, crayons, chalks or painting)* **40-60+ months** *Handles tools, objects, construction and malleable materials safely and with increasing control.* **ELG** *Children show good control and co-ordination in large and small movements. They move confidently in a range of ways, safely negotiating space. They handle equipment and tools effectively, including pencils for writing. (confident and co-ordinated handling of fruit, magnifiers and crayons, chalks, pastels or paintbrushes)*	**UNDERSTANDING THE WORLD**	People and communities	
				The world	**30-50 months** *Can talk about some of the things they have observed such as plants, animals, natural and found objects (children talk about observed fruit)* **40-60+ months** *Looks closely at similarities, differences, patterns and change* **ELG** *Children know about similarities and differences in relation to places, objects, materials and living things. They talk about the features of their own immediate environment and how environments might vary from one another. They make observations of animals and plants and explain why some things occur, and talk about changes. (children observe similarities and differences between the fruits)*
				Technology	
	Health and self-care	**ELG** *Children know the importance for good health of physical exercise, and a healthy diet, and talk about ways to keep healthy and safe. They manage their own basic hygiene and personal needs successfully, including dressing and going to the toilet independently. (understand the importance of a healthy diet and that fruits are a healthy food)*	**EXPRESSIVE ARTS AND DESIGN**	Exploring and using media and materials	**30-50 months** *Explores colour and how colours can be changed (while drawing or painting)* **40-60+ months** *Explores what happens when they mix colours (while using paints, chalks or pastels)* **ELG** *Children sing songs, make music and dance, and experiment with ways of changing them. They safely use and explore a variety of materials, tools and techniques, experimenting with colour, design, texture, form and function. (children explore and experiment with colour, shape and form whist drawing or painting)*
				Being imaginative	**30-50 months** *Captures experiences and responses with a range of media such as paint and other materials (while drawing or painting fruit)* **40-60+ months** *Create simple representations of events, people and objects* **ELG** *Children use what they have learnt about media and materials in original ways, thinking about uses and purposes. They represent their own ideas, thoughts and feelings through design and technology, art, music, dance, role-play and stories. (children explore their representation of fruits through drawing or painting)*
PERSONAL, SOCIAL AND EMOTIONAL DEVELOPMENT	Making relationships	**30-50 months** *Demonstrates friendly behaviour, initiating conversations and forming good relationships with peers and familiar adults (sharing fruits)* **40-60+ months** *Explains own knowledge and understanding, and asks appropriate questions of others (while exploring fruit)* **ELG** *Children play co-operatively, taking turns with others. They take account of one another's ideas about how to organise their activity. They show sensitivity to others' needs and feelings, and form positive relationships with adults and other children. (children play co-operatively taking turns with pastels, crayons, chalks or paints)*			
	Self-confidence and self-awareness	**30-50 months** *Can select and use resources with help (choosing equipment for drawing or painting with help if needed)* **ELG** *Children are confident to try new activities, and say why they like some activities more than others. They are confident to speak in a familiar group, will talk about their ideas, and will choose the resources they need for their chosen activities. They say when they do or don't need help. (children are confident to choose a fruit and corresponding coloured paints or pastels to begin drawing or painting)*			
	Managing feelings and behaviour	**30-50 months** *Begins to accept the needs of others and can take turns and share resources, sometimes with support from others (taking turns sharing of fruit and art equipment)* **ELG** *Children talk about how they and others show feelings, talk about their own and others' behaviour, and its consequences, and know that some behaviour is unacceptable. They work as part of a group or class, and understand and follow the rules. They adjust their behaviour to different situations, and take changes of routine in their stride. (working within the group sometimes sharing a piece of fruit to draw or sketch and keeping focused upon the short activity)*			

Activity guidance

This is a continuous provision activity that aims to develop children's observational skills alongside artistic expression.

Arrange labelled fruit on a tray or in a large basket for the children to touch, smell and observe.

To initiate interest draw the children's attention to the fruits. What do the fruits look like? What colours and shapes can you see? Do the fruits smell? What do the fruits feel like when you touch them?

Suggest the children choose a fruit each to look at carefully and then draw or paint.

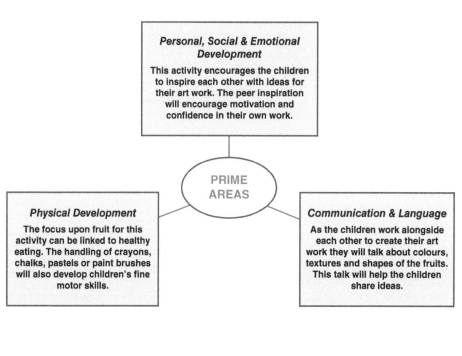

Personal, Social & Emotional Development

This activity encourages the children to inspire each other with ideas for their art work. The peer inspiration will encourage motivation and confidence in their own work.

PRIME AREAS

Physical Development

The focus upon fruit for this activity can be linked to healthy eating. The handling of crayons, chalks, pastels or paint brushes will also develop children's fine motor skills.

Communication & Language

As the children work alongside each other to create their art work they will talk about colours, textures and shapes of the fruits. This talk will help the children share ideas.

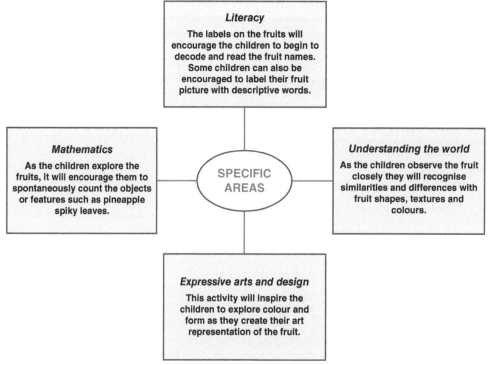

Literacy

The labels on the fruits will encourage the children to begin to decode and read the fruit names. Some children can also be encouraged to label their fruit picture with descriptive words.

SPECIFIC AREAS

Mathematics

As the children explore the fruits, it will encourage them to spontaneously count the objects or features such as pineapple spiky leaves.

Understanding the world

As the children observe the fruit closely they will recognise similarities and differences with fruit shapes, textures and colours.

Expressive arts and design

This activity will inspire the children to explore colour and form as they create their art representation of the fruit.

Possible next steps and opportunities for further development
Printing and moulding

To explore texture further, focus upon creating fruit texture prints or moulds in clay or Play-Doh. Pineapples, galia melons and avocados are good fruits to use for texture. Texture printing can also lead to further art activities such as collage.

Some children will need to keep focusing upon 'texture' to help them develop their sense of touch. The sensory development will also benefit their breadth of descriptive vocabulary.

All senses

Fruits are good for teaching the children about exploring all senses. Through a guided activity, the children can once again observe and touch various fruits but also smell and taste the fruits. They can also explore hearing, as some fruit textures will make a sound if rubbed.

This activity can also include a focus upon guessing (prediction) as the children can use their senses and guess which fruit they link to. Children often need encouragement about guessing (predicting) and need lots of experience with this so they understand that guesses (predictions) may not always be correct and this is part of learning.

Final thoughts and reflections

Reflect upon the importance of developing learning through the senses with young children. Consider how these explorations are essential for perceptual development.

Since there are lots of fruits that many young children will be unfamiliar with, this activity provides an opportunity to develop children's knowledge and understanding of this. The children's unfamiliarity also provides an opportunity for guesses (predictions).

Resource support: *Example accompanying poster*

Sunny summer

During the sunshine of summer, these fruits like to grow...

 watermelons

 cherries

 pineapples

 strawberries

 dragon fruits

 peaches

Activity 4 Rain or shine today?

Activity outline and preparation

This activity encourages the children to role-play as weather forecasters using a large UK map and moveable weather symbols. Children can also take turns 'filming' each other leading the weather forecast using a simple recording device.

For this activity, you will need either a poster or interactive whiteboard large-scale map of the UK, moveable weather symbols and iPads or other recording devices.

Resources

- Map of UK (poster or via interactive whiteboard)

- Weather symbol cards (magnetic or with Blu-tack) to attach to the map – leave some symbols blank to encourage children to add the weather label

- Dry-wipe pens

- iPads or other simple recording devices

Preparation

- Create UK map and print/laminate weather symbols.

- Display the UK map, weather symbols and dry-wipe pens in a tray or basket nearby.

- Ensure iPads or other recording devices are charged and ready to use.

- Download a TV clip of the weather forecast for children to watch.

ESSENTIAL LITERACY AND MATHEMATICS DEVELOPMENT				
PRIME AREAS		Development guidance	SPECIFIC AREAS		Development guidance

PRIME AREAS		Development guidance	SPECIFIC AREAS		Development guidance
COMMUNICATION AND LANGUAGE	Listening and attention	**30-50 months** *Focusing attention - still listen or do, but can shift own attention (while engaged in weather forecast)* **40-60+ months** *Two-channelled attention - can listen and do for a short span (while engaged in weather forecast)*	LITERACY	Reading	**30-50 months** *Recognises familiar words and signs such as own name and advertising logos (recognition of some weather labels, e.g. 'sun', 'rain', with appropriate symbol)* **40-60+ months** *Begins to read words and simple sentences* **ELG** *Children read and understand simple sentences. They use phonic knowledge to decode regular words and read them aloud accurately. They also read some common irregular words. They demonstrate understanding when talking with others about what they have read. (use of phonic knowledge to decode and read some weather labels)*
				Writing	**30-50 months** *Sometimes give meaning to marks as they draw and paint (mark making – adding to weather labels)* **40-60+ months** *Writes own name and other things such as labels (weather labels)*
	Under-standing	**30-50 months** *Understands use of objects (symbols for map and iPads for recording)* **40-60+ months** *Responds to instructions involving two-part sequence. Understands humour, e.g. nonsense rhyme, jokes.* **ELG** *Children follow instructions involving several ideas or actions. They answer 'how' and 'why' questions about their experiences and in response to stories or events. (following ideas and instructions about how to weather forecast)*	MATHEMATICS	Numbers	**30-50 months** *Shows curiosity about numbers by offering comments or asking questions (comments about sun or rain cloud labels)* **40-60+ months** *Uses the language of 'more' and 'fewer' to compare two sets of objects (comments related to number of sun or rain cloud labels while engaged in activity)*
	Speaking	**30-50 months** *Uses talk to connect ideas, explain what is happening and anticipate what might happen next, recall and relive past experiences (talk to connect ideas with weather forecast)* **40-60+ months** *Extends vocabulary, especially by grouping and naming, exploring the meaning and sounds of new words (vocabulary associated with weather)*		Shape, space and measure	**30-50 months** *Uses positional language (while arranging symbols on map)* **ELG** *Children use everyday language to talk about size, weight, capacity, position, distance, time and money to compare quantities and objects and to solve problems. They recognise, create and describe patterns. They explore characteristics of everyday objects and shapes and use mathematical language to describe them. (children use everyday language related to position and distance whilst arranging symbols and engaging with UK map)*

CHARACTERISTICS OF EFFECTIVE LEARNING	Suggested outcomes
Playing and exploring – *engagement*	**Engaging in open-ended weather forecasting**
Active learning – *motivation*	**Maintaining focus on role of weather forecaster, i.e. positioning labels alongside explanation of weather or role as recorder**
Creating and thinking critically – *thinking*	**Making weather predictions**

PRIME AREAS		Development guidance	SPECIFIC AREAS		Development guidance
PHYSICAL DEVELOPMENT	Moving and handling	**30-50 months** *Moves freely and with pleasure and confidence in a range of ways, such as slithering, shuffling, rolling, crawling, walking, running, jumping, skipping, sliding and hopping* (moves freely jumping, walking, shuffling, sliding in front of the map) **40-60+ months** *Experiments with different ways of moving* **ELG** *Children show good control and co-ordination in large and small movements. They move confidently in a range of ways, safely negotiating space. They handle equipment and tools effectively, including pencils for writing.* (good control and co-ordination with large and small movements in front of map)	UNDERSTANDING THE WORLD	People and communities	
				The world	**30-50 months** *Comments on and asks questions about aspects of their familiar world such as the place where they live or the natural world* (weather from natural world) **40-60+ months** *Looks closely at similarities, differences, patterns and change* **ELG** *Children know about similarities and differences in relation to places, objects, materials and living things. They talk about the features of their own immediate environment and how environments might vary from one another. They make observations of animals and plants and explain why some things occur, and talk about changes.* (children know about similarities, differences and patterns in relation to weather changes)
				Technology	**30-50 months** *Knows how to operate simple equipment* (knows how to operate iPad or other simple recording device whilst recording others' weather forecasts) **ELG** *Children recognise that a range of technology is used in places such as homes and schools. They select and use technology for particular purposes.* (understands use of iPads or other recording devices for the purpose of recording others)
	Health and self-care		EXPRESSIVE ARTS AND DESIGN	Exploring and using media and materials	
				Being imaginative	**30-50 months** *Notices what adults do, imitating what is observed and then doing it spontaneously when the adult is not there* (imitating role as weather forecaster after observing TV clip) **ELG** *Children use what they have learnt about media and materials in original ways, thinking about uses and purposes. They represent their own ideas, thoughts and feelings through design and technology, art, music, dance, role-play and stories.* (representing their ideas through role-play as weather forecaster)
PERSONAL, SOCIAL AND EMOTIONAL DEVELOPMENT	Making relationships	**30-50 months** *Initiates play, offering cues to peers to join them* (encouraging others to join in with weather forecasting) **40-60+ months** *Explains own knowledge and understanding, and asks appropriate questions of others* (knowledge and understanding of weather) **ELG** *Children play co-operatively, taking turns with others. They take account of one another's ideas about how to organise their activity. They show sensitivity to others' needs and feelings, and form positive relationships with adults and other children.* (playing co-operatively and taking turns as weather forecaster or recorder)			
	Self-confidence and self-awareness	**30-50 months** *Can select and use resources with help* (selecting labels for map and iPads with help) **ELG** *Children are confident to try new activities, and say why they like some activities more than others. They are confident to speak in a familiar group, will talk about their ideas, and will choose the resources they need for their chosen activities. They say when they do or don't need help.* (confidence to try the roles as weather forecaster or recorder)			
	Managing feelings and behaviour	**30-50 months** *Can usually tolerate delay when needs are not immediately met and understands wishes may not always be met* (toleration of delays with iPad or turns with map) **ELG** *Children talk about how they and others show feelings, talk about their own and others' behaviour, and its consequences, and know that some behaviour is unacceptable. They work as part of a group or class, and understand and follow the rules. They adjust their behaviour to different situations, and take changes of routine in their stride.* (children work as a small group and are sensible whilst recording)			

Activity guidance

This is a continuous provision activity that aims to develop children's understanding of maps and weather through expressive role-play.

Organise the UK map, weather symbol labels and recording devices nearby. The children would benefit from observing a short TV clip of a UK weather forecast before or during participation in this activity.

To initiate interest draw the children's attention to a UK weather forecast TV clip. Ask children to look carefully at the map of the United Kingdom. What do the pictures/symbols mean on the map? Are all the weather pictures/symbols the same on the map?

Remind the children how to capture a video using an iPad or other familiar recording device and ask the children if they could take turns to lead their own weather forecast while other children record.

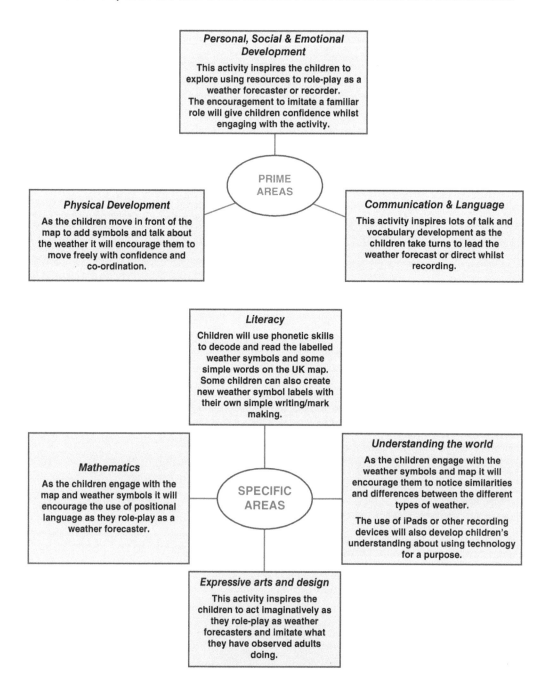

Possible next steps and opportunities for further development

Weather across the world

Children can explore weather forecasting further by looking at the weather in other countries. Focus the children upon a hot country such as Africa and in contrast somewhere cold. Let the children explore weather forecasting once again with different, contrasting maps and symbols.

As children further explore maps, talk to them about North (at the top) and South (near the bottom), so they can begin to add these words to their vocabulary. Not all children will understand and use these new words but this does not matter.

All-weather collages

To consolidate understanding about the different types of weather we experience, encourage the children to engage in creating an all-weather collage. Gather images for the collage from weather photos via home, magazines or downloaded online pictures.

Some children may wish to work on their own all-weather collage while others may want to do this in a group. Explore all options and encourage children to work as they feel comfortable, as this will encourage confidence.

Final thoughts and reflections

Consider how this activity helps develop children's vocabulary and communication skills. It will also encourage the use of specific language as the children focus upon weather and positions on the map.

Reflect upon how this activity helps draw the children's attention to other locations in the UK alongside their familiar home city.

Resource support: *Example weather symbols*

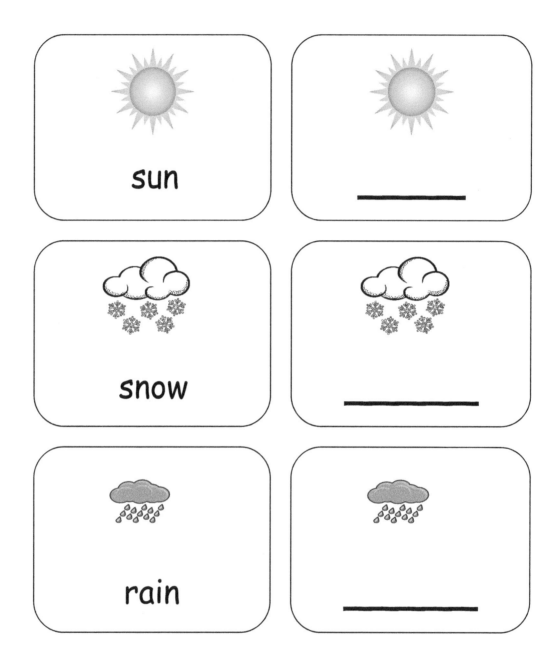

sun

_____

snow

_____

rain

_____

Activity 5 Bee-Bot seasons
Activity outline and preparation

This activity requires the children to explore operating a Bee-Bot floor robot with the aim of moving the robot to a selected season on a floor map.

Since this is a floor activity, it can take place indoors or outdoors but requires a large-scale seasonal floor map. The floor map can display two or all four seasons but does not need detail. As part of the activity, children can add illustrations and mark making to the map to complete it.

Prior to the activity, it would be beneficial if the children have already met Bee-Bot and have a basic understanding about how to move the device forwards and backwards using the arrow buttons and 'GO'.

Resources

- Large-scale floor map
- Bee-Bot floor robot
- Season cards
- Crayons and pencils

Preparation

- Using large pieces of paper create a floor map noting two or all four seasons. Add some 'Start' labels so the children have some structure about where Bee-Bot begins. Aim for the children operating Bee-Bot to move in a simple straight line without turning. This map does not need detail as children can add illustrations and marks as part of the activity.
- Charge the Bee-Bot floor robot.
- Create season cards.

Activity development

ESSENTIAL LITERACY AND MATHEMATICS DEVELOPMENT				
PRIME AREAS		**Development guidance**	**SPECIFIC AREAS**	**Development guidance**
COMMUNICATION AND LANGUAGE	Listening and attention	**30-50 months** *Is able to follow directions (about how to operate Bee-Bot)* **40-60+ months** *Two-channelled attention – can listen and do for a short span* **ELG** Children listen attentively in a range of situations. They listen to stories, accurately anticipating key events and respond to what they hear with relevant comments, questions or actions. They give their attention to what others say and respond appropriately, while engaged in another activity. *(listening to others while operating and simple programming Bee-Bot)*	**LITERACY** — Reading	**30-50 months** *Knows information can be relayed in the form of print (season labels on floor map/cards)* **40-60+ months** *Begins to read words and simple sentence.* **ELG** Children read and understand simple sentences. They use phonic knowledge to decode regular words and read them aloud accurately. They also read some common irregular words. They demonstrate understanding when talking with others about what they have read. *(children use phonic knowledge to decode and read season labels on map/cards and additional words added by other children)*
			Writing	**30-50 months** *Sometimes give meaning to marks as they draw and paint (mark making, adding illustrations and other marks to floor map)* **40-60+ months** *Gives meaning to marks they draw, write and paint* **ELG** Children use their phonic knowledge to write words in ways which match their spoken sounds. They also write some irregular common words. They write simple sentences which can be read by themselves and others. Some words are spelt correctly and others are phonetically plausible. *(illustrations and use of phonics to sound out words added to floor map)*
	Under-standing	**30-50 months** *Understands use of objects (basic understanding of floor robot)* **40-60+ months** *Listens and responds to ideas expressed by others in conversation and discussion (working as a group to operate and programme Bee-Bot)* **ELG** Children follow instructions involving several ideas or actions. They answer 'how' and 'why' questions about their experiences and in response to stories or events. *(children follow ideas and instructions about how to operate Bee-Bot)*	**MATHEMATICS** — Numbers	**30-50 months** *Shows an interest in representing numbers (spontaneous counting as arrow buttons are pressed on Bee-Bot)* **40-60+ months** *Counts actions or objects which cannot be moved (counting actions and pressing arrow buttons to operate Bee-Bot)*
	Speaking	**30-50 months** *Uses talk to connect ideas, explain what is happening and anticipate what might happen next, recall and relive past experiences (group talk to connect ideas about Bee-Bot)* **40-60+ months** *Uses talk to organise, sequence and clarify thinking, ideas, feelings and events (group talk to organise and sequence thinking about how to operate Bee-Bot)*	Shape, space and measure	**30-50 months** *Uses positional language (while talking about the moving Bee-Bot)* **ELG** Children use everyday language to talk about size, weight, capacity, position, distance, time and money to compare quantities and objects and to solve problems. They recognise, create and describe patterns. They explore characteristics of everyday objects and shapes and use mathematical language to describe them. *(children use everyday language related to direction, position and movements whilst talking about Bee-Bot's movements and patterns with programming buttons)*

CHARACTERISTICS OF EFFECTIVE LEARNING	Suggested outcomes
Playing and exploring – *engagement*	**Sustained curiosity while operating Bee-Bot the floor robot**
Active learning – *motivation*	**Bouncing back if challenged when operating Bee-Bot the floor robot**
Creating and thinking critically – *thinking*	**Exploring how to operate Bee-Bot and adapting approach through trial and error**

PRIME AREAS		Development guidance	SPECIFIC AREAS		Development guidance
PHYSICAL DEVELOPMENT	Moving and handling	**30-50 months** Uses one-handed tools and equipment *(pressing buttons to operate Bee-Bot)* **40-60+ months** Handles tools, objects, construction and malleable materials safely and with increasing control. **ELG** Children show good control and co-ordination in large and small movements. They move confidently in a range of ways, safely negotiating space. They handle equipment and tools effectively, including pencils for writing. *(children co-ordinate and operate Bee-Bot confidently)*	UNDERSTANDING THE WORLD	People and communities	
				The world	**30-50 months** Comments and asks questions about aspects of their familiar world such as the place where they live or the natural world *(weather and seasons)* **40-60+ months** Looks closely at similarities, differences, patterns and change. **ELG** Children know about similarities and differences in relation to places, objects, materials and living things. They talk about the features of their own immediate environment and how environments might vary from one another. They make observations of animals and plants and explain why some things occur, and talk about changes. *(children know about similarities and differences between seasons associated with the place they live)*
				Technology	**30-50 months** Knows how to operate simple equipment. Shows skill in making toys work by pressing parts or lifting flaps to achieve effects such as sound, movements or new images *(children show skill as they begin to operate Bee-Bot)* **40-60+ months** Completes a simple program on a computer **ELG** Children recognise that a range of technology is used in places such as homes and schools. They select and use technology for particular purposes. *(selecting and using – programming and using Bee-Bot)*
	Health and self-care		EXPRESSIVE ARTS AND DESIGN	Exploring and using media and materials	
				Being imaginative	
PERSONAL, SOCIAL AND EMOTIONAL DEVELOPMENT	Making relationships	**30-50 months** Keeps play going by responding to what others are saying or doing *(keeps open-ended Bee-Bot exploration going following ideas from others)* **40-60+ months** Explains own knowledge and understanding and asks appropriate questions of others *(knowledge and understanding about how to operate Bee-Bot)* **ELG** Children play co-operatively, taking turns with others. They take account of one another's ideas about how to organise their activity. They show sensitivity to others' needs and feelings, and form positive relationships with adults and other children. *(taking turns to press Bee-Bot buttons)*			
	Self-confidence and self-awareness	**30-50 months** Can select and use resources with help *(having a go at operating Bee-Bot and asking for help if needed)* **ELG** Children are confident to try new activities, and say why they like some activities more than others. They are confident to speak in a familiar group, will talk about their ideas, and will choose the resources they need for their chosen activities. They say when they do or don't need help. *(children are confident to work with Bee-Bot yet ask for help if needed)*			
	Managing feelings and behaviour	**30-50 months** Begins to accept the needs of others and can take turns and share resources, sometimes with support from others *(sharing and taking turns to press buttons on Bee-Bot)* **40-60+ months** Beginning to be able to negotiate and solve problems without aggression **ELG** Children talk about how they and others show feelings, talk about their own and others' behaviour, and its consequences, and know that some behaviour is unacceptable. They work as part of a group or class, and understand and follow the rules. They adjust their behaviour to different situations, and take changes of routine in their stride. *(children work within a group, taking turns and solving problems with Bee-Bot)*			

Activity guidance

This is a continuous provision activity that aims to develop children's understanding of space, direction and movement with the use of technology.

Charge the Bee-Bot floor robot ready for use and lay out the floor map. Organise pencils, crayons or other mark making resources in a basket or tray nearby. Display a stack of season cards on the floor with the map. The children should be encouraged to begin by picking a season card to choose where to send Bee-Bot and then place Bee-Bot on one of the 'start' labels on the floor map.

To initiate interest ask the children if they can remember meeting Bee-Bot and which buttons are pressed to move it forwards and backwards. What does the 'GO' button do? Show the children the floor map with the 'start' labels and explain they will need choose a season card then press Bee-Bot's arrow and go buttons to move it to the matching season on the map.

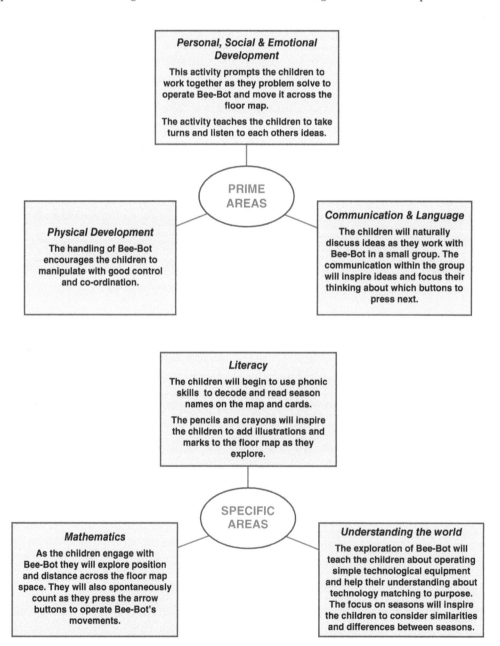

Personal, Social & Emotional Development

This activity prompts the children to work together as they problem solve to operate Bee-Bot and move it across the floor map.

The activity teaches the children to take turns and listen to each others ideas.

PRIME AREAS

Physical Development

The handling of Bee-Bot encourages the children to manipulate with good control and co-ordination.

Communication & Language

The children will naturally discuss ideas as they work with Bee-Bot in a small group. The communication within the group will inspire ideas and focus their thinking about which buttons to press next.

Literacy

The children will begin to use phonic skills to decode and read season names on the map and cards.

The pencils and crayons will inspire the children to add illustrations and marks to the floor map as they explore.

SPECIFIC AREAS

Mathematics

As the children engage with Bee-Bot they will explore position and distance across the floor map space. They will also spontaneously count as they press the arrow buttons to operate Bee-Bot's movements.

Understanding the world

The exploration of Bee-Bot will teach the children about operating simple technological equipment and help their understanding about technology matching to purpose. The focus on seasons will inspire the children to consider similarities and differences between seasons.

Possible next steps and opportunities for further development

Turning around

Explore Bee-Bot's movements further during a guided activity focusing upon turns. Let the children explore moving about and turning and then relate this to the correct operational buttons on Bee-Bot.

Some children will struggle with the idea of turning right or left so before they understand this concept with Bee-Bot they will need to engage in practical activities that help then visualise these movements.

Bee-Bot accessories

Revisit operating Bee-Bot to visit the correct seasons or months of the year using a floor map. This time, place accessories (e.g. sunglasses, sun hat, woolly hat, rain hat) that match a season or month on the map for Bee-Bot to reach and wear. This activity works well after focusing upon turning as the children can revisit the map and operate Bee-Bot.

Bee-Bot directions

As the children gain confidence with Bee-Bot they can begin recording actions for its movements. This can be via a guided activity using simple symbols and numbers.

Children will benefit from recording actions using dry-wipe boards and pens so they can change and edit their ideas. As children record movements, using simple symbols and numbers. They should also be encouraged to move and walk before recording.

Final thoughts and reflections

Consider the links between operating the floor robot and the development of gross motor movement. This activity provides plenty of opportunities for children to visualise and act out gross motor movements before relating these to a floor robot.

Reflect upon the benefit of open exploration with the floor robot. This will provide opportunities for trial and error and develop understanding.

Resource support: *Example season cards*

Go to summer

Go to winter

Activity 6 Outdoor detectives

Activity outline and preparation

This is an outdoor activity that encourages the children to walk around outdoors and discover signs of the season by looking at flowers, trees and leaves. Children can capture what they find through photographs and then record other illustrations and marks on a working wall afterwards.

This activity relies upon an area with trees, bushes and some flowers and is designed as an independent continuous provision activity, but if the outdoor area is not part of the setting and some distance away it will require adult supervision.

Resources

- Magnifying glasses

- iPads or cameras

- Books relating to the season and outdoor plants, trees

- Working wall labelled 'What did I see and solve?' The working wall should begin a blank canvas so children can add illustrations, marks, words or simple sentences as they progress. The working wall should also be a place for children to display any photos captured

- Crayons and pencils

Preparation

- In preparation for the activity, create the working wall with the title 'What did I see and solve?' The working wall should provide lots of blank space for the children to record their ideas freely (see above).

- Charge cameras or iPads.

- Organise magnifying glasses and crayons, pencils.

- Gather books relating to the season, plants and trees to display next to the working wall.

ESSENTIAL LITERACY AND MATHEMATICS DEVELOPMENT				
PRIME AREAS	Development guidance	SPECIFIC AREAS		Development guidance
COMMUNICATION AND LANGUAGE	Listening and attention	**30-50 months** Is able to follow directions (if not intently focused on own choice of activity) *(children follow directions observing within a local area as an outdoor detective)* **40-60+ months** *Two-channelled attention - can listen and do for short span* **ELG** *Children listen attentively in a range of situations. They listen to stories, accurately anticipating key events and respond to what they hear with relevant comments, questions or actions. They give their attention to what others say and respond appropriately, while engaged in another activity. (simultaneous listening and observing as outdoor detective)*	LITERACY	Reading	**30-50 months** Shows interest in illustrations and print in books and print in the environment. Looks at books independently Handles books carefully. Holds books the correct way up and turns pages *(season books on display with working wall)* **40-60+ months** Enjoys an increasing range of books Knows that information can be retrieved from books and computers. **ELG** *Children read and understand simple sentences. They use phonic knowledge to decode regular words and read them aloud accurately. They also read some common irregular words. They demonstrate understanding when talking with others about what they have read. (reading and understanding simple words or sentences in season books on display)*
				Writing	**30-50 months** Sometimes give meaning to marks as they draw and paint. Ascribes meaning to marks that they see in different places *(illustrations and marks added to working wall)* **40-60+ months** Gives meaning to marks they make as they draw, write and paint. Uses some clearly identifiable letters to communicate meaning, representing some sounds correctly and in sequence. **ELG** *Children use their phonic knowledge to write words in ways which match their spoken sounds. They also write some irregular common words. They write simple sentences which can be read by themselves and others. Some words are spelt correctly and others are phonetically plausible. (children add illustrations, and use phonic knowledge to add marks and simple words to working wall)*
	Understanding	**30-50 months** Understands use of objects *(magnifying glasses, cameras and iPads for capturing images outside)* **40-60+ months** Responds to instructions involving a two-part sequence. Understands humour e.g. nonsense rhymes, jokes. **ELG** *Children follow instructions involving several ideas or actions. They answer 'how' and 'why' questions about their experiences and in response to stories or events. (children follow guidance about how to be an outdoor detective - observe, capture images, record on working wall)*	MATHEMATICS	Numbers	**30-50 months** Uses some number names and number language spontaneously *(spontaneous counting whilst exploring e.g. leaves and flowers)* **40-60+ months** Counts actions or objects that cannot be moved *(counting as exploring, e.g. leaves, trees, flowers)*
	Speaking	**30-50 months** Builds up vocabulary that that reflects the breadth of their experiences *(vocabulary related to seasons, plants, trees)* **40-60+ months** Extends vocabulary, especially by grouping and naming, exploring the meaning and sounds of new words *(new vocabulary related to seasons, plants, trees)* **ELG** *Children express themselves effectively, showing awareness of listeners' needs. They use past, present and future forms accurately when talking about events that have happened or are to happen in the future. They develop their own narratives and explanations by connecting ideas or events. (children express themselves effectively whilst exploring as outdoor detectives)*		Shape, space and measure	**30-50 months** Shows an interest in shape and space by playing with shapes or making arrangements with objects *(shows an interest in shapes whilst exploring outdoors)* **40-60+ months** Can describe their relative position such as 'behind' or 'next to' *(while exploring location of trees, plants outside)* **ELG** *Children use everyday language to talk about size, weight, capacity, position, distance, time and money to compare quantities and objects and to solve problems. They recognise, create and describe patterns. They explore characteristics of everyday objects and shapes and use mathematical language to describe them. (children use everyday and mathematical language whilst observing leaf, petal shapes outdoors)*

CHARACTERISTICS OF EFFECTIVE LEARNING	Suggested outcomes
Playing and exploring – *engagement*	**Using the senses of sight, touch, smell and hearing to explore the outdoors**
Active learning – *motivation*	**Paying close attention to detail while observing outdoors**
Creating and thinking critically – *thinking*	**Making links and noticing patterns outdoors**

PRIME AREAS		Development guidance	SPECIFIC AREAS		Development guidance
PHYSICAL DEVELOPMENT	Moving and handling	**30-50 months** Uses one-handed tools and equipment *(magnifiers, cameras, iPads)* **40-60+ months** Handles tools, objects, construction and malleable materials safely and with increasing control. *(magnifiers, cameras, iPads)* **ELG** Children show good control and co-ordination in large and small movements. They move confidently in a range of ways, safely negotiating space. They handle equipment and tools effectively, including pencils for writing. *(well handled, good control of magnifying glasses, iPads or cameras)*	**UNDERSTANDING THE WORLD**	People and communities	
				The world	**30-50 months** Comments on and asks questions about aspects of their familiar world such as the place where they live or the natural world Can talk about some things they have observed such as plants, animals, natural and found objects *(while exploring as outdoor detectives)* Developing an understanding of growth, decay and changes over time *(if children explore being outdoor detectives more than once)* **40-60+ months** Look closely at similarities, differences, patterns and change *(outside as detectives)* **ELG** Children know about similarities and differences in relation to places, objects, materials and living things. They talk about the features of their own immediate environment and how environments might vary from one another. They make observations of animals and plants and explain why some things occur, and talk about changes. *(observation of similarities and differences with plants and living things outdoors)*
				Technology	**30-50 months** Knows how to operate simple equipment *(cameras or iPads)* **ELG** Children recognise that a range of technology is used in places such as homes and schools. They select and use technology for particular purposes. *(selecting and using cameras or iPads for purpose – capturing images from outdoors)*
	Health and self-care		**EXPRESSIVE ARTS AND DESIGN**	Exploring and using media and materials	
				Being imaginative	
PERSONAL, SOCIAL AND EMOTIONAL DEVELOPMENT	Making relationships	**30-50 months** Keeps play going by responding to what others are saying or doing *(continue interest as outdoor detective by responding to others' ideas and actions)* **40-60+ months** Explains own knowledge and understanding and asks appropriate questions of others *(while observing outdoors and adding to working wall)* **ELG** Children play co-operatively, taking turns with others. They take account of one another's ideas about how to organise their activity. They show sensitivity to others' needs and feelings, and form positive relationships with adults and other children. *(taking turns with magnifiers, iPads or cameras and observing whilst sharing ideas)*			
	Self-confidence and self-awareness	**30-50 months** Can select and use resources with help *(asking for help with cameras, iPads if needed)* **40-60+ months** Confident to speak to others about own needs, wants, interests, opinions *(seeking help outdoors if needed)* **ELG** Children are confident to try new activities, and say why they like some activities more than others. They are confident to speak in a familiar group, will talk about their ideas, and will choose the resources they need for their chosen activities. They say when they do or don't need help. *(children are confident using resources to support and record observing)*			
	Managing feelings and behaviour	**30-50 months** Can usually tolerate delay when needs are not immediately met and understands wishes may not always be met *(while sharing resources and cameras/iPads)* **ELG** Children talk about how they and others show feelings, talk about their own and others' behaviour, and its consequences, and know that some behaviour is unacceptable. They work as part of a group or class, and understand and follow the rules. They adjust their behaviour to different situations, and take changes of routine in their stride. *(children explore sensibly as a group sharing resources and following activity guidance whilst outside)*			

Activity guidance

This is a continuous provision activity that aims to develop children's observations of nature outdoors in relation to the season.

Ensure the working wall is ready for use with crayons and pencils nearby and seasonal books on display. Charge cameras and/or iPads ready for use and organise magnifiers for children to take outdoors with them. Print any photos after the activity ready for children to add to the working wall.

To initiate interest gather children by the working wall and books on display. Encourage children to look through books and look for images of the season (spring, summer, autumn, winter – whichever season is the focus). What kinds of things may we find in spring/summer/autumn/winter? How can we look carefully to find clues of the season? Can you be detectives and look carefully for clues of spring/summer/autumn/winter)?

Once children have explored for a short while, return to the activity to encourage children to record illustrations, marks or words about what they have discovered on the working wall.

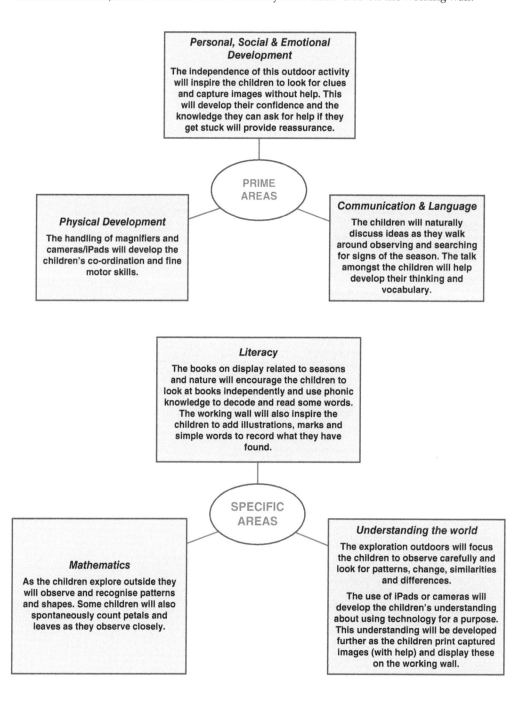

Personal, Social & Emotional Development

The independence of this outdoor activity will inspire the children to look for clues and capture images without help. This will develop their confidence and the knowledge they can ask for help if they get stuck will provide reassurance.

PRIME AREAS

Physical Development

The handling of magnifiers and cameras/iPads will develop the children's co-ordination and fine motor skills.

Communication & Language

The children will naturally discuss ideas as they walk around observing and searching for signs of the season. The talk amongst the children will help develop their thinking and vocabulary.

Literacy

The books on display related to seasons and nature will encourage the children to look at books independently and use phonic knowledge to decode and read some words. The working wall will also inspire the children to add illustrations, marks and simple words to record what they have found.

SPECIFIC AREAS

Mathematics

As the children explore outside they will observe and recognise patterns and shapes. Some children will also spontaneously count petals and leaves as they observe closely.

Understanding the world

The exploration outdoors will focus the children to observe carefully and look for patterns, change, similarities and differences.

The use of iPads or cameras will develop the children's understanding about using technology for a purpose. This understanding will be developed further as the children print captured images (with help) and display these on the working wall.

Possible next steps and opportunities for further development
Seasonal book

Repeat the exploration outdoors for more than one season. Transfer working wall information (for each season) to a class 'seasonal book' with supplementary photos, illustrations and mark makings from home too. Aim for collating information from two opposite seasons of the year, e.g. summer and winter or autumn and spring.

Asking for example illustrations, photos and mark makings from home too will help cement the children's understanding about the season and encourage the children to explore and observe at home too.

Planting for the next season

Explorations outside during autumn or spring can also lead to a focus upon planning for the new season through planting. Autumn explorations can plant for spring as spring explorations can plant for summer. This activity encourages the children to think about and verbalise/illustrate their guesses (predictions). What will the planted bulbs look like once in bloom?

Opportunities for predictions (guessing) will help the children build upon observations and experiences they have already gained as outdoor detectives. Encourage children to discuss their predictions at home too and then capture these via illustrations and simple words and sentences once back in the setting.

Final thoughts and reflections

The primary science national curriculum has strong links with observing the natural world outdoors. Therefore this activity lays very firm foundations for children's future learning in primary science.

Consider the impact of repeating this outdoor detective activity more than once. The repeated observation of the same area but during a different season will help develop the children's attention to detail.

CHAPTER 5

LEARNING THREAD
A PLACE WE CALL HOME

A Place We Call Home

In this chapter

In this chapter, you will find activities related to 'homes'. This learning thread links to:

- nature and the outdoors through activities such as 'Book into the bug hotel' and 'I spy an animal home'

- exploration and logic through activities such as 'Ice homes' and 'Solve, match, unlock!'

- personal happy memories through activities such as 'I can catch a dream'

- comforts of individual homes through activities such as 'My family home is special'.

The activities in this chapter will help you to work towards:

- developing children to make links between their worlds inside, outside and beyond while building an awareness of others

- personalising experiences for children as they relate to their own homes, families and traditions as well as outdoor spaces in their school/setting and home locality.

Activities

	Activity	Page	Provision
1	Ice homes	155	Continuous provision indoors or outdoors
2	My family home is special	161	Continuous provision indoors or outdoors
3	I can catch a dream	167	Continuous provision indoors or outdoors
4	Solve, match, unlock!	173	Continuous provision indoors or outdoors
5	I spy an animal home	179	Continuous provision outdoors
6	Book into the bug hotel	185	Continuous provision outdoors

Role-play area links:

- Estate agents

- Building site

- Traditional 'home corner' - to develop further, link to a celebration at that time and decorate the home corner accordingly.

- 'Homes' from familiar shared stories - igloo, lighthouse, cave, witch's house, castle, palace

Activity 1 Ice homes

Activity outline and preparation

This activity involves the children melting pre-frozen ice blocks that contain Duplo blocks. Once the Duplo blocks have melted from the ice, the children can build a simple house with the blocks they retrieve.

Instruction prompts that prompt thinking as opposed to directing it will help focus the children with their ideas while melting and subsequent building.

Resources

- Duplo blocks

- Plastic containers for freezing Duplo (small plastic lunch boxes with divided sections are ideal)

- Plastic spoons, paint brushes

- Sugar, salt, flour (in shaker containers), warm and cold water bottles – empty washing-up bottles work well

- Beakers, funnels, wide plastic tubes and other pouring equipment

Preparation

- Freeze individual Duplo blocks in plastic containers.

- Set up in empty water or tuff tray.

- Display printed instruction prompts.

- Display printed images of completed Duplo houses (as the activity progresses over several days, replace these images with photos of children's Duplo house building)

- Evaluation notice board set up.

- Gather some towels or paper towels to use if needed. The activity can soon make the surrounding floor slippery and wet if several children in succession choose the activity.

Activity development

ESSENTIAL LITERACY AND MATHEMATICS DEVELOPMENT				
PRIME AREAS		**Development guidance**	**SPECIFIC AREAS**		**Development guidance**

PRIME AREAS		Development guidance	SPECIFIC AREAS		Development guidance
COMMUNICATION AND LANGUAGE	Listening and attention	**30-50 months** *Listens to others one to one or in small groups when conversation interests them (while ice is melting and building)* **ELG** *Children listen attentively in a range of situations. They listen to stories, accurately anticipating key events and respond to what they hear with relevant comments, questions or actions. They give their attention to what others say and respond appropriately, while engaged in another activity. (simultaneous listening to others whilst melting and building)*	LITERACY	Reading	**30-50 months** *Knows information can be relayed in the form of print (follows basic instruction prompts)* **40-60+ months** *Begins to read words and simple sentences.* **ELG** *Children read and understand simple sentences. They use phonic knowledge to decode regular words and read them aloud accurately. They also read some common irregular words. They demonstrate understanding when talking with others about what they have read. (use of phonic knowledge to decode and read simple words and sentences on instruction prompts)*
				Writing	**30-50 months** *Sometimes give meaning to marks as they draw and paint (evaluation picture with some mark making)* **40-60+ months** *Attempts to write short sentences in meaningful contexts (evaluation picture with a sentence)*
	Understanding	**30-50 months** *Understands use of objects (equipment for melting)* **ELG** *Children follow instructions involving several ideas or actions. They answer 'how' and 'why' questions about their experiences and in response to stories or events. (able to follow simple instruction prompts for melting)*	MATHEMATICS	Numbers	**30-50 months** *Shows curiosity about numbers by offering comments or asking questions (comments about numbers on Duplo bricks)* **40-60+ months** *Recognises numerals 1 o 5 (on Duplo bricks; numbers beyond 5 also displayed)*
	Speaking	**30-50 months** *Uses vocabulary focused on objects and people that are of particular importance to them (children use vocabulary related to equipment, melting and Duplo building)* **40-60+ months** *Uses talk to organise, sequence and clarify thinking, ideas, feelings and events (while melting and building)*		Shape, space and measure	**30-50 months** *Shows an interest in shape and space by playing with shapes or making arrangements with objects (shapes and arrangements when Duplo building)* **ELG** *Children use everyday language to talk about size, weight, capacity, position, distance, time and money to compare quantities and objects and to solve problems. They recognise, create and describe patterns. They explore characteristics of everyday objects and shapes and use mathematical language to describe them. (children use everyday and mathematical language whilst building a Duplo house after melting ice).*

CHARACTERISTICS OF EFFECTIVE LEARNING	Suggested outcomes
Playing and exploring – *engagement*	**Finding out what can melt ice and learning from discoveries**
Active learning – *motivation*	**Concentrating and persisting with melting ice blocks to free Duplo blocks and begin building**
Creating and thinking critically – *thinking*	**Choosing their own route to melting ice blocks from equipment on offer**

PRIME AREAS		Development guidance	SPECIFIC AREAS		Development guidance
PHYSICAL DEVELOPMENT	Moving and handling	**30-50 months** Uses one-handed tools and equipment (simple equipment melting ice) **40-60+ months** Uses simple tools to effect changes to materials (equipment for melting ice)	UNDERSTANDING THE WORLD	People and communities	
				The world	**30-50 months** Talks about why things happen and how things work (initial ideas about melting) **ELG** Children know about similarities and differences in relation to places, objects, materials and living things. They talk about the features of their own immediate environment and how environments might vary from one another. They make observations of animals and plants and explain why some things occur, and talk about changes. (children can recognise the similarities and differences with effects of substances to melt ice. They also can talk about changes with the ice as it melts)
				Technology	
	Health and self-care	**30-50 months** Understands that equipment and tools have to be used safely (safely using tools to melt ice) **40-60+ months** Practises some appropriate safety measures without direct supervision (safely using tools to melt ice)	EXPRESSIVE ARTS AND DESIGN	Exploring and using media and materials	**30-50 months** Uses various construction materials (Duplo building) **40-60+ months** Constructs with a purpose in mind, using a variety of resources (use of different shaped and sized Duplo bricks to build house)
				Being imaginative	
PERSONAL, SOCIAL AND EMOTIONAL DEVELOPMENT	Making relationships	**30-50 months** Demonstrates friendly behaviour, initiating conversations and forming good relationships with peers and familiar adults (sharing resources and equipment whilst melting ice and then building) **40-60+ months** Takes steps to resolve conflicts with other children (taking turns, settling disputes over equipment)			
	Self-confidence and self-awareness	**30-50 months** Confident to talk to other children when playing, and will communicate freely about home and community (confidently discussing ideas about melting/building) **ELG** Children are confident to try new activities, and say why they like some activities more than others. They are confident to speak in a familiar group, will talk about their ideas, and will choose the resources they need for their chosen activities. They say when they do or don't need help. (children are confident to select resources for melting and building without help).			
	Managing feelings and behaviour	**30-50 months** Begins to accept the needs of others and can take turns and share resources, sometimes with support from others (taking turns and sharing equipment with melting and building) **40-60+ months** Beginning to be able to negotiate and solve problems without aggression (working within the group to negotiate equipment use and sharing ideas)			

Activity guidance

This is a continuous provision activity that aims to inspire independent discovery and problem-solving.

Set up the separate blocks of frozen Duplo pieces in an empty water or tuff tray. Place equipment for melting next to the tray and display instruction prompts and images of Duplo house building next to the activity. Set up an evaluation noticeboard where children will be encouraged to draw or write a simple sentence about what they used to melt the ice.

To initiate interest ask the children what they think is within the ice blocks. How can we melt the ice to see inside? What could we do with the Duplo once all the blocks have been melted?

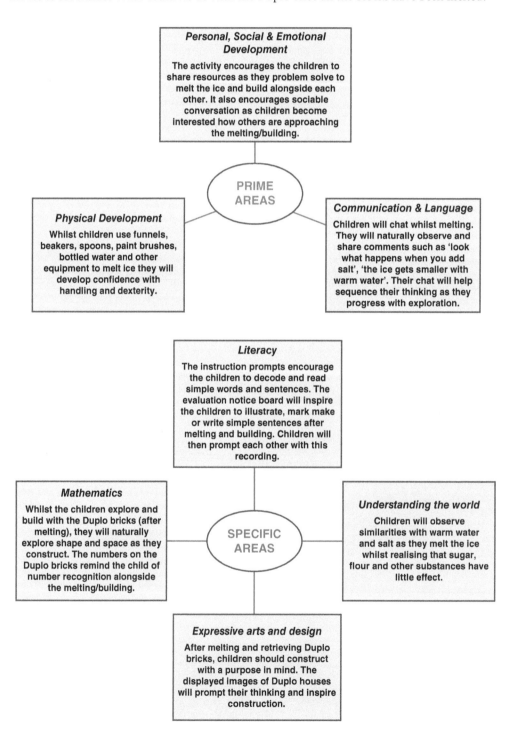

Personal, Social & Emotional Development

The activity encourages the children to share resources as they problem solve to melt the ice and build alongside each other. It also encourages sociable conversation as children become interested how others are approaching the melting/building.

PRIME AREAS

Physical Development

Whilst children use funnels, beakers, spoons, paint brushes, bottled water and other equipment to melt ice they will develop confidence with handling and dexterity.

Communication & Language

Children will chat whilst melting. They will naturally observe and share comments such as 'look what happens when you add salt', 'the ice gets smaller with warm water'. Their chat will help sequence their thinking as they progress with exploration.

Literacy

The instruction prompts encourage the children to decode and read simple words and sentences. The evaluation notice board will inspire the children to illustrate, mark make or write simple sentences after melting and building. Children will then prompt each other with this recording.

Mathematics

Whilst the children explore and build with the Duplo bricks (after melting), they will naturally explore shape and space as they construct. The numbers on the Duplo bricks remind the child of number recognition alongside the melting/building.

SPECIFIC AREAS

Understanding the world

Children will observe similarities with warm water and salt as they melt the ice whilst realising that sugar, flour and other substances have little effect.

Expressive arts and design

After melting and retrieving Duplo bricks, children should construct with a purpose in mind. The displayed images of Duplo houses will prompt their thinking and inspire construction.

Possible next steps and opportunities for further development

Investigate with coloured water

Children can further explore the role of water in the melting process by placing the frozen ice blocks into a tray of filled coloured water. During this activity, the children will observe floating and quick changes in the ice blocks that will be further visualised by the use of food colouring in the water.

Sensory play

Children can explore frozen cubes via sensory exploration. Fill ice cube tray sections with items such as sequins, glitter or rice and add coloured or plain water, freeze, pop out and go!

Some children will notice how the ice blocks float differently as they begin to melt and may verbalise this. Other children will not notice such differences but will explore the sensory sequins and glitter as the ice cubes melt and release.

Exploration of reversible change

Children can explore how to refreeze Duplo blocks, guided through this process during a group activity or teachable moment. This exploration provides many opportunities for prediction and group discussion.

Those children with developed thinking will make the connection between melting and refreezing which will lay foundations for an understanding of reversible changes. Other children will not make the connection but will observe the process and offer ideas and possibly some 'guesses'.

Final thoughts and reflections

These early explorations with melting ice will help to lay the foundations for future teaching and learning about material change of state, including reversible changes.

Consider how to develop the children's vocabulary while they are exploring melting ice. How could vocabulary become visual to support this process?

Resource support: *Instruction prompts*

Can you melt the ice with water?

Can you melt the ice with sugar or salt? sugar

What happens to the ice when you add flour?

When you free the duplo blocks, can you build a house?

Activity 2 My family home is special

Activity outline and preparation

This activity builds upon the links between home and setting as the children share their experiences from home. The children are encouraged to bring in a photo from home that illustrates family time. This may involve celebrating a tradition, special family moment or key event from their lives so far. The photo can be a physical printed photo or parents can email a photo that the children can then print out with support.

Once children have a photo to work with, the activity encourages the children to show alongside the photo illustrations, marks, words or simple sentences using a home-shaped template.

Resources

- Home templates for children to add to

- Washing line and pegs

- Pencils, crayons, glue, scissors

Preparation

- Ask parents to send in a printed or electronic family photo.

- Print any electronic photos with the children.

- Create a home shaped template for children to add photo and illustrations, words or sentences.

- Prepare washing line at children's eye level to display completed examples.

Activity development

ESSENTIAL LITERACY AND MATHEMATICS DEVELOPMENT				
PRIME AREAS		**Development guidance**	**SPECIFIC AREAS**	**Development guidance**
COMMUNICATION AND LANGUAGE	Listening and attention	**30-50 months** *Listens to stories with increasing attention and recall (listens to shared stories from home)* **ELG** *Children listen attentively in a range of situations. They listen to stories, accurately anticipating key events and respond to what they hear with relevant comments, questions or actions. They give their attention to what others say and respond appropriately, while engaged in another activity. (children listen to each other's shared stories from home)*	LITERACY — Reading	**30-50 months** *Recognises familiar words and signs such as own name and advertising logos (recognises familiar words such as mum, dad, from others' displayed work)* **40-60+ months** *Begins to read words and simple sentences (from others' displayed work)*
			LITERACY — Writing	**30-50 months** *Sometimes give meaning to marks as they draw and paint (illustrations and marks alongside photo)* **ELG** *Children use their phonic knowledge to write words in ways which match their spoken sounds. They also write some irregular common words. They write simple sentences which can be read by themselves and others. Some words are spelt correctly and others are phonetically plausible. (children use their phonic knowledge to write words alongside displayed photo)*
	Understanding	**30-50 months** *Beginning to understand 'why' and 'how' questions (questions related to shared family stories)* **40-60+ months** *Listens and responds to ideas expressed by others in conversation or discussion (related to family stories)*	MATHEMATICS — Numbers	**30-50 months** *Shows an interest in numerals in the environment (numbers on home front doors)* **40-60+ months** *Recognises some numerals of personal significance (numbers on front doors, own front door number which may go beyond 20)*
	Speaking	**30-50 months** *Can retell a simple past event in correct order (shared stories from home)* **40-60+ months** *Uses talk to organise, sequence and clarify thinking, ideas, feelings and events (shared stories from home)*	MATHEMATICS — Shape, space and measure	**30-50 months** *Shows interest in shapes in the environment (house, door shapes displayed)* **ELG** *Children use everyday language to talk about size, weight, capacity, position, distance, time and money to compare quantities and objects and to solve problems. They recognise, create and describe patterns. They explore characteristics of everyday objects and shapes and use mathematical language to describe them. (children use everyday language related to time as they talk about past family events related to display)*

CHARACTERISTICS OF EFFECTIVE LEARNING	Suggested Outcomes
Playing and exploring – *engagement*	Showing curiosity about their own and other's family events
Active learning – *motivation*	Paying attention to detail as they label their family photo with illustrations, words and/ or simple sentences
Creating and thinking critically – *thinking*	Making links and noticing similarities between their home experiences

PRIME AREAS		Development guidance	SPECIFIC AREAS		Development guidance
PHYSICAL DEVELOPMENT	Moving and handling	**30-50 months** *Use one-handed tools and equipment (scissors and glue)* **ELG** Children show good control and co-ordination in large and small movements. They move confidently in a range of ways, safely negotiating space. They handle equipment and tools effectively, including pencils for writing. *(children show good control and co-ordination as they add illustrations, marks, words alongside photo)*	**UNDERSTANDING THE WORLD**	People and communities	**30-50 months** *Recognises and describes special times or events for family or friends (illustrated photo)* **40-60+ months** *Enjoys joining in with family customs and routines* **ELG** Children talk about past and present events in their own lives and in the lives of family members. They know that other children don't always enjoy the same things, and are sensitive to this. They know about similarities and differences between themselves and others, and among families, communities and traditions. *(children talk about and their family photo with a past or present family event from their life)*
				The world	
				Technology	**30-50 months** *Knows how to operate simple equipment (with help, print a photo for display)* **ELG** Children recognise that a range of technology is used in places such as homes and schools. They select and use technology for particular purposes. *(understand how photos can be printed from the computer and have experience of this alongside an adult).*
	Health and self-care	**30-50 months** *Understands that equipment and tools have to be used safely (safely using scissors)* **40-60+ months** *Practises some appropriate safety measures without direct supervision (safely using scissors)*	**EXPRESSIVE ARTS AND DESIGN**	Exploring and using media and materials	
				Being imaginative	**30-50 months** *Captures experiences and responses with a range of media, such as music, dance and paint and other materials or words (captured response about family times via illustrations and marks alongside photo)* **40-60+ months** *Creates simple representations of events, people and objects (simple representation via displayed photo with attached illustration, marks, words)*
PERSONAL, SOCIAL AND EMOTIONAL DEVELOPMENT	Making relationships	**30-50 months** Demonstrates friendly behaviour, initiating conversations and forming good relationships with peers and familiar adults *(friendly behaviour sharing resources and showing interest in each other's photos)* **ELG** Children play co-operatively, taking turns with others. They take account of one another's ideas about how to organise their activity. They show sensitivity to others' needs and feelings, and form positive relationships with adults and other children. *(children show sensitivity for other's feelings in relation to different family photos and stories)*			
	Self-confidence and self-awareness	**30-50 months** *Can select and use activities and resources with help (help printing photo if photo sent via email)* **ELG** Children are confident to try new activities, and say why they like some activities more than others. They are confident to speak in a familiar group, will talk about their ideas, and will choose the resources they need for their chosen activities. They say when they do or don't need help. *(children confidently discuss their home photo whilst completing activity)*			
	Managing feelings and behaviour	**30-50 months** *Aware of own feelings and knows that some actions and words can hurt other's feelings (sensitive to other's family photos or stories)* **40-60+ months** *Understands that own actions can affect other people, for example, becomes upset when trying to comfort another child when they realise they have upset them (understanding that negative comments about other's home or family can hurt)*			

Activity guidance

This is a continuous provision activity that aims to develop awareness of others.

Following requests for family photos and opportunities for children to show and discuss the photos with others, the continuous provision activity can begin. It would also be useful to model the home template with the children to ensure they understand how the photo and template relate.

To *initiate interest* ask the children to talk about their photo and how this can be shared with others.

As the children complete their template by adding their photo and illustrations, marks and words the work becomes part of an ongoing interactive display via the washing line. This will inspire others to also complete the activity and encourage children to read other's contributions.

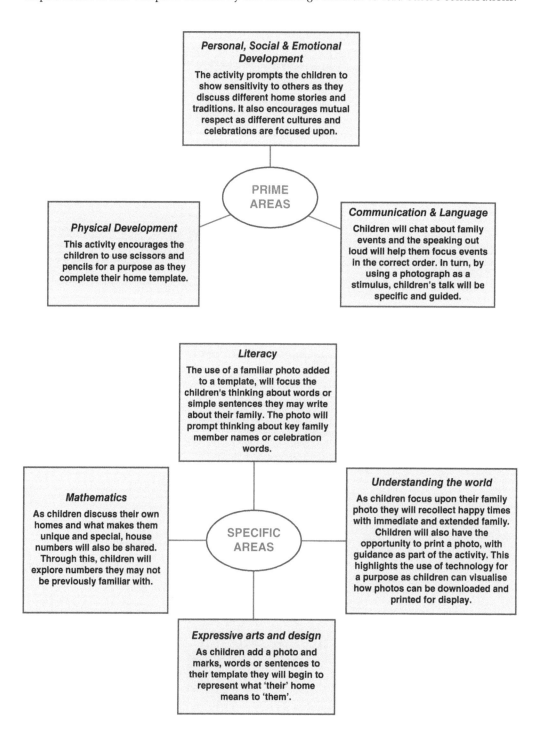

Personal, Social & Emotional Development

The activity prompts the children to show sensitivity to others as they discuss different home stories and traditions. It also encourages mutual respect as different cultures and celebrations are focused upon.

PRIME AREAS

Physical Development

This activity encourages the children to use scissors and pencils for a purpose as they complete their home template.

Communication & Language

Children will chat about family events and the speaking out loud will help them focus events in the correct order. In turn, by using a photograph as a stimulus, children's talk will be specific and guided.

Literacy

The use of a familiar photo added to a template, will focus the children's thinking about words or simple sentences they may write about their family. The photo will prompt thinking about key family member names or celebration words.

Mathematics

As children discuss their own homes and what makes them unique and special, house numbers will also be shared. Through this, children will explore numbers they may not be previously familiar with.

SPECIFIC AREAS

Understanding the world

As children focus upon their family photo they will recollect happy times with immediate and extended family. Children will also have the opportunity to print a photo, with guidance as part of the activity. This highlights the use of technology for a purpose as children can visualise how photos can be downloaded and printed for display.

Expressive arts and design

As children add a photo and marks, words or sentences to their template they will begin to represent what 'their' home means to 'them'.

Possible next steps and opportunities for further development

Recorded memories

Children can capture ideas in more detail about a special family event via a recording. Using a tablet or other technological device to capture children speaking will encourage the children to share further detail they are unable to write down.

The children's differing speaking and listening ability will be apparent here. Some children will confidently discuss family events with good detail and sequence where others will be more reticent and may need to answer questions posed by an adult.

Birthday celebrations

Children can repeat this activity with a different focus. A birthday photograph from a party, celebration or actual birth day (for those who do not celebrate birthdays) can be brought in and then displayed on a cake template with additional illustrations, words and/or sentences.

Final thoughts and reflections

Reflect upon how the links between homes and school/setting could develop further though this activity. Contemplate visitors, historical photographs, parent contributions and electronic family photo albums.

Consider the impact of opportunities for talk during this activity. The familiarity of discussing families, homes and happy family celebrations will include all children. Familiarity often develops confidence and those children usually more reticent can be encouraged to talk about what is familiar to them.

Resource support: *Example home template*

Activity 3 I can catch a dream

Activity outline and preparation

This activity inspires the children to create a dream catcher with sequins, feathers, stickers and wool. It builds upon the links between home and setting as the children recollect and share ideas about their bedtime routines and favourite dreams. It is a creative activity but also one that links to home routines and aims to highlight the links between good sleep and good health.

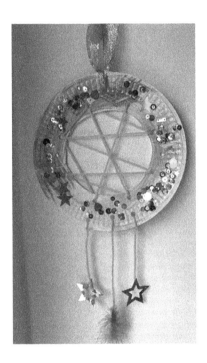

Resources

- Pencils, crayons, glue, scissors

- Pre-cut (use paper plates) and pre-threaded (for 30-50 months) dream catcher bases

- Sequins, beads, feathers, glitter, stickers, wool strings

- Glue, scissors, crayons, pencils

Preparation

- Create a 'model' dream catcher to share with children and display to inspire others.

- Pre-cut the centre from paper plates and punch holes around the side. Pre-thread for younger children or those unable to thread wool through holes.

Activity development

ESSENTIAL LITERACY AND MATHEMATICS DEVELOPMENT				
PRIME AREAS		**Development guidance**	**SPECIFIC AREAS**	**Development guidance**
COMMUNICATION AND LANGUAGE	Listening and attention	**30-50 months** *Listens to stories with increasing attention and recall (dream stories)* **ELG** *Children listen attentively in a range of situations. They listen to stories, accurately anticipating key events and respond to what they hear with relevant comments, questions or actions. They give their attention to what others say and respond appropriately, while engaged in another activity. (children listen and respond to shared dream stories)*	LITERACY / Reading	**30-50 months** *Knows that print carries meaning and, in English, is read from left to right and top to bottom (understanding special purpose of words on dream catcher)* **ELG** *Children read and understand simple sentences. They use phonic knowledge to decode regular words and read them aloud accurately. They also read some common irregular words. They demonstrate understanding when talking with others about what they have read. (children use phonic knowledge to read some words on displayed dream catchers)*
			Writing	**30-50 months** *Sometimes give meaning to marks as they draw and paint (marks added to dream catcher)* **ELG** *Children use their phonic knowledge to write words in ways which match their spoken sounds. They also write some irregular common words. They write simple sentences which can be read by themselves and others. Some words are spelt correctly and others are phonetically plausible. (children use phonic knowledge to sound out and write simple words on dream catchers)*
	Understanding	**30-50 months** *Understands use of objects (equipment for making dream catcher)* **40-60+ months** *Listens and responds to ideas expressed by others in conversation or discussion (listening and responding to dream stories)*	MATHEMATICS / Numbers	**30-50 months** *Shows an interest in representing numbers (beginning to count resources as added to dream catcher)* **40-60+ months** *Counts an irregular arrangement of up to ten objects (sorting through and counting resources as adding to dream catcher)*
	Speaking	**30-50 months** *Uses talk to connect ideas, explain what is happening and anticipate what might happen next, recall and relive past experiences (talk to connect ideas whilst recalling a recent dream)* **ELG** *Children express themselves effectively, showing awareness of listeners' needs. They use past, present and future forms accurately when talking about events that have happened or are to happen in the future. They develop their own narratives and explanations by connecting ideas or events. (children express themselves clearly as they share their dreams and events in sequence)*	Shape, space and measure	**30- 50 months** *Uses shapes appropriately for tasks (choosing and using resources for dream catcher)* **ELG** *Children use everyday language to talk about size, weight, capacity, position, distance, time and money to compare quantities and objects and to solve problems. They recognise, create and describe patterns. They explore characteristics of everyday objects and shapes and use mathematical language to describe them. (children recognise and explore patterns, whilst creating dream catcher)*

CHARACTERISTICS OF EFFECTIVE LEARNING	Suggested outcomes
Playing and exploring – *engagement*	Being willing to have a go and create own dream catcher
Active learning – *motivation*	To keep focused and trying while creating dream catcher
Creating and thinking critically – *thinking*	Enjoying creating their own dream catcher that will be unique to them

PRIME AREAS		Development guidance	SPECIFIC AREAS		Development guidance
PHYSICAL DEVELOPMENT	Moving and handling	**30-50 months** *Uses one-handed tools and equipment (while decorating dream catcher)* **ELG** *Children show good control and co-ordination in large and small movements. They move confidently in a range of ways, safely negotiating space. They handle equipment and tools effectively, including pencils for writing. (children show good control and co-ordination whilst cutting and decorating their dream catcher)*	UNDERSTANDING THE WORLD	People and communities	**30-50 months** *Shows interest in the lives of people who are familiar to them (shared stories about home bedtime routines)* **ELG** *Children talk about past and present events in their own lives and in the lives of family members. They know that other children don't always enjoy the same things, and are sensitive to this. They know about similarities and differences between themselves and others, and among families, communities and traditions. (through talk children make links with dream catchers and own home bedtime routines)*
				The world	
				Technology	
	Health and self-care	**30-50 months** *Understands that equipment and tools have to be used safely (while making dream catcher)* **40-60+ months** *Shows some understanding that good practices with regard to exercise, eating, sleeping and hygiene can contribute to good health (children understand the links between the dream catcher and sleep for good health)*	EXPRESSIVE ARTS AND DESIGN	Exploring and using media and materials	**30-50 months** *Beginning to be interested in and describe the texture of things (exploration of colour and texture while making dream catcher)* **40-60+ months** *Selects tools and techniques needed to shape, assemble and join materials they are using* *Constructs with a purpose in mind, using a variety of resources (clear understanding of purpose of dream catcher)*
				Being imaginative	**30-50 months** *Develops preferences for forms of expression (choosing their colours and materials for dream catcher)* **40-60+ months** *Chooses particular colours for a purpose (calm colours for dream catcher)*
PERSONAL, SOCIAL AND EMOTIONAL DEVELOPMENT	Making relationships	**30-50 months** *Demonstrates friendly behaviour, initiating conversations and forming good relationships with peers and familiar adults (demonstrating friendly behaviour whilst sharing resources and creating dream catcher)* **40-60+ months** *Taking steps to resolve conflicts with others (taking turns, disputes over resources)*			
	Self-confidence and self-awareness	**30-50 months** *Enjoys responsibility of carrying out small tasks (choosing own resources to create dream catcher)* **ELG** *Children are confident to try new activities, and say why they like some activities more than others. They are confident to speak in a familiar group, will talk about their ideas, and will choose the resources they need for their chosen activities. They say when they do or don't need help. (children are confident selecting resources for their dream catcher without help)*			
	Managing feelings and behaviour	**30-50 months** *Begins to accept the needs of others and can take turns and share resources sometimes with support from others (sharing resources and taking turns whilst creating dream catcher)* **40-60+ months** *Beginning to be able to negotiate and solve problems without aggression (working within the group to negotiate resources and sharing ideas)*			

Activity guidance

This is a continuous provision activity that aims to develop awareness about the links between good sleep and good health.

Prior to this activity during continuous provision, it would be helpful if children could discuss their favourite dream during group time or a teachable moment. This will encourage the children to focus upon dreams, why we dream and what can help us relax and dream.

To initiate interest show the children the model dream catcher and explain its role. 'If this can help me sleep and dream could one do the same for you?'

Model how resources such as feathers and sequins can be attached and encourage the children to choose textures and colours that they prefer.

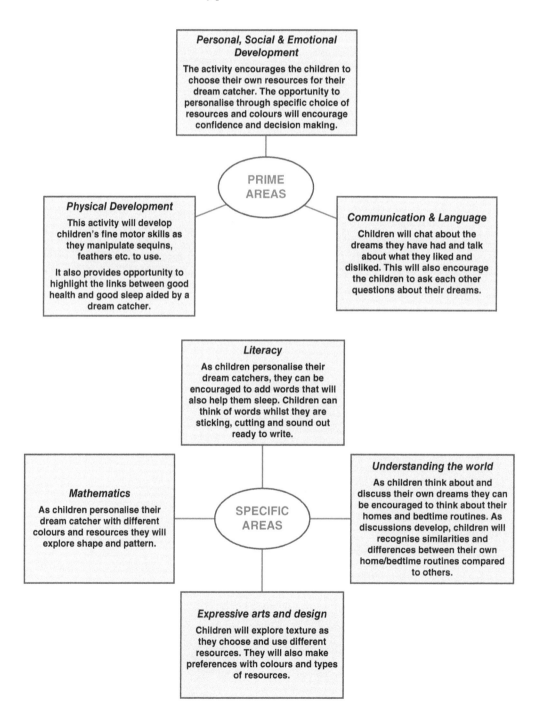

Personal, Social & Emotional Development

The activity encourages the children to choose their own resources for their dream catcher. The opportunity to personalise through specific choice of resources and colours will encourage confidence and decision making.

PRIME AREAS

Physical Development

This activity will develop children's fine motor skills as they manipulate sequins, feathers etc. to use.

It also provides opportunity to highlight the links between good health and good sleep aided by a dream catcher.

Communication & Language

Children will chat about the dreams they have had and talk about what they liked and disliked. This will also encourage the children to ask each other questions about their dreams.

Literacy

As children personalise their dream catchers, they can be encouraged to add words that will also help them sleep. Children can think of words whilst they are sticking, cutting and sound out ready to write.

SPECIFIC AREAS

Mathematics

As children personalise their dream catcher with different colours and resources they will explore shape and pattern.

Understanding the world

As children think about and discuss their own dreams they can be encouraged to think about their homes and bedtime routines. As discussions develop, children will recognise similarities and differences between their own home/bedtime routines compared to others.

Expressive arts and design

Children will explore texture as they choose and use different resources. They will also make preferences with colours and types of resources.

Possible next steps and opportunities for further development

Dream words

Encourage children to add 'dream words' or marks to their catcher once it is complete. Ask the children to suggest 'whisper' words that they think could link to their dreams.

Dream collector

Once the children have taken their dream catcher home, invite children to share new dreams that have been 'caught'. Children can be encouraged to record an illustration with marks or an illustration with key words and sentence of their dream. Keep a 'Dream Collector' book in the class/setting to capture these recordings for all to see and share.

Some children will confidently add illustrations with marks or key words to the 'Dream Collector' book. Others will be more hesitant but be able to verbalise ideas instead. In time, more children may add to the book as they observe and copy others.

Final thoughts and reflections

This activity has strong personal, social and emotional development links. Therefore opportunities to address worries or 'bad dreams' could develop through open ended circle time activities alongside or following this activity.

Consider exploring relaxation through simple yoga as a physical activity related to creating dream catchers. Do the children understand the concept of relaxation? If so, evaluate whether the children are able to connect relaxation and healthy sleep.

Activity 4 Solve, match and unlock!

Activity outline and preparation

This activity encourages the children to open locks with keys after solving simple mathematical sums. It builds upon the links between home and setting as the children recognise that homes have locks for a purpose. It also encourages children to understand how keys and locks work as simple tools that we use at home.

This activity will help develop number recognition for those children working at 30–50 month goals, as these children match single-digit numerals on locks to corresponding keys/doors.

For those children working at 40–60+ months, there is an opportunity to solve simple addition and subtraction sums on locks and match to corresponding keys with displayed answers.

Resources

- Door and gate display
- Keys and locks (labelled with sums and answers)
- Dry-wipe pens
- Familiar counting apparatus for those children solving addition or subtraction sums

Preparation

- Create a doors and gates display which will form part of this activity. Display different coloured and shaped doors/gates. Ensure the door/ gate names are displayed on dry wipe card so children can change them. Numbers on the doors and gates should also match numbers on keys.

- Organise keys and matching locks. Add numerals or sums (depending upon age-appropriate outcomes/goals) onto locks and number answers to keys.

Activity development

ESSENTIAL LITERACY AND MATHEMATICS DEVELOPMENT				
PRIME AREAS		**Development guidance**	**SPECIFIC AREAS**	**Development guidance**
COMMUNICATION AND LANGUAGE	Listening and attention	**30-50 months** *Is able to follow directions (of simple match, open challenge)* **ELG** *Children listen attentively in a range of situations. They listen to stories, accurately anticipating key events and respond to what they hear with relevant comments, questions or actions. They give their attention to what others say and respond appropriately, while engaged in another activity. (children listen to other's ideas whilst completing sum, match, open activity)*	LITERACY	Reading	**30-50 months** *Recognises familiar words and signs such as own name and advertising logos (children may recognise some familiar names on door and gate display)* **ELG** *Children read and understand simple sentences. They use phonic knowledge to decode regular words and read them aloud accurately. They also read some common irregular words. They demonstrate understanding when talking with others about what they have read. (children use phonic knowledge to decode and read some names on door and gate display.)*
				Writing	**30-50 months** *Sometimes give meaning to marks as they draw and paint (mark making on door and gate display)* **40-60+ months** *Uses some clearly identifiable letters to communicate meaning, representing some sounds correctly in sequence* **ELG** *Children use their phonic knowledge to write words in ways which match their spoken sounds. They also write some irregular common words. They write simple sentences which can be read by themselves and others. Some words are spelt correctly and others are phonetically plausible. (children use phonic knowledge to sound out and write new names on door and gate display)*
	Understanding	**30-50 months** *Understands use of objects (use of keys to open locks)* **40-60+ months** *Listens and responds to ideas expressed by others in conversation or discussion (thoughts about solving the sums)*	MATHEMATICS	Numbers	**30-50 months** *Shows an interest in number problems (match of numbers between keys and locks)* **ELG** *Children count reliably with numbers from one to 20, place them in order and say which number is one more or one less than a given number. Using quantities and objects, they add and subtract two single-digit numbers and count on or back to find the answer. They solve problems, including doubling, halving and sharing. (children add and subtract two single-digit numbers with sum, match, open activity)*
	Speaking	**30-50 months** *Uses vocabulary focused upon objects and people that are of particular importance to them (vocabulary related to task numbers, locks and keys)* **40-60+ months** *Uses talk to organise, sequence and clarify thinking, ideas, feelings and events (children use talk to sequence and clarify thinking whilst completing the sum, match, open activity)*		Shape, space and measure	**30-50 months** *Shows awareness of similarities of shapes in the environment (different shapes of doors and gates)* **ELG** *Children use everyday language to talk about size, weight, capacity, position, distance, time and money to compare quantities and objects and to solve problems. They recognise, create and describe patterns. They explore characteristics of everyday objects and shapes and use mathematical language to describe them. (children use everyday language to talk about size, position and observe shapes and patterns of keys)*

CHARACTERISTICS OF EFFECTIVE LEARNING	Suggested outcomes
Playing and exploring – *engagement*	**Willing to have a go at sum, match, open**
Active learning – *motivation*	**Being involved and concentrating during sum, match and open sequence**
Creating and thinking critically – *thinking*	**Making links between actions and solving the problems**

PRIME AREAS		Development guidance	SPECIFIC AREAS		Development guidance
PHYSICAL DEVELOPMENT	Moving and handling	**30-50 months** *Uses one-handed tools and equipment (use of keys and locks)* **40-60+ months** *Handles tools, objects, construction and malleable materials safely and with increasing control.* ***ELG** Children show good control and co-ordination in large and small movements. They move confidently in a range of ways, safely negotiating space. They handle equipment and tools effectively, including pencils for writing. (good co-ordination and control operating keys and locks)*	**UNDERSTANDING THE WORLD**	People and communities	**30-50 months** *Shows interest in the lives of people who are familiar to them (keys and locks in homes and other familiar homes)* ***ELG** Children talk about past and present events in their own lives and in the lives of family members. They know that other children don't always enjoy the same things, and are sensitive to this. They know about similarities and differences between themselves and others, and among families, communities and traditions. (children talk about their own lives, homes, keys and locks they have at home or other family homes)*
				The world	
				Technology	
	Health and self-care	**30-50 months** *Understands that equipment and tools have to be used safely (safely using keys and locks)* **40-60+ months** *Practises some appropriate safety measures without direct supervision (safely using keys and locks)*	**EXPRESSIVE ARTS AND DESIGN**	Exploring and using media and materials	**30-50 months** *Realises tools can be used for a purpose (purpose of keys and locks)* ***ELG** Children sing songs, make music and dance, and experiment with ways of changing them. They safely use and explore a variety of materials, tools and techniques, experimenting with colour, design, texture, form and function. (children safely explore tools and techniques as they operate keys and locks)*
				Being imaginative	
PERSONAL, SOCIAL AND EMOTIONAL DEVELOPMENT	Making relationships	**30-50 months** *Keeps play going by responding to what others are saying or doing (group solving of key and lock problem)* ***ELG** Children play co-operatively, taking turns with others. They take account of one another's ideas about how to organise their activity. They show sensitivity to others' needs and feelings, and form positive relationships with adults and other children. (children play co-operatively sharing keys and locks in turn)*			
	Self-confidence and self-awareness	**30-50 months** *Enjoys responsibility of carrying out small tasks (locks and keys)* ***ELG** Children are confident to try new activities, and say why they like some activities more than others. They are confident to speak in a familiar group, will talk about their ideas, and will choose the resources they need for their chosen activities. They say when they do or don't need help. (children are confident selecting, operating keys and locks with little help)*			
	Managing feelings and behaviour	**30-50 months** *Begins to accept the needs of others and can take turns and share resources, sometimes with support from others (taking turns with the keys and locks)* **40-60+ months** *Beginning to be able to negotiate and solve problems without aggression (working within the group to negotiate keys/locks and sharing ideas)*			

Activity guidance

This is a continuous provision activity that aims to develop the children's number and problem-solving skills.

Set up the displayed doors and gates alongside baskets of labelled locks and keys. Ensure familiar counting apparatus is also available for those children wishing to use while solving simple additions and subtractions. The bright doors and gate display will already generate interest among the children. As this is an explore, discover and solve activity – refrain from modelling 'how' to open a lock with the key as many will discover this themselves through trial and error.

To initiate interest encourage the children to look at the numbered/named doors and gate display. Draw attention to the baskets of keys and locks and the different numeral/sum labels.

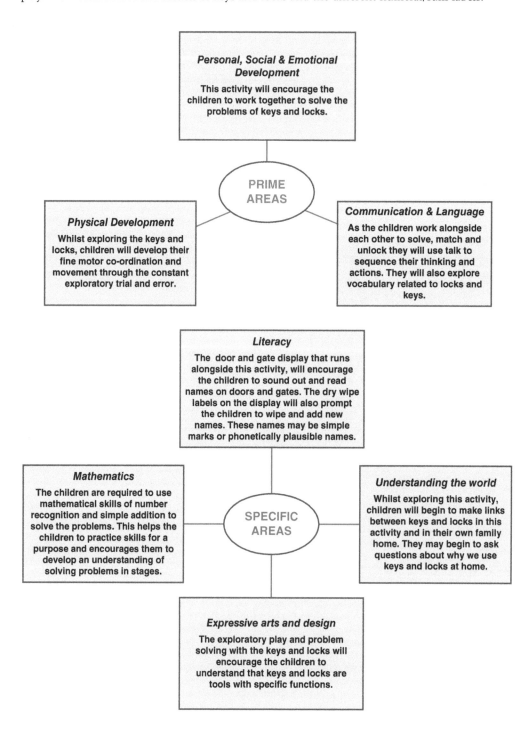

Personal, Social & Emotional Development
This activity will encourage the children to work together to solve the problems of keys and locks.

PRIME AREAS

Physical Development
Whilst exploring the keys and locks, children will develop their fine motor co-ordination and movement through the constant exploratory trial and error.

Communication & Language
As the children work alongside each other to solve, match and unlock they will use talk to sequence their thinking and actions. They will also explore vocabulary related to locks and keys.

Literacy
The door and gate display that runs alongside this activity, will encourage the children to sound out and read names on doors and gates. The dry wipe labels on the display will also prompt the children to wipe and add new names. These names may be simple marks or phonetically plausible names.

Mathematics
The children are required to use mathematical skills of number recognition and simple addition to solve the problems. This helps the children to practice skills for a purpose and encourages them to develop an understanding of solving problems in stages.

SPECIFIC AREAS

Understanding the world
Whilst exploring this activity, children will begin to make links between keys and locks in this activity and in their own family home. They may begin to ask questions about why we use keys and locks at home.

Expressive arts and design
The exploratory play and problem solving with the keys and locks will encourage the children to understand that keys and locks are tools with specific functions.

Possible next steps and opportunities for further development

Key patterns

Encourage children to observe different shaped/sized keys closely and recognise the different key patterns. Explore further through rubbings, printing and Play-Doh.

Some children will be able to recognise differences in the shapes and sizes of different keys and be able to verbalise these. Other children will observe these differences but not recognise them. Experiencing the shape and size of the keys through rubbings, prints and Play-Doh will help these children recognise the differences through exploration.

Treasure boxes

Develop the keys and locks idea further using boxes with locks. Attach longer questions (related to other operations in Mathematics or other areas e.g. word questions in Literacy) to keys via small bags with directions to another box containing an answer.

Final thoughts and reflections

Consider the children's understanding about why we need keys and locks. Have they seen keys and locks at home and why do we need them? Alongside this activity, the children need to make connections between objects from the world around us and their purpose.

Reflect upon the value of the problem-solving within a familiar context with this activity. Children will continue to progress and develop with this skill throughout their education following essential foundations laid in early years.

Activity 5 I spy an animal home

Activity outline and preparation

This activity is an outdoor activity that requires the children to search for and scan pre-organised QR codes to answer a simple question or find out basic information. Children can complete the trail within the school grounds, local park or nearby woodland area and it will raise the children's interest in the world around them.

To complete this activity, children need to be familiar with using a tablet (with installed QR code reader) to position, point and scan a displayed QR code. If children are unfamiliar with this skill, they will need to spend some guided time prior to this activity to understand how to scan a QR code.

This activity introduces children to different mini-beasts and the term 'habitats' as a word used to describe a home.

Resources

- Printed, numbered QR codes to display (laminated if possible)
- Tablets or iPads with QR code reader installed
- Charged tablets or iPads
- Recording sheets or blank paper and clip boards
- Pencils or crayons

Preparation

- Locate different animal homes around the school grounds, local park or woodland area. Look for fallen logs, rocks, piles of leaves and under bushes to locate animals (mini-beasts) such as snails, slugs, woodlice, spiders, ants, etc.

- Once located, create a record for you to follow noting the habitat locations and list animals (mini-beasts) found.

- Locate photos or simple websites online that relate to the animals (mini-beasts) you have located in your locality. Using a QR code generator app, create single QR codes that will take the children to a photo or simple website about selected animals (mini-beasts).

- Print out created QR codes and add a repetitive question (for 30–50 months) such as 'who lives here?' or a simple question (for 40–60+ months) such as 'how many legs does this mini-beast have?' Children can then use retrieved information via the QR code to answer.

Activity development

ESSENTIAL LITERACY AND MATHEMATICS DEVELOPMENT				
PRIME AREAS		Development guidance	SPECIFIC AREAS	Development guidance
COMMUNICATION AND LANGUAGE	Listening and attention	**30-50 months** *Is able to follow directions (seek and follow some of the QR codes)* **40-60+ months** *Two-channelled attention - can listen and do for short span* **ELG** *Children listen attentively in a range of situations. They listen to stories, accurately anticipating key events and respond to what they hear with relevant comments, questions or actions. They give their attention to what others say and respond appropriately, while engaged in another activity. (children give their attention to what others say as they complete the QR code trail)*	LITERACY — Reading	**30-50 months** *Recognises familiar words and signs such as own name and advertising logos (recognises simple familiar words within repeated simple questions alongside QR code – Who lives in here?)* **40-60+ months** *Begins to read words and simple sentences* **ELG** *Children read and understand simple sentences. They use phonic knowledge to decode regular words and read them aloud accurately. They also read some common irregular words. They demonstrate understanding when talking with others about what they have read. (children use phonic knowledge to decode simple words and sentences alongside QR code)*
			Writing	**30-50 months** *Sometimes give meaning to marks as they draw and paint (children use illustrations and marks to record findings during trail)* **40-60+ months** *Uses some clearly identifiable letters to communicate meaning, representing some sounds correctly in sequence* **ELG** *Children use their phonic knowledge to write words in ways which match their spoken sounds. They also write some irregular common words. They write simple sentences which can be read by themselves and others. Some words are spelt correctly and others are phonetically plausible. (children use their phonic knowledge to sound out and write words to record findings during trail)*
	Understanding	**30-50 months** *Understands use of objects (use of tablet to read QR codes)* **40-60+ months** *Listens and responds to ideas expressed by others in conversation or discussion* **ELG** *Children follow instructions involving several ideas or actions. They answer 'how' and 'why' questions about their experiences and in response to stories or events. (children follow simple instructions whilst completing QR code trail)*	MATHEMATICS — Numbers	**30-50 months** *Shows an interest in numerals in the environment (notices numbered 1-5 QR codes)* **40-60+ months** *Recognises numerals 1-5* *(follows QR code numbers 1-5 and beyond in sequence)*
	Speaking	**30-50 months** *Uses vocabulary focused upon objects and people that are of particular importance to them (vocabulary related to outdoor nature discoveries whilst engaging in the QR code trail)* **40-60+ months** *Uses talk to organise, sequence and clarify thinking, ideas, feelings and events.* **ELG** *Children express themselves effectively, showing awareness of listeners' needs. They use past, present and future forms accurately when talking about events that have happened or are to happen in the future. They develop their own narratives and explanations by connecting ideas or events. (children express themselves and use talk to connect their ideas whilst completing the QR code trail)*	Shape, space and measure	**30-50 months** *Shows awareness of similarities of shapes in the environment (uses shape words while talking about animal homes)* **40-60+ months** *Can describe their relative position such as 'behind' or 'next to'* **ELG** *Children use everyday language to talk about size, weight, capacity, position, distance, time and money to compare quantities and objects and to solve problems. They recognise, create and describe patterns. They explore characteristics of everyday objects and shapes and use mathematical language to describe them. (children use everyday language to talk about size, position, distance to compare quantities and objects whilst engaging in QR code trail)*

CHARACTERISTICS OF EFFECTIVE LEARNING	Suggested outcomes
Playing and exploring – *engagement*	**Finding out and exploring, using technology to develop thinking**
Active learning – *motivation*	**Persistence with tablet as the device reads QR codes**
Creating and thinking critically – *thinking*	**Making links between animals and their homes outdoors**

PRIME AREAS		Development guidance	SPECIFIC AREAS		Development guidance
PHYSICAL DEVELOPMENT	Moving and handling	**30-50 months** *Moves freely and with pleasure and confidence in a range of ways, such as slithering, shuffling, rolling, crawling, walking, running, jumping, skipping, sliding and hopping (children move freely and with confidence whilst outside completing the QR code trail)* **40-60+ months** *Handles tools, objects, construction and malleable materials safely and with increasing control.* **ELG** *Children show good control and co-ordination in large and small movements. They move confidently in a range of ways, safely negotiating space. They handle equipment and tools effectively, including pencils for writing. (children show confidence and control handling tablet whilst scanning QR codes)*	UNDERSTANDING THE WORLD	People and communities	
				The world	**30-50 months** *Can talk about some of the things they have observed such as plants, animals, natural and found objects.* *Shows care and concern for living things and the environment (children talk about what they observe whilst showing care and concern for these things after and during QR code trail)* **ELG** *Children know about similarities and differences in relation to places, objects, materials and living things. They talk about the features of their own immediate environment and how environments might vary from one another. They make observations of animals and plants and explain why some things occur, and talk about changes. (children know about similarities and differences with plants and animals they observe during the QR code trail)*
				Technology	**30-50 months** *Knows how to operate simple equipment (children able to operate tablet with guidance)* **ELG** *Children recognise that a range of technology is used in places such as homes and schools. They select and use technology for particular purposes. (children understand the purpose of an iPad/tablet alongside the QR codes to support animal trail)*
	Health and self-care	**30-50 months** *Can usually manage washing and drying hands (wash hands after prompt following exploring animal homes outside)* **40-60+ months** *Shows understanding of how to transport and store equipment safely (while using tablets outside)* **ELG** *Children know the importance for good health of physical exercise, and a healthy diet, and talk about ways to keep healthy and safe. They manage their own basic hygiene and personal needs successfully, including dressing and going to the toilet independently. (children wash their hands after exploring animal homes outside and have some understanding about why)*	EXPRESSIVE ARTS AND DESIGN	Exploring and using media and materials	
				Being imaginative	
PERSONAL, SOCIAL AND EMOTIONAL DEVELOPMENT	Making relationships	**30-50 months** *Demonstrates friendly behaviour, initiating conversations and forming good relationships with peers and familiar adults (children show friendly behaviour and work with others, sharing tablet during trail)* **40-60+ months** *Explains own knowledge and understanding and asks appropriate questions of others (while engaging in QR code trail)* **ELG** *Children play co-operatively, taking turns with others. They take account of one another's ideas about how to organise their activity. They show sensitivity to others' needs and feelings, and form positive relationships with adults and other children. (children show friendly behaviour and work with others, sharing tablet during trail)*			
	Self-confidence and self-awareness	**30-50 months** *Shows confidence in asking adults for help (asking for help during trail if unsure)* **ELG** *Children are confident to try new activities, and say why they like some activities more than others. They are confident to speak in a familiar group, will talk about their ideas, and will choose the resources they need for their chosen activities. They say when they do or don't need help. (children are confident to try the activity and ask for help during trail if needed)*			
	Managing feelings and behaviour	**30-50 months** *Begins to accept the needs of others and can take turns and share resources, sometimes with support from others (children take turns with iPad/ tablet)* **ELG** *Children talk about how they and others show feelings, talk about their own and others' behaviour, and its consequences, and know that some behaviour is unacceptable. They work as part of a group or class, and understand and follow the rules. They adjust their behaviour to different situations, and take changes of routine in their stride. (children behave sensibly and keep focused whilst engaging in QR code trail)*			

Activity guidance

This is a continuous provision activity that aims to develop the children's awareness of the world around them while simultaneously using technology.

An adult will need to supervise this activity if the location of animal homes (habitats) is far from the setting. However, this is for supervision only and children should be encouraged to attempt this continuous provision activity without constant adult guidance.

Set up the created QR codes outdoors, using your original notes and records regarding located habitats.

To initiate interest ask the children if they can 'I spy' any possible animal homes. Remind the children to scan the nearby QR code to find out information about the animal in the home.

During or following the activity, encourage the children to illustrate and add marks or words and sentences about animals (mini-beasts) found in the different locations.

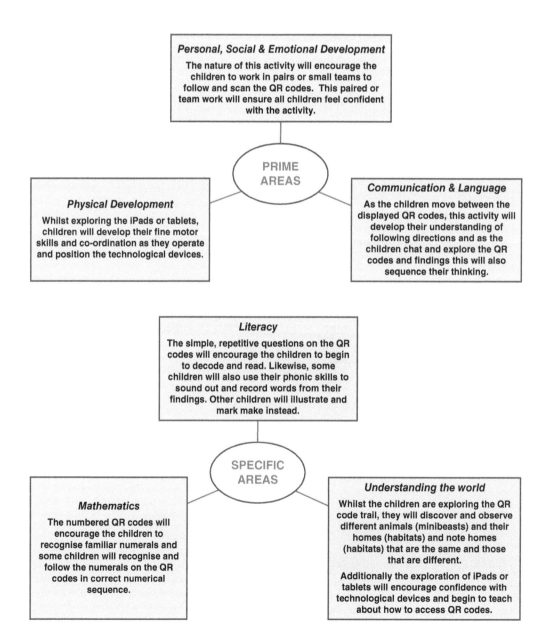

Personal, Social & Emotional Development
The nature of this activity will encourage the children to work in pairs or small teams to follow and scan the QR codes. This paired or team work will ensure all children feel confident with the activity.

PRIME AREAS

Physical Development
Whilst exploring the iPads or tablets, children will develop their fine motor skills and co-ordination as they operate and position the technological devices.

Communication & Language
As the children move between the displayed QR codes, this activity will develop their understanding of following directions and as the children chat and explore the QR codes and findings this will also sequence their thinking.

Literacy
The simple, repetitive questions on the QR codes will encourage the children to begin to decode and read. Likewise, some children will also use their phonic skills to sound out and record words from their findings. Other children will illustrate and mark make instead.

SPECIFIC AREAS

Mathematics
The numbered QR codes will encourage the children to recognise familiar numerals and some children will recognise and follow the numerals on the QR codes in correct numerical sequence.

Understanding the world
Whilst the children are exploring the QR code trail, they will discover and observe different animals (minibeasts) and their homes (habitats) and note homes (habitats) that are the same and those that are different.

Additionally the exploration of iPads or tablets will encourage confidence with technological devices and begin to teach about how to access QR codes.

Possible next steps and opportunities for further development

Further QR code trails

Children can engage with further QR coding through trails of discovery across all areas. Some further ideas include using QR codes to support the discovery of seasons, materials around us, number recognition, shapes in the environment and word discovery.

For those children who lacked confidence with QR coding during the initial activity, the repetitive approach (with a different focus) will really help. These children will probably hang back and observe initially but through further opportunity will gain confidence to have a go!

Home projects

Encourage children to continue the 'I spy' discovery in their own locality at home. What animals (mini-beasts) live near you? Encourage the children to take photos of newly discovered animals (mini-beasts) and their homes (habitats) to share within the setting.

Some children will need more input to identify animals (mini-beasts) and their homes (habitats) so further exploration at home will help them make these connections. Other children will show more confidence and ability with this recognition, so the explorations at home will help them make further connections such as which animals share the same home (habitat).

New homes

Children can develop their understanding about animal (mini-beast) homes (habitats) further by creating new homes. This can lead to other activities such as nest and bug hotel building, which is the focus for the next activity in this chapter.

Final thoughts and reflections

Reflect upon the impact of simultaneous learning that this activity develops. Technology is used as a tool to enhance learning and not distract from it. Consider other ideas about how technology can enhance a learning activity already taking place.

Consider how the simple explorations of animal homes (habitats) lays foundations for future teaching and learning about habitats, microhabitats and ecosystems within the primary science curriculum.

Resource support: *Creating QR codes*

- Before setting up QR codes, search for relevant, age-appropriate websites, YouTube videos, plain text, photos, Google map locations, etc. that you wish to use to support your activity.

- Use a QR code generator to create the QR codes for the internet links. There are many free QR code generator websites on the internet.

- Using the QR code generator, fill in the appropriate information (selected website, plain text, photos, YouTube videos, etc.) to generate the QR code.

- Once generated, the QR codes will be ready to download and print to use.

- Before printing, it is useful to download the QR code and add a question that will prompt the children. For younger children, these questions will be repetitive but older EY children may cope with differing simple questions.

Who lives here?

Activity 6 Book into the bug hotel

Activity outline and preparation

This activity is an outdoor activity that encourages the children to use cardboard boxes, tubes and other resources to make a basic bug hotel for insects. If the children have already focused upon animals (mini-beasts) and their homes, this activity follows on well and it raises the children's interest in the world around them.

In preparation for this activity, ask the children to bring in cardboard cereal boxes of different sizes (small boxes such as toothpaste boxes or mini cereal boxes are good to fit within the bigger box), tubes (not toilet rolls) and newspapers as well as natural objects such as twigs and pine cones.

Resources

- Different sized cereal boxes, cardboard tubes, newspapers
- Pine cones, twigs, bark pieces and other natural objects – ensure these are all washed and dried before use
- Photographs of completed bug hotels to display
- Scissors, pencils
- Dry-wipe pens
- 'Bug hotel check-in board' – use a paper covered noticeboard, small dry-wipe board or interactive whiteboard
- Bug hotel directive illustrations
- Bin liners – once children have completed their bug hotel, bin liners are good for adding an outside coating to help waterproof the cardboard. An adult can add this after the activity using strips of liner and glue

Preparation

- Collect cardboard resources and natural objects (wash and dry first) and store these in different display boxes or baskets so the children have freedom to select from a variety of organised objects and resources.
- Print photos of pre-constructed bug hotel/s to display and inspire the children. Printed photos can be changed as children begin making the bug hotels.
- Print directions to display that inspire the children with ideas.
- Create a 'Bug hotel check-in board' as part of the activity for children to complete lists via illustrations, mark making or simple sentences about who has 'checked in' to their hotel.

Activity development

ESSENTIAL LITERACY AND MATHEMATICS DEVELOPMENT				
PRIME AREAS		**Development guidance**	**SPECIFIC AREAS**	**Development guidance**
COMMUNICATION AND LANGUAGE	Listening and attention	**30-50 months** Listens to others one to one or in small groups when conversation interests them *(while bug hotel building)* **40-60+ months** Two-channelled attention - can listen and do for short span **ELG** *Children listen attentively in a range of situations. They listen to stories, accurately anticipating key events and respond to what they hear with relevant comments, questions or actions. They give their attention to what others say and respond appropriately, while engaged in another activity. (children give their attention to what others say and respond whilst constructing bug hotel)*	**LITERACY** — Reading	**30-50 months** Knows print carries meaning and, in English, is read from left to right *(reading of some words with bug hotel directive illustrations)* **40-60+ months** Begins to read words and simple sentences **ELG** *Children read and understand simple sentences. They use phonic knowledge to decode regular words and read them aloud accurately. They also read some common irregular words. They demonstrate understanding when talking with others about what they have read (children use their phonic knowledge to decode simple words/sentences with bug hotel directive illustrations)*
			Writing	**30-50 months** Sometimes give meaning to marks as they draw and paint *(children use simple marks or illustrations to record who has checked into the bug hotel)* **40-60+ months** Uses some clearly identifiable letters to communicate meaning, representing some sounds correctly in sequence **ELG** *Children use their phonic knowledge to write words in ways which match their spoken sounds. They also write some irregular common words. They write simple sentences which can be read by themselves and others. Some words are spelt correctly and others are phonetically plausible. (children write simple word or sentences to record who has checked into the bug hotel)*
	Understanding	**30-50 months** Understands use of objects *(resources for bug hotel)* **40-60+ months** Listens and responds to ideas expressed by others in conversation or discussion **ELG** *Children follow instructions involving several ideas or actions. They answer 'how' and 'why' questions about their experiences and in response to stories or events. (children follow visual directions whilst building bug hotel)*	**MATHEMATICS** — Numbers	**30-50 months** Shows an interest in representing numbers *(begins to count some sections of bug hotel)* **40-60+ months** Counts objects to 10, and beginning to count beyond 10 *(counts sections of bug hotel)*
	Speaking	**30-50 months** Uses talk to connect ideas, explain what is happening and anticipate what might happen next, recall and relive past experiences. Uses vocabulary focused upon objects and people that are of particular importance to them *(using talk to connect ideas and vocabulary focused upon bug hotel building)* **40-60+ months** Uses talk to organise, sequence and clarify thinking, ideas, feelings and events **ELG** *Children express themselves effectively, showing awareness of listeners' needs. They use past, present and future forms accurately when talking about events that have happened or are to happen in the future. They develop their own narratives and explanations by connecting ideas or events. (children express themselves about ideas related to bug hotel building)*	Shape, space and measure	**30-50 months** Uses shapes appropriately for tasks *(uses largely appropriate shapes when building bug hotel)* **40-60+ months** Uses familiar objects and common shapes to create and recreate patterns and build models *(appropriate shapes when building bug hotel)*

CHARACTERISTICS OF EFFECTIVE LEARNING	Suggested outcomes
Playing and exploring – *engagement*	**Exploring the different resources and making a decision about what to choose and use to construct the bug hotel**
Active learning – *motivation*	**Concentrating and trialling with different shapes, e.g. fitting tubes within box**
Creating and thinking critically – *thinking*	**Choosing their own resources when building the bug hotel based on their own experiences, thoughts and ideas**

PRIME AREAS		Development guidance	SPECIFIC AREAS		Development guidance
PHYSICAL DEVELOPMENT	Moving and handling	**30-50 months** *Uses one-handed tools and equipment (while constructing bug hotel)* **40-60+ months** *Handles tools, objects, construction and malleable materials safely and with increasing control.* **ELG** *children show good control and co-ordination in large and small movements. They move confidently in a range of ways, safely negotiating space. They handle equipment and tools effectively, including pencils for writing. (children show good co-ordination and control with tools while constructing bug hotel)*	UNDERSTANDING THE WORLD	People and communities	
				The world	**30-50 months** *Shows care and concern for living things and the environment (understands the need for constructing bug hotel)* **ELG** *Children know about similarities and differences in relation to places, objects, materials and living things. They talk about the features of their own immediate environment and how environments might vary from one another. They make observations of animals and plants and explain why some things occur, and talk about changes. (children know about similarities and differences in relation to materials and objects they use for the bug hotel)*
				Technology	
	Health and self-care	**30-50 months** *Understands that equipment and tools have to be used safely (while using scissors to construct bug hotel)* **40-60+ months** *Shows understanding of how to transport and store equipment safely (while using equipment such as scissors to construct bug hotel)*	EXPRESSIVE ARTS AND DESIGN	Exploring and using media and materials	**30-50 months** *Joins construction pieces together to build and balance (while constructing bug hotel)* **40-60+ months** *Constructs with a purpose in mind using a variety of resources* **ELG** *Children sing songs, make music and dance, and experiment with ways of changing them. They safely use and explore a variety of materials, tools and techniques, experimenting with colour, design, texture, form and function. (children explore materials, tools and techniques whilst experimenting with design, texture and form to create their bug hotel)*
				Being imaginative	
PERSONAL, SOCIAL AND EMOTIONAL DEVELOPMENT	Making relationships	**30-50 months** *Demonstrates friendly behaviour, initiating conversations and forming good relationships with peers and familiar adults (children work as a team or in pairs, sharing resources and ideas whilst building bug hotel)* **40-60+ months** *Initiates conversations, attends to and takes account of what others say* **ELG** *Children play co-operatively, taking turns with others. They take account of one another's ideas about how to organise their activity. They show sensitivity to others' needs and feelings, and form positive relationships with adults and other children. (children play co-operatively, taking turns with ideas and resources whilst building bug hotel)*			
	Self-confidence and self-awareness	**30-50 months** *Can select and use activities and resources with help. (constructing bug hotel with available resources and some help if needed.)* **ELG** *Children are confident to try new activities, and say why they like some activities more than others. They are confident to speak in a familiar group, will talk about their ideas, and will choose the resources they need for their chosen activities. They say when they do or don't need help. (children are confident to try and build a bug hotel and choose available resources when constructing)*			
	Managing feelings and behaviour	**30-50 months** *Begins to accept the needs of others and can take turns and share resources. (children take turns and share resources whilst constructing bug hotel)* **40-60+ months** *Beginning to be able to negotiate and solve problems without aggression* **ELG** *Children talk about how they and others show feelings, talk about their own and others' behaviour, and its consequences, and know that some behaviour is unacceptable. They work as part of a group or class, and understand and follow the rules. They adjust their behaviour to different situations, and take changes of routine in their stride. (children play sensibly and keep focused upon constructing bug hotel with others opposed to playing with resources.)*			

Activity guidance

This is a continuous provision activity that aims to develop the children's awareness of the world around them.

Organise the collected cardboard boxes, tubes, newspapers (some torn and scrunched pieces) and natural objects into different boxes so the children are free to view and choose from the various items. Display the photos of constructed bug hotels to inspire the children and stir their thinking. This will also guide the children into choosing a 'box' to begin building their bug hotel and give their construction structure.

Display the directive illustrations to prompt the children. These illustrations will encourage the children to think about placing items within items, e.g. pine cones and twigs inside cardboard tubes.

To initiate interest ask the children to look at the illustrated directions and examples or photos of bug hotel WAGOLLs (What A Good One Looks Like) and ask them to think about creating a bug hotel of their own that has different spaces for various animas (mini-beasts) to come and stay.

Following the activity, encourage the children to illustrate and add marks or words and sentences to the 'Bug hotel check-in board'.

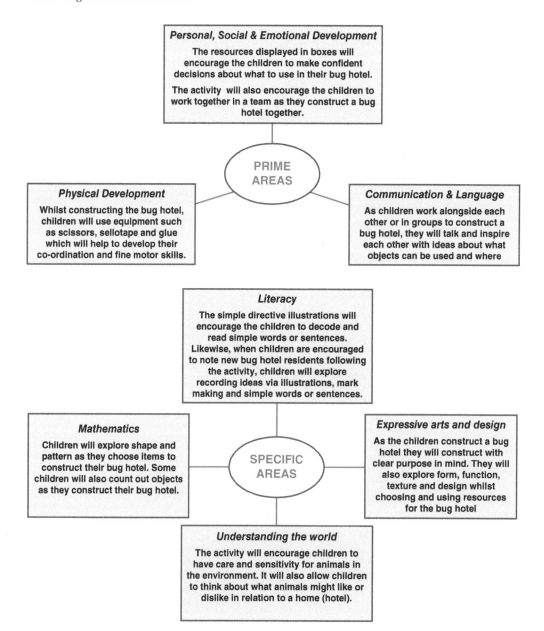

Possible next steps and opportunities for further development

Giving nature a home

Make links with the RSPB giving nature a home website so the children can learn more facts about nature and create other nature homes.

Butterfly diner

Continuing the nature theme, guide the children to plant a patch of flowers for butterflies during the summer months. As part of this activity, children can create simple painted signs or labels to display with the colourful flowers.

This activity will ignite interest in further planting or recognition of some flowers for some children alongside an interest in butterflies. Other children will participate in the activity but develop less interest with connecting ideas. For these children, it is an idea to make links with observing and investigating at home, for example being a 'butterfly detective' to spot butterflies outside their home and note their colours and patterns.

Final thoughts and reflections

Consider how this activity helps build children's thinking about constructing with a purpose in mind. Reflect upon the idea of 'purpose' and the links to learning. Are the children more motivated when there is an end purpose?

Reflect upon the need to teach young children about care for the environment and sensitivity for creatures within it. Consider how home-setting/school links could be used to develop this further.

Resource support: *Example bug hotel directive illustrations*

You could add tubes or small boxes to your bug hotel box

Try adding scrunched paper to make the tubes cosy

Bugs may like some added twigs, bark or pine cones too

Index

Index